EXPERIENCE AND CONCEPTUAL ACTIVITY

A Philosophical Essay Based Upon the Writings of A. N. Whitehead

The M.I.T. Press
Massachusetts Institute of Technology
Cambridge, Massachusetts, and London, England

ACE

Long ago interest in A. N. Whitehead's philosophical ideas induced me to formulate a summary which might advance the understanding of these ideas. The appeal of Whitehead's philosophy is its basic assumption that the Universe is driven by the combined outcome of effects having their origin in the past and anticipations directed toward future possibilities. The elaboration of this point of view opens the way to a world picture in which valuation can find a status along with causal relationship. It gives a place to conceptual activity as a fundamental feature in the entire universe, and it can synthesize domains in which modern man often feels himself involved in great dilemmas. The picture constitutes a radical departure from the causality principle as it is accepted in physics, where the only relationship recognized is that from past to present (whether fully determinate or statistical) with the exclusion of all forms of expectation and valuation.

The exposition in Whitehead's books is not easy to follow, as a consequence of the wealth of thoughts compressed into almost every paragraph. Moreover, Whitehead's mode of presentation underwent some changes in the course of the years. It is hoped, therefore, that a new presentation of this philosophy in a concise form can fulfil a useful purpose.

In developing his ideas, Whitehead had to criticize many current views and to point out limitations in man's theorizing which are not always properly recognized. This is a matter of much importance, since the limitations involved in the generally accepted scientific world picture make themselves felt whenever results and methods of the physical sciences come into contact with problems and needs of human society. Many

iii

of Whitehead's observations in this connection touch upon the problem of life, a topic of critical importance for our attitude with regard to nature. While this topic is often mentioned in Whitehead's books, it is not treated in detail. Nevertheless, his statements on this topic are so closely related to the basic trend of his metaphysics that a presentation of his ideas would be incomplete and pointless if the issue were not clearly faced. Much attention has therefore been given to it, particularly in the second half of the essay. I have attempted to present some further developments of this topic.

The main thesis is that life cannot be completely described or analyzed in terms which have fixed meanings in the vocabulary of physics and mathematics. There are essential features of life which do not have an unambiguous relationship to states of matter or of fields that can be objectively characterized. Their explanation requires reference to subjective features. Within ourselves we experience that these features involve expectations and valuations. It is the key of the philosophy here presented to consider expectations and valuations not as accidental byproducts of physical states of matter, but as essential aspects of functioning. Without the assumption of features beyond physical relationship there is no room for the concept of an "organism," since this term, like "organization," has a meaning only when we accept a reference to purposes. It is a term which cannot find a basis in the language of physics, and consequently, there is no way to understand life in this language. Certain authors have used terms like "complexity" to catch something of the aspects which are peculiar to life. Following Whitehead, I prefer to use the term "conceptual activity," in order to denote something much more explicit than just complexity: it indicates that a notion of concepts is involved, that is, the notion of recognizing forms of relationship, pointing to aims and choices.

The study of life as a phenomenon of nature should begin with notions of conceptual activity, anticipation, aim, choice, freedom, and even such a notion as play, in order to derive from these the features of material structure, chemical reactions, motion, reproduction, carriers of heredity, mutation, evolution. It is suggested that such a method will ultimately prove to be more illuminating and logical than starting from the material apparatus and the metabolic processes of life and describing them from a purely physical point of view, in the vague (and actually vain) hope that personality, consciousness, and the sense of freedom may somehow arise from the physical scheme.

In order to make the philosophical picture consistent and fruitful, we need the basic doctrine that conceptual activity is a fundamental feature of the Universe. Living matter is not just ordinary matter plus conceptual activity added to it. The functioning of the entire Universe is the outcome of conceptual activity; the presence of matter, the division between life and nonlife, and the emergence of material structures carrying life are results of its mode of operation.

When discussing the problem of life from the point of view indicated in the preceding paragraphs, one enters into a difficult and controversial domain of biological science. Readers may argue that this is reintroducing ideas of vitalism or of holism, or what other names have been used for notions now discarded by the majority of biologists and physicists. However, statements concerning the need for consideration of new forms of relationship in biology, reaching beyond those which can be expressed in the terminology of physics, are appearing in the scientific literature of the present day. Some biologists are explicitly referring to Whitehead's thoughts as presenting a possible new way of approach. On the other hand, those discussions in the literature on organic evolution and on the origin of life which attempt to limit themselves to purely physical processes often introduce expectations which are not fully analyzed and which on closer inspection appear to have a shaky foundation. Needless to say, the picture which is proposed in this essay does not discard the great importance of the discoveries of modern biochemistry and biophysics, but it attempts to find a way for their integration within a wider scheme.

The picture developed in the essay at the same time offers another perspective: it constitutes a background against which the relation between scientific knowledge in general and the value judgments of human life can be projected. The doctrine presented by Whitehead bridges the dichotomy of our thinking with regard to scientific results on the one hand and values on the other hand. It establishes a connection between scientific analysis and the expression of values in life and in art. It breaks through the idea of a universe moving according to inexorable laws devised for the behavior of matter. Since the picture considers both the physical world and our lives within it as manifestations of an all pervading conceptual activity, it puts us in the midst of all that happens. It can serve as a foundation for a way of thinking that does not oppose man to nature but connects him closely with her. It asks for universality in our search for truth instead of compartmentalization. It may give guidance in our attempts to harmonize our experiences and our conceptions, and it stresses that knowledge must not be disconnected from responsibility. The picture therefore directs itself to all those working in science or in domains of human relationship who are concerned about that which is sometimes called "the two cultures of our age." By giving a primary position to conceptual activity a way may be found for integrating human creativity and human aspirations with the findings of scientific investigation without surrendering ourselves to a social order completely ruled by technology and machinery. New ideas may spring up with regard to the philosophy of science. In a sense the picture contains a profession of faith. These are some of the consequences which come forward from an attempt to extend the principle of causality beyond its meaning in physics in the way indicated by Whitehead.

The origin of this attempt to present Whitehead's ideas and to discuss some of their applications goes back to studies which started about 1935. A few partial presentations have been given in publications which appeared in the Netherlands and in talks before small groups of scientists and others.

Exchange of opinion with many friends and colleagues naturally has had its influence upon my thinking and my interests, but the responsibility for the contents of the essay rests with me. It would be too much to mention the names of all those with whom I have spoken about this topic during the many years. I will restrict myself here to the names of L. G. M. Baas Becking, H. J. Jordan, A. J. Kluyver, H. A. Kramers, H. R. Kruyt, J. H. F. Umbgrove in the Netherlands, none of whom is still living; to those of Mr. Albert K. Herling, Greenbelt, Maryland, Dr. Martin A. Garstens, Silver Spring, Maryland, Mr. Milton Rogers, Baltimore, Maryland, and Dr. Thomas L. Lincoln, Institute for Fluid Dynamics and Applied Mathematics of the University of Maryland, who have read large parts of the manuscript when it was approaching its final state, and who in many discussions have given advice and inspiration; to Dr. C. B. van Niel, Pacific Grove, California, Dr. L. Edelstein, Rockefeller Institute, New York, and Dr. V. Lowe, The Johns Hopkins University, Baltimore, Maryland. My warm thanks are directed to them, but my indebtedness also goes to many others with whom I have spoken or corresponded, and who have helped by their interest and sympathy, or who by their teaching have contributed to form my mind. They have belonged to the circle of my parental home, to schools, to the University of Leiden, the Technical University of Delft, the Royal Netherlands Academy of Sciences in Amsterdam; still others belong to the University of Maryland and the Paint Branch Unitarian Church. In addition to them I wish to thank my wife deeply for all her support and her never-failing interest, and also to thank her who was before her and passed away. Finally I thank the office staff of the Institute for Fluid Dynamics and Applied Mathematics for much help in typing the manuscript.

College Park, Maryland   J. M. B.
June 1965

CONTENTS

EXPERIENCE AND CONCEPTUAL ACTIVITY

A Philosophical Essay Based Upon the Writings of A. N. Whitehead

INTRODUCTION

As stated in the Preface, the purpose of this essay is to outline a system of thought in which notions concerning values can find a place along with the ideas of causal relationship that are applied in the physical sciences. The essential doctrine of this system, which is taken from the metaphysical picture developed by Alfred North Whitehead in several of his books, is the assumption that in every act occurring in the universe experience derived from that which has gone before is integrated with conceptions concerning possibilities in the future.

The first three chapters of the essay attempt to present an account of the main features of Whitehead's philosophy which have a bearing upon this assumption. The later chapters are applications of the notions developed to the description of the phenomena exhibited by material, nonliving systems, as well as to the description of those observed in living beings.

A major purpose of the essay is a discussion of the problem of whether the phenomena of life can be completely reduced to consequences of the laws of physics, or whether the concept of values, such as we believe to experience within ourselves, must supplement the physical relations in order that a satisfactory explanation of life shall become possible.

An indication may be given of the background against which the presentation must be seen.

Every form of philosophy is an attempt to bring into an ordered picture the information we have collected about the phenomena around us and inside us. The data taken into consideration may cover a wider or a more restricted domain, but the ultimate aim is to embrace as much as possible of that which is believed to be of relevance. Evidently, in each type of philosophy there will be elements of emphasis depending upon the society in which the author is living, as well as upon features of his personal experience; this explains why systems of philosophy may come and go during the course of history. Nevertheless, there are central questions which do not cease to exert an attraction upon every thinker and which will be studied again and again.

The object of the following considerations is to find a basis which may throw light simultaneously upon the physical relations between material phenomena, known through external observation and scientific analysis, and upon the awareness of values and purposes, which is characteristic for our thinking. There is a gap between these two domains of experience, to which attention has been drawn by various authors. The fact that this gap is not adequately bridged has many effects upon the development of present society. Thinking derived from the physical sciences is increasingly exerting influence in domains far beyond the original realm of physics. It has become an influence in human life and is dangerous, because the far reaching development in technological power which is taking place around us is not accompanied by a simultaneously expanding vision of the aims toward which the life of mankind can be directed.

The natural sciences have developed from a mode of investigation in which we have detached ourselves from the phenomena of nature in order to observe them as outsiders who are not personally involved. This has enabled us to become experts in analyzing every phenomenon into separate aspects, each of which as far as possible is considered in isolation. Recombination follows at a later stage. In our approach attention is directed to the establishment of relationships which can be expressed in sharply defined terms, preferably in quantitative form. Often it is taken as an important characteristic of a scientific description that it can be given in mathematical terms.

In framing scientific descriptions the general trend is to look for causal relationship, that is, for relations which connect present happenings and situations with past situations. Sometimes it is possible to express these relations in a fully determinate form; more often we must revert to statistical relations. Nevertheless, it is always relationship pointing from a past to the present. In order to establish such relationship with as much certainty as possible, we need to repeat observations, since this is our only means for separating that which we consider to be essential relations from what is termed accidental. As objective observers, that is, as outsiders, we have no means to find out whether anything may have been important from an inside, subjective point of view. Hence, in principle, the physical sciences must deal with phenomena which can occur repeatedly, and unique occurrences can be fitted into the frame only when they can be related to repeatedly occurring situations.

It is not necessary to expand upon the power which this method of approach has proved to possess. The method is the daily work of the scientist, and everyone knows how much it has helped man to unravel what we call the laws of nature. It has provided mankind with almost unlimited means for making use of natural resources.

Nowhere in the physical sciences is there anything which tells us what to do. I mean "what to do" in an absolute sense, for science can help us to find out how to proceed when some goal has been taken in view. But science itself does not give direction for choosing goals. Indeed, the notion of purpose is a notion outside the domain and the language of physics. Neither is there in physics anything of the qualifying notions, the values, which come into play when we think about purposes. The terms "beautiful," "ugly," "useful," "noxious," "good," "bad," "responsibility," "personality" never enter into description as used by the physicist. From the physical point of view the birth of a living organism and its decay are equally interesting instances of rearrangement of atoms and molecules. There is from this physical point of view no reason why life should be ranked as more important than crystallization or the motion of celestial bodies. Physics does not give an answer, for example, to the question of whether or not it may be desirable to endanger all life upon the earth by spreading a high intensity of radioactivity through the atmosphere. In the picture of physics every arrangement of particles or radiation fields has the same weight as any other arrangement. Nor is there any principle which induces us to consider one group of particles to be more important than any other group; for nature is a whole, and poisons and balms are equally important.

As is well known, ideas and methods derived from the physical and chemical sciences at present are penetrating into biology with great success. The advances made in the analysis of phenomena of assimilation and dissimilation, in the synthesis of organic compounds, in heredity, genetics, and many other topics are very large. They are so far-reaching that certain physicists and biologists are trying to make us believe that life is just another property of matter and that almost complete understanding of its intricacies is around the corner. If we progress still further along the present road, they would have us believe that the whole development of living beings will be understood from a knowledge of the laws of behavior of atoms, electrons, photons, and perhaps other elementary particles.

This seems to imply that our notion of being persons who form judgments about our experiences and who have intentions is no more than an accompanying effect, a reflection from states of motion of atoms or wave fields. Continuing in this train of thought, some physicists expect that scientists will soon succeed in creating living beings or at least some form of life. One cannot dismiss the possibility of such a performance right away. Also there is no doubt that our thoughts and feelings must be intimately connected with phenomena of atoms and molecules and electrons within the nervous system and in other parts of the body. But when it is said that we soon shall be able to create life, real promising life, then the problem becomes insistent: is molecular motion all that we find in life?

When it is stated that life can be expected to arise as a property of matter, provided that it is of sufficient complexity, one must ask: which properties of matter are meant in this sentence? Otherwise the statement does not have a clear meaning. The qualification which seems to be implied is that life should be understood as a result of those properties of matter which are described by present day physics and its allied sciences (plus their probable extension which will come through further research), as there is no other set of properties sufficiently well defined to be brought into the picture. Against this I would observe that if the development of physics keeps to its fundamental concept that there is nothing else than states of particles and of fields, and that situations at the present instant must be understood exclusively by reference to data concerning the past location and motion of particles and fields, without admitting any notion of purpose or of value, then there is no element in the description which provides us with the means of discussing ourselves as persons, that is, as subjects who have experiences which we associate with values.

The fact that we are subjects having experiences which we associate with values is of the utmost importance in our personal and social life. It is recognized in literature, in art, in religion, but it is entirely left out in discussions concerning the physical basis of life. I am convinced that values, intentions, anticipation are not features of human life alone. I therefore believe that biological research cannot come to terms with life unless it recognizes the effectiveness of such features in the activities of living organisms.

Undoubtedly there are great difficulties in our way when we attempt to bring values and intentions into our considerations. We are directly acquainted with values only in our personal lives. We have no certain data about other life. Nevertheless, that which we experience in our human life must have evolved from features to be found in animals. There are definite indications that some of the higher mammals and perhaps some birds can have "personal" feelings and hopes, and I believe that primitive forms of these feelings are present also in so-called lower forms of life down the entire scale. I cannot accept that there is an absolute gap between human life and all other life, and, with full recognition of the immense distance man has advanced in his emergence from other types of primates, I believe that his achievements have been built up by elaborating material already present. Neither can I accept that there is a gap at some other point in the evolutionary ladder. Thus far we have not found out whether in forms of life distant from human life there can be occasion to recognize effects connected with some form of subjectivity or with an association of experience with values; but it has been observed that even types of animals low on the scale can be trained when to expect unpleasant experiences.

Another difficulty is that our terminology is insufficient. We must attempt to get away from our human notions of values and of subjectivity toward more elementary and more fundamental urges before we shall be able to attack such problems properly. Also, these notions may not be amenable to the known and usual forms of analysis and of mathematical treatment. Perhaps they cannot always be properly supported by repeated observation or measurement. The very method of objective research may drive them out of sight.

A point upon which we can fix attention, however, is that we, human beings, can *discuss* physical situations and experience and that we are conscious of doing this. We can take experience apart; we can analyze the phenomena we are observing; we form abstract ideas concerning types of order and other aspects of relationship; we can imagine physical situations which were not experienced. It is this discussion which makes physics possible as a domain of human thinking, but at the same time *the discussion and the thinking is outside the picture we build up with it:* it is a metaphysics. We are facing here a somewhat similar situation as is met in mathematics where metamathematics is needed to discuss its logical structure. We cannot build a picture and at the same time put into it the act of discussing the picture.

The picture of physics does not in itself contain anything which embodies the notion of a subject integrating its experience with abstract notions and with values. In the picture of physics, as said before, all molecules, all fields, etc., form a whole. A form of motion or any other situation is not built up as it is in our thinking by the superposition of what physicists may term elementary effects. It appears immediately as a total effect, no matter how accidental or minute certain driving or resisting forces may look when we introduce them into our equations. When we make a demarcation in the field or in material systems to render the analysis more transparent for our understanding, we can speak of action and reaction, but again it is *we* who have introduced the dividing line. There is in the picture of physics nowhere a group of atoms having the notion of constituting an "I" or a "we" in opposition to what does not share that particular notion. Hence, to define such terms as "person," "environment," "death," we need concepts which are outside the realm of physics: these are metaphysical terms. When use is made of such terms, we must be aware of the extension of terminology which is involved in them.

The typical features of our thinking, the notion of value, the notions of purpose and of intention, of responsibility and of having a task, are observational facts, as real as the facts which physics has discovered in the relations between particles and fields. The two types of facts belong to different categories, which thus far appear to be unconnected. I do not believe that the idea of responsibility can be deduced from any formalism of physics, and I reject any world picture which puts this notion on a secondary plane. The two sets of features which we call "conceptual" and "physical" undoubtedly must have relations to each other, and each part of our thinking will be intimately connected with physical occurrences. However, it is not possible that this is a connection which completely fits the present picture of physics. The best thing that we can do is to make use of a wider picture, and the conceptual and the physical features must find a place as complementary aspects of that wider picture. This is meant somewhat in the same sense as in quantum mechanics the particle picture and the wave picture are complementary. There is — this should be kept in mind — no direct analogy between the two cases, but the example of quantum mechanics can teach the usefulness of complementary aspects.

The most consistent attempt to construct a coherent metaphysical picture aiming at a view of the universe which combines the two aspects of which we must be constantly aware is that which has been developed by *Alfred North Whitehead*. In this picture the notion is brought forward and extensively discussed that there is a form of coordination in the universe which reaches beyond the postulates of physics. The basic relations of physics, as well as the conceptual phenomena of our thinking, are considered as derivatives of this more fundamental coordination. The picture does not give an explanation of the ultimate nature of things: to expect that would be a utopian notion which can never be realized. It must be constructed out of the data of our experience by a process of extrapolation, and it will remain "provisional," open to continuous reconstruction. Nevertheless, although the question of ultimate knowledge must be left aside, we can attempt to develop the picture in such a way that it will illuminate many relations which otherwise seem to be at variance with one another.

Fundamental in this picture is a step beyond causality in the physical sense. This is embodied in the idea that the functioning of the universe must be conceived as an immense complex of "events" or "processes," each coming to its own conclusion and at the same time furnishing the basis for the development of still more processes so that there will never be an end to this vast progression. In each process influences derived from the outcome of past events act together with forms of valuation directed toward an immediate future. Note that I do not say "derived from a future" but "aiming at a future": that means, having some inkling that a future will follow and that its structure will have an importance with reference to which each process must shape itself.

The influences derived from past processes constitute the "experience" of the developing process, the ground from which it arises. They determine the form of causality which we attempt to disentangle when we carry out physical investigations. The influences of valuations directed toward the future are an anticipation of possibilities and result in a decision between possibilities. It is thus assumed that the experience derived from the past does not completely direct the developing process; and it is also assumed that this incompleteness does not lead to mere statistical randomness, but that there is room for some coordinative activity of a nature not described by physical theory. It is not assumed that this is a far-reaching coordination working toward some preconceived plan. It operates in small steps, with a limited outlook. But the point is that in each process there is a slight form of evaluation, although it is of a nature far removed from the concepts of value which we entertain in our minds. In essence each process is therefore a unique occurrence never to be repeated precisely in the same way.

It is true that in many complexes of processes the conceptual elements, to all our knowledge, seem to have little correlation between one process and the next and produce no more than what an outsider calls random effects. In consequence of this lack of correlation the conceptual elements become unobservable for an outside observer. That which he can investigate is only the remaining average influence derived from the outcome of past processes. The study of these influences is the domain of the physical sciences.

From this point of view the existence of matter is a result of persistent repetition of certain patterns in complexes of processes, which for long stretches of time seem to conform to statistical rules of unchanging character. This is the case when there is absence of correlated influence of conceptual elements so that there is no evidence of any spontaneity. *Matter in this way expresses traditions.* Matter is a set of habits of the universe. It is these habits which are studied in physics.

Although the possibility of long persistent repetition must be connected with a fundamental feature of the universe, the habits themselves are not fundamental things. This means that the so-called properties of matter are not final expressions of fundamental properties of the universe. They are important and useful, but it would be short-sighted to believe that there is nothing other than habits. The circumstance that it is relatively easy to study habits should not blind us to the possibility of deviations. We must therefore not consider the properties of matter as eternal: there may come a change, perhaps even in those properties which we summarize under the heading "properties of space and time."

The deviations to which I have alluded can gain a special importance when they are connected with a new conceptual form, a new anticipation of possibilities strong enough to be retained in subsequent processes. There is then, to use a modern term, a "breakthrough" of the statistical habits, from whence a new line of development starts depending upon a correlation between the conceptual elements in successive processes.

It is here that I look for the essential features of life. Habits are not life. The essential character of life must not be sought in its reproduction, in so far as this can be explained physically as a perfected form of crystallization. The essence of life is the possibility of again and again making new evaluations and inducing new starts based upon these. Specifically, I mean that some new evaluation ultimately can lead to a new arrangement of electrons or atoms, for instance, within the possibilities left open by the indeterminacy of the quantum rules. This will occur if the new evaluation has given unequal weights to situations which formerly were counted as equivalent. When this new evaluation appears to be persistent, it can lead to the development of some new structure, ensuring the new distribution of weights from then on by physical, *i.e.*, material means. Much of that which follows in the behavior of the new structure will then come again under the heading of habits, but what has happened is that a new tradition has been started, linked with the existing habits. Using a broad generalization, I would say that it is a feature of life to create new traditions, or in other words, to create a new apparatus, to "create matter," which must ensure the functioning of some important new chain of processes. In physiological and biochemical investigations one studies these apparatus, and one usually reasons as if this is all that is to be seen. The real feature of life, however, is not so much in the regular functioning of the apparatus as in its first appearance. Evidently it is far more difficult to observe this appearance than it is to investigate what is continually repeated.

Thus, in this picture, *life is coordination of spontaneity.* The more extensive the coordination in conceptual activity, the fuller the life. Another way to express this is to say: *life is a struggle against mere randomness.*

These ideas must be kept in mind when discussing the origin of life. I do not deny that life, in the history of the earth, may have become recognizable as such in a gradual way. Physical situations, perhaps ultraviolet light bombarding the primeval atmosphere and the ocean of the earth in the presence of solid surfaces or flakes which could act as a support, may have led to occasions where some form of valuation could operate and remain influential more persistently than elsewhere. But the apparent continuity from a state where life was not recognizable toward one where life is found is not based upon an explanation of life as resulting from "properties of matter." It is the other way round: there is a coordination more fundamental than the properties of matter, and matter is only a solidified product of traditions, whereas life is the form in which fluidity has been preserved. Life at the same time builds itself a material apparatus to protect this fluidity.

If it is thought that many features introduced into the picture which has been sketched in the preceding lines are strange, it should not be forgotten that much of the present structure of physics is similarly beyond imagination. Physical theory started from observations, and scientists constructed pictures behind these observations, using concepts of molecules, atoms, fields, quanta and the like. Gradually these have found general acceptance, but at the same time they have moved further and further away from the common things around us. Quantum physics contains a vast amount of notions which are beyond anything we can see before us. We have learned to be content with the idea that there is a definite unit of electric charge, but what this is is an utter mystery. We accept that the effect of a magnetic field upon a moving charge is in a direction perpendicular to the direction of motion as well as to the magnetic field lines, but what structure there is in space to guarantee these directional relations is utterly unknown. We accept quantum conditions, of fundamental importance for all that which exists, which are expressed by "noncommutative multiplication," and so it goes on. Along with mathematical relations we accept certain qualitative notions to introduce the differences between mass, electric charge, magnetic effects, radiation fields. Actually these notions are not more than rules for calculation with quantities occurring in our equations. We consider these rules to be an expression of causality, but this in itself is no more than a name. The primary notions escape us, and they are not less strange than the assumption that there may be still other coordinating principles beyond those recognized in physics. There is observational evidence for such other coordinating principles: we observe the relevance of values in our own lives, and there are many indications for their effectiveness in other living beings.

The physical sciences are based upon the restrictive assumption that values are irrelevant in physical phenomena. Whitehead's picture is the wider one, embracing the picture of physics as a special case, while at the same time opening the way to the understanding of combined physical and conceptual effects in living beings. This will be set forth in the main text of the essay.

It is possible that the introduction of notions of conceptual activity and of valuation in every process of the universe and, consequently, of an all pervading creativity (see Chapter 1) will be considered as a return to ideas which scientific research was believed to have discredited and abandoned. It may appear to be a return to a kind of "divine providence." It is true that the assumption has been introduced as a result of not being satisfied with the picture of the physical sciences when applied to the entirety of the phenomena of life. But it is based upon the conviction that we can find out something about this creativity by starting from observation. Otherwise it would not be helpful as a basis for explanation. The difference between this view and physics is a difference of emphasis.

It is not supposed that this creativity bears in itself a predetermined purpose which has worked continuously toward a definite end. It operates in small steps, and "chance" (we have no other term) has always played a large part in its achievements. But it is presumed that inherent in each step there is something having the nature of an evaluation of possibilities, and that this evaluation can produce a bias so that "chance" leads to less randomness than it would do on purely physical grounds. In this respect we may find a kind of similarity with human history. Every man and woman can make no more than incidental decisions, depending a great deal on personal chances and having only a very limited view of what may happen in the future. Out of these decisions the course of history evolves; it cannot be predicted, but tendencies can nevertheless become apparent, depending upon certain trends in the set of values our society cherishes. "Providence" therefore is not an appropriate term for the doctrine that is proposed, since it carries a notion of far-sightedness and far-reaching purposiveness which cannot be introduced as a fundamental notion.

The fundamental feature of the conceptual activity in a process can be termed "appreciation of contrasts," an awareness that in the experience out of which the process arises there is a contrast accompanied by an urge "to do something about this contrast," to express it in some form which can serve as basis for the experience of other processes. The awareness of a contrast is the root of all creative action.

Let me come back to the qualification "divine." I believe that ethical values are the outcome of the creative urge after an extensive development. It must be expected that some root of this aspect of life will be present already in the more primitive forms of creativity. What form this root should have I cannot say. But it does not seem acceptable that ethical values should be something apart, given only to man. I believe that some preparation of these values is active already in certain higher animals. The word "divine" might then point to the fact that in creativity there is inherent a possibility for arriving at the conception of ethical ideals.

In so far as ethical values become effective, one may be inclined to speak of an "awareness of God." But the ideas of God or of a Creator involve many aspects of deeply personal and emotional nature. I shall use them very seldom. Everyone must work out for himself what will be most appropriate to his or her needs in this respect.

Attention to the presence of a creative element pervading the entire universe may help us to find a bridge between "the two different cultures of our age." It may help us to arrive at a synthesis of science and technology with that part of our thinking that struggles with the problem: where do we go? We are the most advanced outcome of a process which has been operating during stretches of time and space of cosmic extent, and we must be extremely careful in handling both the natural resources of the earth and its living species. Cosmic exploration and travel are putting before us new responsibilities.

The pages to follow will put the picture in a systematic form. The picture is based upon the ideas set forth by A. N.

Whitehead in his books *Science and the Modern World, Process and Reality, Adventures of Ideas,* and *Modes of Thought* (see the bibliography given under "References and Notes"). In presenting an account of these ideas a certain personal interpretation cannot be avoided. Whitehead's books are difficult to read, and parts of *Process and Reality* are elaborated to such an extent that one may lose track. Moreover, Whitehead was building and rebuilding, and his mode of expression shows differences from book to book. I have deliberately left aside the discussion of the nature of God, as well as many developments bearing upon the theory of feelings (see *Process and Reality,* Part III). If my presentation is not judged to be what Whitehead may have had in mind, it must be considered as my elaboration of a set of ideas for which I am indebted to Whitehead, but for which I am responsible. References to the relevant passages in the books just mentioned will be given extensively in the text and may help the reader to find his own way in Whitehead's scheme of thinking. References are also given to other books consulted and to scientific papers.

The exposition will be given in the form of sections containing statements, digressions on terms used in these statements, and discussions of the reasons which have led to their formulation. Although the scheme in the first three chapters may somewhat resemble the disposition followed in Spinoza's *Ethica,* the sections are not meant as a deductive system, moving from theorem to theorem. Their only purpose is to present a gradual unfolding of the doctrine and its implications. For these chapters, Part III of *Adventures of Ideas,* entitled "Philosophical," has been most helpful.

The following chapters present applications of the picture. Chapter 4, "Matter," discusses some of the basic ideas of physics in order to confront them with points of view developed in Whitehead's scheme. Some properties of material systems have been mentioned which are of importance for a comparison with features presented by living bodies, to be considered later. This chapter is followed by an Appendix, in which some of the notions incorporated in the philosophical system and their application to physical concepts have been reconsidered, starting from the question whether the present laws of physical theory may themselves have a history behind them.

In Chapter 5, "Life as a Coordination of Initiatives," the new point of view concerning life has been developed. The discussion first follows the main lines of thought found in Whitehead's books. This is supplemented by the analysis of a simple model for something living, which provided the possibility of introducing various biological concepts on the basis of a comparison with the idea of "strategies" as applied in games. The chapter is followed by an Appendix containing a discussion of problems raised by automatic machines, which have started to exercise a large influence in technology as well as in attitudes with regard to various biological problems.

In view of the importance which is given to the principle of "natural selection" in biological evolution, this concept has been discussed in Chapter 6, together with some other questions connected with it.

Finally, in a "Retrospect" the main ideas of the philosophical system have been summarized once more. It is hoped that the partial repetition to be found in the expositions of, first, Chapters 1 through 3, next, the Appendix to Chapter 4, and, finally, the Retrospect will be helpful to the reader, and that the discussions of various fundamental ideas from different angles may supplement one another.

The picture is not completed. I am well aware that many problems have remained unanswered and will require further investigation. This holds with regard to both the physical side and the biological side of the picture. Many additional assumptions must be introduced and worked out. I hope that the problems encountered here will find interest, and that ways may be found to attack them.

1

THE PRINCIPLE OF CREATIVITY

§ *1.*

We are part of the universe, a universe in which change and development never end. To give expression to an awareness of certain relations, a vision of some form of order, a feeling for a value asking for realization, is the urge which drives each step in this development. Every expression reached gives rise to new relations which are added to the relations already existing. Together with these predecessors they act as the source of a new urge toward the recognition of a new relation. We use the term "realization" for the expression of a relation, since its expression has the consequence that it has become something that can be experienced and thus has become real.

There is no end to this continuous progression toward new realizations. Neither is there a single direction of advance: the steps form a connected pattern, branching out and converging again, embracing infinitely numerous strands of connected relations. We look upon these steps as the most fundamental reality of the universe. This is the basis of our philosophy. Out of them all phenomena develop, both those commonly described as the properties of material systems, and those which we observe in living beings, reaching upwards to what we find in ourselves as consciousness, the conviction of acting with a purpose and having responsibility for our actions.

This view of the development of the universe is summarized in the thesis: *The ultimate and fundamental reality*

*of the universe is a multiple and never ending complex of
processes developing out of one another.*

In this statement the phrase "ultimate and fundamental"
has been used to indicate a starting point. The term "reality"
must be understood as indicating the essence and the functioning of the universe. It should not be taken as descriptive
of a static character, as "being" in itself; it is meant to stress
the never ending chain of steps always going on. The word
"multiple" indicates that the chain is not a single one, but
that there is a complex network with ramifications everywhere. The term "process" has been chosen rather than "step"
or "occasion" to indicate the fundamental unit in order to
stress that each advance in itself is a complex instance of
functioning.[1] Various aspects of this functioning will be described in the following sections. The genetic relation between
successive processes, expressed in the words "developing out
of one another," will be considered in Chapter 2. The term
"process" must be understood as an ultimate unit: there are
no fractional processes.

§ 2.

*Each process is a mode of functioning which arises out of
the experience of existing facts, establishing a new fact by
expressing a relation recognized as a feature of value in the
experience.*

A "fact" is the result in which the relation recognized in
a process has been expressed. A fact, once established, remains
forever and is unchangeable.[2]

Each process thus has two aspects: it is a becoming in
which the recognition of the relation takes form; and it is
the realization of the relation as a definite fact. The becoming,
the growth of the process, is felt as the *subjective* form of the
process; the fact in which the process ends will be material
for the experience of other processes and thus can be known
objectively. The process is a totality of becoming and expressing; these aspects should not be construed in the sense that

one is believed to follow upon the other in temporal order according to any physical time scale. At the present stage of our considerations we have not yet reached the notion of physical time; the problem of time will be the subject of §§ 18ff. and 49.

The phrase "experience of existing facts" indicates that the origin of each new process is found in the results of preceding processes. This is the basis for the interconnectedness of the universe. There are no detached parts of the universe, nor isolated regions unconnected with other parts. The statement forms the basis for a type or order, although this is not to be taken as a simple serial order: we have already stressed the multiple connectivity of the pattern which constitutes the developing universe. Some aspects of the connection will be considered in §§ 17ff.

In the opening statement of § 1 we accepted never ending advance as a fundamental feature of the universe. The universe thus is always new, and each experience is something unique which can never be completely repeated. In this feature is also embodied the doctrine that the universe is infinite.[3]

§ 3.

The phrase "a relation which is recognized," and the terms "value," "expression," "realization," which have been connected with the notion of experience, denote features of conceptual activity present in each process. The following comments elucidate the meaning of these terms.

The possibility of experience must be accepted as a fundamental notion; this is suggested by our personal experience as well as by scientific investigation and by the circumstance that we can bring order and system into our experience. It is evident that each experience comes to us in a definite form, emphasizing some aspect of relationship which has impressed us in the thing experienced. This form always contains subjective features: our experience is processed through activities of our body and our mind; hence, for each human being experience is something personal which has its own peculiar character. The assumption that experience will have an individual and special character not only within ourselves, but in every happening of the universe, is an extension of this assertion, necessary to make understandable the multiform differences in the types of reactions following upon the experience.

This assumption leads to the doctrine that in each process experience is clad in a form peculiar to *that* process and to no other process. It will be necessary to consider to what degree this idea is compatible with the regularities which we observe in the physical world, regularities which make possible the persistence of material objects, as, for instance, atoms and electrons, and the existence of causal laws (see § 37 and Chapter 4).

The terms "value" and "realization" intend to bring into evidence the subjective character of the form in which experience functions in a process. The term "value" is used to indicate an awareness of possibilities for the immediate future, a point which will be discussed in § 8. The term "realization" has been introduced in order to stress that each process is a form of activity leading to a result that can be material for other experience. The subjective aspect of the experience from the point of view of this activity is the urge to express, to realize something which will have objective importance in a future, and, in particular, to realize *that* aspect which has acquired relevance in *that* particular process.

The reader should not be shocked by the way in which the term "value" is taken as a fundamental notion, while nothing is stated about some "thing" or some "being" making value judgments. Nor is anything said about a scale of values. The further discussion will give more content to the term. It should not be forgotten that in physical science many terms are taken for granted in a similar way, for instance, "attraction" or "repulsion" between electric charges, or quantum rules such as Pauli's principle which "forbids" that two electrons move in the same quantum state with the same spin. Such statements are accepted as points of departure for the construction of important chains of reasoning. We have learned that often it is more profitable, that is, more illuminating to follow up their consequences than to ask for a mechanism leading to attraction or leading to the separation of quantum states. The open-minded scientist remains aware of the provisional nature of all such statements and is prepared to accept their replacement when it is found that the chains of reasoning built upon them do not furnish a satisfactory description of observed facts. There have been periods in the history of physics and in the development of certain theories in which this provisional nature was forgotten, and in which the abstractions of physics, meant only as working tools, have been considered as absolute realities. In a great deal of the nineteenth century this was the case, for instance, with the idea of the existence of isolated particles, the idea that space and time had existence independent of matter, and the idea that absolutely sharp location in space and time was conceivable.

Some notion of the provisional character of these ideas can be obtained if we think of the surface of the ocean and take the crests of the waves visible upon it as separate entities, as a kind of bodies, and then attempt to work out a theory of their behavior, their growth and decay, the effects of collisions between them, etc. Such a theory must become insufficient at certain points since we know that waves are the consequence of motions in the water of the ocean, which must be considered in its entirety in order to arrive at a full understanding of the behavior of the surface. In a similar way it may be that what have been called "particles" are no more than particularly conspicuous manifestations of the behavior of a kind of substratum.

Thus it may also come forward that the notion of the entities considered in the present form of physics as happenings devoid of any purpose and not involving a notion of value is no more than a useful abstraction in a certain domain of analysis, viz., that part which pertains to nonliving matter, whereas it is too limited to be applied to life. The terms used in physics are insufficient for the description of the idea of personality or of the contrast between a subject and its surroundings; neither do they give a basis for explaining the part played by spiritual aspirations in the activity of our minds. By taking "valuation" as a fundamental notion we reach a point of view from which this "other half of our world" may acquire a better perspective so that it can be investigated along its own lines and still be organically connected with the physical side of the world.

There is, of course, a difference in so far as the terms introduced in physics are amenable to mathematical expression and form the basis for a highly exact structure with numerous occasions for precise internal as well as for external observational checking. This is not the case with the notion of value. Perhaps the word "not" should be read as "not yet" in so far as the possibility of checking is considered. But it is probable that mathematics can be applied only in those circumstances where predictable recurrences are found, and where the notion of a certain multitude of identical things has use. The discussion of the notion of value is primarily connected with the notion of unique occurrences: indeed the "value" accorded to an occasion gives the character of uniqueness to that occasion. Hence a discussion of the notions of value and purpose may require another type of logic in which quantitative relationships (even the possibility of arranging notions into a serial relationship) do not play a part.

That we do not as yet have a method for a systematic elaboration of these metaphysical notions does not mean that a more or less consistent logic of values and of purposes will never be possible. We are in need of some logic of this nature, and it should be developed along lines, which, notwithstanding their difference from the methods of physics and mathematics, still shall have points of contact with the results of physics. This will be the only way to find guidance in the problem: what are we to do with our scientific knowledge?

§ 4.

We shall use the term "conception" to mean the way in which experience is active in a process that is growing into a fact. Conception is both the awareness and the expression of the relation which appeared in the experience, or, as we shall say, which was conceived in the experience. Conception must not be considered as a purely passive reaction to the facts which form the starting point of the experience. In other words: *The form of the conception is not completely determined by the mere facts.*[4]

This doctrine is connected with the circumstance that in the facts, which can be known objectively, the subjective aspect of the preceding processes is lost. The new process must find a new subjective form. In this respect each process has a certain *conceptual autonomy*. A limitation of this autonomy will be considered in § 17.

If one should accept the opposite idea, one arrives at a determinism which is expressly refuted here. It would lead to the idea that no single process could distinguish itself from other processes by something specific for *that* process; hence, all processes should be considered as "modes" of a single "substance," in the sense in which Spinoza uses this word. The philosophy presented here, on the contrary, stresses the doctrine that each process has something specific which functions in that process only and in no other process.

The doctrine introduces a *principle of creativity*, which we take as an ultimate category in our picture of processes developing out of each other.[5]

§ 5. Creativity

In stating the principle of creativity we accept as fundamental and unseparable features of the universe:

Activity — the ever newly recurring urge toward growth, arising out of experience;

Creativity (in a more restricted sense) — the urge to realize a relation, conceived in the experience as something new and valuable;

Individuality — the realization of the conception in a fact, which introduces the discreteness (if we should use physical terms: a "quantization") of the experience, while at the same time procuring a starting point for conception in a subsequent experience.

The discreteness provides the "points of rest" in which value can find expression. In a world picture based on the assumption of a perfectly continuous functioning, such as was presented in the classical physics of the nineteenth century, there are no points of rest which distinguish themselves from other instants. In such a picture there is no room for a conception, nor for the notion of an individual, nor for the contrast between a subject and its surroundings. The doctrine of discreteness consequently is intimately connected with the doctrine that value is a fundamental feature in the functioning of the universe.

In a way this doctrine may suggest a relation between quantum theory and the emergence of spiritual aspirations in our minds, but one must be careful with such notions which easily lead to unfruitful speculations. Nonetheless, the notion obtains a pregnant aspect if we take it as indicating that there is a connection between quantization, the possibility of life, and the emergence of human ideals.

§ 6.

The experience out of which a new process starts embraces all that which was before that process. The meaning of the words "that which was before that process" will be considered in § 20. The basis for the unity in the cosmos is the never ceasing occurrence of attempts toward a synthesis of experience. Through this fundamental feature all is connected with all. Whitehead expresses this in the statements:

"The world expands through recurrent unification of itself, each, by the addition of itself, automatically recreating the multiplicity anew."

"The universe is always one, since there is no surveying it except from an actual entity which unifies it. Also the universe is always new, since the immediate actual entity is the superject of feelings which are essentially novelties."[6]

A consequence of this doctrine is that there is no irrationality in the universe, meaning that nowhere are there things which cannot in some way be compared, and that nowhere is there an absolute freedom or lawlessness. Another consequence is that the universe is open for analysis, that it can be understood, in the sense that over and over again we can form an idea, a view, and a judgment concerning that which we experience.

The universe, however, is *transcendent* in the sense that in every instance of experience the universe is accepted from a particular subjective point of view. *It is always conceived under a certain perspective* which is proper to the particular process and which never can embrace all parts of the experience with the same clarity. In every conception there are relevant notions appearing with more or less distinction against a background which fades away into obscurity (compare § 14).

The limitation to what can be expressed in a single fact, that is, in the outcome of a single process, is the ground for the emergence of new conceptions and thus of new processes. Each is a renewed attempt to grasp relationship; each arises out of dissatisfaction with the result obtained before. Through this there is a never ending recurrence of attempts, in the hope that along some lines there may be reached an advance toward richer, more embracing expressions. It is this principle which is behind the statement of § 2, and in particular behind the last words of that section: that the universe is infinite.

A comparison may be inserted with some features of Indian thinking. The principle of creativity, as formulated in § 5, might be compared with Atman, the Self; the expressions reached in the facts to which all processes must lead constitute Maya, the world of phenomena or appearances in their endless variety, each illuminating certain features of the universe, none of them giving full expression, each being limited. However, the line of thought presented here does not pretend to lead us away from the consideration of facts toward a unique contemplation of the Self, of which it is said: "The Self is to be described as *not this, not that.* It is incomprehensible, for it cannot be comprehended; undecaying, for it never decays; unattached, for it never attaches itself; unfettered, for it is never bound." There is some parallelism, but not a complete one. Neither does the following sentence, lofty as it may be, reflect our attitude: "He who has realized eternal Truth does not see death, nor illness, nor pain; he sees everything as the Self, and obtains all."[7] On the contrary, it is a feature of our Western way of thinking to attach great importance to the appearances, to the facts: our life, our thoughts, our hope and our glory are in them, and they are not less venerable to us than the underlying creativity. We do not wish to overlook pain and death; we wish to understand something about them and through that we hope to alleviate some pains and terrors.

But what has been stated before contains a warning: no fact, no theory, no dogma can express God's truth fully and finally.

§ 7.

It is necessary to observe that where we have been speaking of the "recognition" or the "conception" of a relation, of an "awareness" of a value, and of an urge to express what has been conceived, the idea of consciousness should be left aside. Consciousness as we experience it within our minds must be the result of extremely complicated connections in the nervous system of what we call highly developed organisms. This is evident from the fact that we perceive less and less of it when we go to organisms further down from us in the scale of evolution.

Consciousness is one of the highest forms in the functioning of nervous perceptive systems; its role increases with the progress of our development. Even within ourselves it is not continually present; it operates with flashes and disappears. An important part of the processes of mental character do not penetrate into our consciousness. It would therefore be entirely wrong to consider consciousness, in the sense in which we apply this term to our own minds, as a feature of a fundamental process.[8] This is the reason for the introduction of the terms "awareness," "conception," "to conceive," in order to indicate a more vague notion which shall retain its importance when every form of consciousness is absent. This notion at the same time involves something of a tendency, of an urge, of being drawn or driven to something, an "appetition." Again, one should not think here of a material tendency, an attraction to be explained in the terms of physics; what is meant is something of much more fundamental character.[9]

§ 8.

The awareness of a value is inseparably connected with the awareness of a possibility, that is, an *anticipation of the circumstance that the fact in which the conception expresses itself will be material for experience in other processes and thus will have meaning for the future.* This anticipation is just as fundamental as is the experience of past facts; the two are inseparably interwoven in the urge to express the conception.

In this way our philosophical picture presents an extension of the doctrine of physics which recognizes only determining influences coming from the past.[10] It should be noted that our picture assigns to this anticipation a role different from that played by the influences deriving from experience. In the anticipation there are no influences from the not yet existing future; there is no more than an awareness that the experience is not fully determinative but leaves some latitude for possible modes of expression which will have consequences. When the process has come to its termination and has become a fact, a decision has been taken within the extent of this latitude, as was mentioned before in § 4. In § 17 a principle will be introduced which provides a partial link between the decisions in successive processes.

§ 9.

An elementary awareness of value can be interpreted as an *appreciation of certain contrasts*. The term contrast here can be taken in its simple direct sense; a discussion of the contents of this term will be given in §§ 13 and 14. To be aware of a value means that something is recognized as being of particular relevance, something present in the relations existing between experienced facts but nevertheless not counted in the analysis as given by objective scientific investigation.

From the point of view of physics there is no difference in importance or in meaning between large and small, between concentration or dispersion, or between the manifold configurations which can be presented by the molecules of a gas. From the point of view of physics the processes which occur during the decay of a corpse are not less important or less meaningful than those which occur within a living organism. From the point of view of physics there is no distinction between a "message" and "background noise." From the point of view of physics the development of life on the earth is not more remarkable than the appearance of crystals or of wave patterns.

The distinction between forms of order so that they can be studied and the distinction between living and nonliving are distinctions introduced as results of conceptual activity. They are expressions of our faculty of observing and evaluating. It is through them that science is possible, but they derive from a type of coordination added to that furnished by the notions of physics. They belong to "metaphysics," in the same sense as there is "metamathematics" to provide a background for the discussion of mathematical concepts. Our discussions of the term "value" are an attempt to achieve some understanding of this metaphysical coordination.

§ 10.

The notion of value, which thus far has been used without further qualification, must be construed in such a sense that it will entail elements out of which a great variety of aspects can develop. This will usually not appear within a single process; its full development will only be reached in particular complexes of processes, the nature of which will be discussed in Chapter 3. But it is necessary to state that a richness of qualities can evolve out of the fundamental notion. Beauty is one of them. At the same time it must be stated that amidst these qualities there are features which can develop into an *awareness of value in an ethical sense,* pointing to a *distinction between good and bad.*

The distinction between good and bad is not a clear cut one. Almost never in our lives can we reach unequivocal decisions. The judgment about what is good and what is bad in particular cases — and particular cases are the ones that matter — changes with people and changes with the times. Sometimes it may look as if there is no sure principle and as if the distinction solely derives from some code of behavior. It has been attempted to define "good" by a reference to certain objectively describable data concerning facts, e.g., by defining it as the greatest well-being for the greatest number of people. But the definition of "well-being" is subject to an endless variety of opinions, and to consider the well-being of a larger number of people as the more desirable thing is a choice made by human beings while the question why we should do so remains unanswered.

We reach a more honest point of view when we accept that ethical values, like other values, have their roots in fundamental aspects of the notion of value as it functions throughout the universe. We can then assume that one of the features of human life is the urge to discover more and more about these values and to state them in forms which appeal to all men and women. Our doctrine consequently is: the conviction of a sense in life, of having a task, of being obliged to strive for what is good, of having responsibility derives from some fundamental principle of the universe. Having regard to its vagueness, we say that there is a fundamental "polarization," and that, although its precise projection upon our deeds is never fully evident and must be sought and guessed at the cost of great exertion, the sign of the polarization cannot be reversed.

It is not suggested that an ethical aspect is always discernible in the conception of value as it evolves in a single process. It may be so far in the background as to be practically unrecognizable, and it needs the cooperation of extensive complexes of processes to bring an ethical aspect into the foreground.[11] The same holds for that aspect of value which we call beauty.

To this must be added that the notion of ethical values in the form in which it has developed thus far in our minds does not necessarily represent the only possible form of development. Although we have confidence in the sign of the polarization, there may be various directions of projection, and perhaps we exemplify only a particular one of these. We cannot exclude the possibility that in other parts of the universe different developments may have taken place. But we shall assume that in whatever form it may have developed the notion of ethical value is fundamentally connected with the creativity of the universe.

It is of importance to note how intimately the ethical urge operating within us is connected with the urge to be active, to develop, to expand, to investigate, to understand, and often to dominate. Ethical values contain much more than a code of behavior; they are interwoven with a vision of a future and constitute the source of power from which derives the greater part of our creative work. This is the basis for our conviction that a fundamental principle of the universe is operating through us. No doubt most of it has developed along lines of trial and error; but there has always been some awareness of the polarization, which has helped us to distinguish between errors and more promising results.

One may consider the awareness of value as the experience of God. This may be an appropriate expression to suggest the depth of the notion we are attempting to catch. But the term "God" embodies many different aspects and touches so deeply upon the most intimate feelings of every individual person that it would lead to difficulties to refer to it as a means for explanation. The place which should be given to God must remain a subject for decision by each person for himself. We add that the awareness of value should not be construed as a form of "Providence."

§ 11.

The fundamental doctrine according to which each process arises out of experience of existing facts, and at the same time is directed toward the expression of a relation conceived in this experience, can be summarized in the words: *Each process is a totality of experience and conception.*

Experience is that element which is taken from the past. It provides the connection with what has preceded and is the root of all *causal relationship.* The conception, embodying what has been described in §§ 3, 4, 8, 9, and 10, is an awareness of a future; hence it contains a *finalistic* or teleological element. All processes in the universe are directed by conceptions concerning a future just as they are dependent upon experience of what has preceded.[12]

The use of the word "totality" (or "a whole") is intentional. To speak of a "synthesis" of experience and conception might evoke the idea that experience and conception would represent two features, each given by itself and then juxtaposed and coupled in a process. On the contrary, each process is a single happening, a whole, and the terms "experience" and "conception" refer to two aspects of this single happening. Experience refers to the objectively describable features of the connection which the process has with its past; conception refers to the subjective development which contains an anticipation of the future. Making use of a term developed in theoretical physics, we may describe these two aspects as being complementary to each other.[13]

It must be stressed that this in no way assumes that there is some predetermined purpose governing all processes in the entire universe. Nothing is known to us about such an ultimate purpose beyond that which has been considered in § 10 concerning our awareness of value in the ethical sense. Our personal experience shows that nowhere is there more than a dim awareness of some possible future. The vision of a future may become wider and to a certain degree more probable in the results obtained in complexes of cooperating processes, but it always loses itself in vagueness beyond a certain distance.

§ 12.

In this and the following three sections, some features of the internal development of a process will be considered.[14]

Several times we have used the term "to be aware of" or "to recognize" certain relations in what is experienced. This can be described by saying that in each process the reaction to facts is expressed in certain forms of relatedness. The *forms of relatedness* or forms of definiteness can be considered for themselves; they can then be denoted as *ideals, universals,* or *eternal objects,* terms which are all names for forms of relatedness.[15]

Ideals have a status different from those of processes and of facts. Processes are occasions of functioning and constitute actuality. Facts once having occurred exist forever. Ideals have a meaning only when they enter into conceptions. However, ideals can be considered in abstract form, and hence they have a status outside the temporal and spatial relations of phenomena: it is for this reason that they are called "eternal objects." The important point is that *eternal objects can have relations amongst themselves,* which are exemplified in the outcome of a process if they have entered into the conception driving that process. It is the power of the human mind that it can recognize these relations in the exemplifications and can abstract them from the particular form of occurrence. Starting from such recognitions the human mind has built up systematic pictures which are continually extended of the relations between eternal objects. The fact that this is possible demonstrates the existence of coordination in the universe.

Particular relations between ideals lie at the basis of those relationships which are studied in the physical sciences (some of these are mentioned in §§ 17, 34, and 41). The most fundamental discovery of man in this domain has been that relations deduced from other relations by means of mathematical reasoning can often find exemplification as well. Thus theoretical science can find practical application.[16]

Other relations are considered in esthetics. A further group is considered in theology. Also here, deduction by means of reasoning is to some extent possible although this has not reached such elaborate constructions as are found in the physical sciences. Nevertheless, what has been recognized is sufficiently impressive to show that the coordinations existing in the universe embrace more than the domain covered by the physical sciences.

Returning to the development of a process, one can say that each process is a reaction to facts together with a reaction to ideals. In the development of a process novel relations may play a part, relations particular for that process and consequently not having the status of eternal objects.

Reactions may also be called *"prehensions,"* indicating that something is taken into account, is apprehended. This need not always involve acceptance; on the contrary, there may be rejection. Thus we can distinguish between positive and negative prehensions. A "positive prehension" is a reaction, either to a fact or to an ideal, of such nature that this fact or this ideal will play an active part in the growth of the process. If it is strong enough, it acts as a spotlight. A "negative prehension" is a reaction in which a fact or an ideal is driven back, is suppressed. Then it no longer plays a conspicuous positive part in the growth of the process, although it is somewhere present in the background.[17]

§ 13.

The conception, which represents the subjective aspect of a process, can be of greater or lesser complexity. Its character develops through the acceptance of certain elements of the experience and the rejection of other elements, through the recognition of contrasts and of similarities, through the use of conjunctions (syntheses) and disjunctions (separations). All this can happen repeatedly, and conjunctions and disjunctions already obtained can be used again, combined into new forms, contrasted, or even rejected. This can be a highly elaborate procedure. One might expect that in general such a development will lead to more fully worked out, more mature conceptions, but this need not be the case in all circumstances.

The notion of a *"contrast"* is important and meaningful in the analysis of the development of a conception.[18] It indicates that elements of the experience which differ amongst themselves are seen in a certain relationship. They appear neither as contradictory nor as completely unrelated. We can state that *a conception is an urge to combine a number of contrasts into an organized relationship.* This type of combining will be termed an *integration of prehensions,* since it is not a simple summation (juxtaposition) but a summation in which the elements are provided with weight factors (in part these may be negative factors indicating rejection) and are brought into a pattern of relationship.

When the conception has achieved the combination of all the positively prehended elements of the experience and of the relevant ideals into a single pattern of relationship and has expressed this relationship in a fact, the process has reached its interior satisfaction. With this achievement the conception is no longer a subjective feature; there remains only the fact in which the relation has been laid down.

§ 14.

In opposition to the relation indicated by the term "contrast" there can be featureless monotony when no differences are felt in the elements of experience; or chaotic multiformity when no relationship is felt, and the various elements of the experience lead to urges obstructing and annihilating one another.

It is never possible to combine all particularities of the experience into a single contrast or into a single harmonically related pattern of contrasts. There are always particularities which are rejected and lost from sight. Hence: *Each contrast, each conception, represents the universe from a certain perspective.* The term harmony is used here to indicate an important coordination of contrasts. The value of a conception is determined by the amount of creative work that has been performed in arriving at its final form. A valuable conception combines harmony with richness of expression for all the positively prehended elements of the experience, which are seen with great clarity before a background of vagueness.

The terms used here can be applied for a classification of perspectives:

(*a*) Rich or elaborate — when a great number of contrasts are brought into a harmonic relationship.

(*b*) Limited or narrow — when many details have been rejected and thus are left out of the picture.

(*c*) Vague or superficial — when too many details have been lumped together without further distinction.

When awareness recognizes only very little above chaotic multiformity, the perspective is trivial or poor; little creative work has been done in such a case.

Conceptions in which intensive contradictions are left unsolved give the impression of evil.[19] When a conception embraces a positive prehension of an awareness of ethical values, the satisfaction of that conception will contain an awareness of something good.

§ 15.

The origin of every conception is found in the awareness of a contradiction between elements of the experience and in the awareness that this contradiction can be transformed into a contrast, that is, *into a meaningful relation.* This transformation is the creative work performed by the process.

The urge toward the resolution of contradictions into contrasts and toward their expression into definite facts is the driving force of each process. It is at the same time the feature which governs the integration of the various prehensions with its conjunctions, disjunctions, and rejections until a result is obtained which brings satisfaction.[20] This doctrine might be compared with the dialectic doctrine which seeks the urge for evolution of the universe in the relation between ultimate opposites. We have used the term "contrast" as a much more fruitful notion than that of ultimate opposites.

The term "satisfaction" used here (introduced previously at the end of § 13) carries in it the roots of what in higher forms of development constitutes something like "enjoyment" as a result of mutual reinforcement (see § 16 and Chapter 3).

We experience various aspects of the features governing the interior development of a process within ourselves when we consider in which way the conception of some aim can give us the means to find and to carry through all the steps necessary to reach the goal. Under the influence of the conception various features acquire mutually supporting aspects: they stimulate and determine each other and lead to the establishment of a pattern of harmonious relatedness. We have the experience of definite interior laws which make the development determinate; and we feel enjoyment, sometimes very deeply, when the result is attained. This is evident in all artistic creation, and creative work in common life is not different from it. The same holds, of course, for creative work in science and in social matters.

It may be repeated that the importance of a process, the creative work performed in it, is found in the decisions concerning what shall be included in a contrast and what shall be left out. The circumstance that not all decisions need be expressed, and that in human work they often may be unconscious, does not necessarily detract from the importance.

2

COORDINATION IN THE DEVELOPING COMPLEX OF PROCESSES

In this chapter we analyse some aspects of the connections found in the developing complex of processes which constitutes the universe. Two principles of general character will be considered first (§§ 16 and 17). The rest of the chapter presents a discussion of the basic forms of arrangement in the multiply connected pattern. In Chapter 3 this is followed by a study of systems of coordinated processes, the so-called societies of processes.

§ 16. *Mutual reinforcement of prehensions resulting from facts of similar character*

In the development of a conception an important role can be performed by the circumstance that experiences obtained from a plurality of existing facts of similar character may be prehended with nearly equal subjective forms. When this is the case, these subjective forms can be integrated into a complex awareness of great intensity, presenting the aspect of a single relation.[21] If the number of similar facts is large, this complex awareness can become so strong that it leads to the elimination of many other features which were present in the experience of these facts. This postulate of reinforcement combined with elimination of unconformable and consequently "undesired" features is of basic importance for the existence of matter (compare § 38).

The phenomenon has some distant analogy with what is called "mass-psychosis," an enormous reinforcement of some idea in consequence of the simultaneous presence of a great number of people all in the same mood, often leading to the impossibility of bringing any other thought to their consciousness (even including one's own, perhaps).

§ 17. Continuity of subjective form

In every process the initial experience of an immediately preceding process is prehended *in a subjective form which presents a certain measure of continuity with the subjective form of the preceding process.*[22]

This postulate states that the subjective form of the first phase of any process bears a close relation to the subjective forms of the process or perhaps several processes which have immediately preceded the one under consideration. (We cannot exclude that there may be more than one immediately preceding process since there is no unique serial development of processes but rather ramifications and convergences.) The postulate introduces the assumption that every process experiences from its immediate predecessor(s) something more than that which is given by the objective facts which resulted from these processes: *the experience of the immediate past contains more than mere physical experience of past facts.* It should be understood that immediate transmission of subjective form will become less and less important when we recede further and further back into the past, so that there remains only objective (physical) transmission except in so far as a transmission of subjective form is carried along by the intermediate processes. Within ourselves we experience this continuity as direct consciousness of our immediate past. Because of it we identify ourselves with the selves of a few instants ago and thus also with the selves which we remember from the more distant past.[23]

The continuity of subjective form in the first phase of the interior development of a process does not prevent the integration of new elements with it in further stages or the rejection of elements of the original subjective form. This freedom for further integration guarantees the conceptual autonomy of the process, which has been asserted in § 4, and which makes it possible for each process to experience the past with its own subjective form so that there is room for initiative.

To summarize: The doctrine that each process arises out of the experience of past facts expresses the basis for the existence of causal relationship, as has been stated in §§ 6 and 11. The postulate of subjective continuity influences the form in which causality comes to effect. This postulate provides the basis for the existence of traditions and of matter.

§ 18. Basic forms of arrangement

The results of modern science have established that the particular forms in which we experience time and space are dependent upon the behavior of matter. We cannot consider these particular forms as primary aspects of the universe. Nevertheless, there must be certain fundamental aspects in the arrangement of processes and in their connections, which are basic for the appearance of time and space in the way they have become known to us through personal observation and through the methods of physical measurement. These fundamental features must express both progress and togetherness. We shall denote them as *progressive relations* and *coordinative relations,* respectively. These relations are forms of definiteness (see § 12) which enter into the conception of every process together with the experienced facts.

As distinct from the fundamental progressive relations and coordinative relations we shall use the terms *"time"* and *"space"* for those forms of definiteness which have been abstracted from experience and have been made more precise with the aid of the methods and principles of physics. These forms are obtained from relations observed between sets of facts.

The interior development of a process, the conception with its integrations, cannot be considered as happening in the scale of time which is constructed from physical observation.

The interior development can only be experienced subjectively in its actual happening. If one wishes to apply a temporal notion to this development, it is necessary to revert to something which is different from physical time and which moreover has a specific character for each separate process. We may use the term *"duration"* or *"interior duration."*[24]

When it is attempted to compare the interior duration of a process with a physical time scale, no unambiguous correspondence can be found. Any attempt to locate the occurrence of some phase of a process on a physical time scale requires an "observation," that is, a new process must be brought to completion, a process which has experience both of the process under consideration and of other processes observed in fixing the time scale. This completion of a new process interrupts and upsets the development of the original process. Consequently, one must expect that the resulting location will be subject to a measure of uncertainty (compare § 43).

§ *19.*

The point raised in the last paragraph of the preceding section leads to the question of whether all processes should be considered as being completely exterior to one another, or whether there can be overlapping. The terms "exterior to one another" and "overlapping" as used here can have a meaning only for observation from the outside, that is, when it is attempted to relate the development of processes to a time scale constructed by means of physical experiments and their analysis. Such observation is always performed from a certain perspective and the results are influenced by the perspective chosen. It cannot be excluded that in such a perspective overlapping may be noticed.

From the subjective point of view, on the other hand, each process is a unit. Other processes do not enter by other means than by that which is expressed in the terms: experience of past processes, continuity of subjective form, and anticipation of a future. As mentioned before, these terms describe possible prehensions of other processes in the subjective aspects of the process under consideration. From the subjective point of view all processes are exterior to one another.[25]

§ 20.

We return to the progressive relations which may exist between processes. The only datum which can be applied is the experience a process has from other processes. On the basis of this datum we introduce the definition: If in the experience of a process, for example the process "B," a part is played by experience which "B" has from another process "A," *the process "A" is in the past of "B."* Conversely, *the process "B" is in the future of "A."*

This is a revision of what was stated in § 6 in so far as the meaning of the terms "past" and "future" are now fixed by a reference to a relation of experience. The relation of experience is considered to be fundamental and is not deduced from other notions. The most important feature in this connection is the relation with the immediate past through the continuity of subjective form.

"Past" and "future" thus are not defined with reference to a physical time scale. The definition fixes at the same time the meaning of the terms "to precede" and "to follow." It will be noticed that the relation is not symmetric: when "A" is in the past of "B," "B" is not in the past of "A" but is in the future of "A." The relation is transitive: when "A" is in the past of "B," the past of "A" is also in the past of "B." An important point is that the relation can be inapplicable: it is possible that neither of the two processes "A" and "B" has experience of the other one. This possibility will be considered in the next section.

The words "processes developing out of one another" used in the doctrine of section I must now be understood in the sense that each process develops from certain preceding processes from which it has experience. It should not be thought that each process has experience from all other processes.

The latter point of view would be incompatible with the doctrine of conceptual autonomy in each process and would give no possibility for evolution. The notion of evolution has in it the idea of a direction of advance and requires independence from what the future may contain. On the contrary, the future depends upon present decisions.

We repeat once more that the definition adopted here stresses the *fundamental asymmetry between past and future,* a feature which is inherent to the basic doctrine of § 1.

§ 21.

When two processes are considered, for example "A" and "B," it is not necessary either that "B" has experience of "A" or that "A" has experience of "B." It is possible, as mentioned in the previous section, that *neither of them has experience of the other.* When this is the case we call the two processes "coexistent."[26]

The possibility of coexistence is taken over from physical theory, in particular from the theory of relativity. In that theory it is based upon the doctrine that causal relations can never be propagated with a speed larger than the speed of light (that is, the speed of propagation of electromagnetic phenomena). The physical idea of propagation, however, is not a fundamental notion in the philosophy here presented: it is a derived notion abstracted from the results of the transmission of experience in certain chains of processes amenable to physical investigation. "Speed of propagation" is a notion still further away from primary notions. Hence, although the idea has been taken over from physical theory, the terms "past," "future," "coexistence" are not based upon a description in terms of physics. They represent fundamental relations of arrangement in the universe, immediately connected with the possibility of experience and of absence of experience. The physical relations are a distant consequence of the fundamental relations.

It should be noted that the philosophy developed here does

not give a rule from which one can determine in which case there can be experience and in which case there will not be. What can be experienced can only be found out from experience itself. When experiences occur repeatedly, rules can be made: this is what physics does. But however large the domain of applicability of the rules with regard to phenomena occurring repeatedly, we must not turn them into a dogma but must leave open the possibility that something unexpected always can turn up.

§ 22.

Processes which between themselves exhibit the relation of past and future are *genetically related to each other.* An equivalent statement is: *there exists an effective causal relationship* between such processes. The relationship can be described by saying that *the past of a process is immanent in that process.* The immanence is given on one hand by the experience of past facts and on the other hand by the continuity of the subjective form of the experience, as explained in § 17.

The converse of the immanence of the past is *an anticipation of a future.* This anticipation (mentioned previously in § 8) is: (*a*) an awareness that the developing process, once it becomes a fact, will be of importance for a future and will introduce some causal relations into that future; (*b*) an awareness of various possibilities for these causal relations, so that there is room for a set of suppositions. The anticipation has the same actuality in a process as the immanence of the past. Without the awareness of a future there would be no driving force urging the process to its conclusion, and thus no real functioning.

The following point must be noted: *No two processes can fully have the same past;* and *no two processes have fully the same future.* Given any pair of processes, one can point out elements, in each of the two processes, which have no meaning for the constitution of the other process.[27]

§ 23.

Between coexistent processes there can be a *coordinative relationship*. This relationship is of indirect nature. It must be deduced either from the circumstance that there are common elements in the pasts of the two processes considered (in other words, the processes must have some elements of experience in common) or from the circumstance that the processes can be experienced together in certain future processes.

When a certain process has a dominating experience of some type of order, expressed by a group of processes in its past (the possibility of such dominating experience has been pointed out in § 16), it must be assumed that *an anticipation of the transmission of that order to all processes arising from that past will be active in the conception of that process*. This means that in the conception of that process there will be *an awareness of a coexistent world* in which this order finds expression.

It is in this way that the "coexistent world" can have a meaning in a conception, although the coexistent world is not itself a part of the experience out of which the conception has arisen. The coexistent world appears as *an extrapolation from the past*. It figures as the passive carrier of certain relations and qualities. The laws of physics are such relations, and temporal and spatial relationship represent two examples.[28] There is no causal dependence upon the coexistent world. This is a ground for freedom, that is, for the autonomy of each new conception: what happens somewhere does not immediately introduce conditions for all other processes.[29]

§ 24.

A *"complex"* or a *"nexus"* of processes is a collection of processes which exert a common function in the conception of some process arising from an experience of which these processes form a part. The complex is experienced as a group, or rather as a unit (compare again § 16). The way in which the processes enter into the group can be considered as a synthesis, a juxtaposition: the group can always be analyzed into separate elements (separate facts or groups of facts).[30]

The notion of complexes of processes is a feature entering into the integration discussed in § 13. Complexes function as objective data for certain prehensions.

§ 25.

Two particular types of complexes are as follows:

(*a*) *Purely Progressive Complexes*: any two processes of such a complex exhibit the relation of past and future. In such a complex there is a single line of genetic relationship and thus a single serial order. Coexistent processes are completely lacking in the complex.

(*b*) *Purely Coordinative Complexes*: these are defined by the condition that no two processes of the complex are in genetic relationship so that all processes are coexistent with reference to one another.

Many other types of complexes can be imagined.

§ 26.

Two processes which are genetically related will be called *contiguous* when there are no processes which follow upon one of them (that is, which are in the future of this process) and which at the same time precede the other process (form a part of the past of the other process).

A purely progressive complex of processes, as defined in the preceding section, will be called *uninterrupted* if each process of the complex is contiguous to a preceding process as well as to a following process (with the exception that the first and the last process of the complex are contiguous each on one side only, the first one on the side of the future and the last one on the side of the past). This definition implies that in a purely progressive complex there is an un-ambiguous serial order, as mentioned in § 25.

Two coexistent processes, for example "A" and "B," can be called contiguous when it is impossible to find a process which is coexistent with both "A" and "B" and at the same time has a past embracing all processes common to the past of "A" and the past of "B." Contiguity in coordinative respect thus can be defined only in an indirect way by means of a reference to the past. This is an example of the statement made in § 23 concerning relations in the coexistent world.[31]

3

SOCIETIES OF PROCESSES

§ 27.

Thus far we have mainly considered the individual processes which represent the basic steps in the development of the universe. We now turn attention to the way in which conceptions can gain dominant influence. This occurs through the cooperative efforts which are found in a particular type of complexes of processes, to be called societies of processes.[32]

A *society of processes* is a complex of processes (compare § 24) satisfying the following conditions:

(*a*) There is present a particular feature (or group of features) having significance in the conceptions of all processes of the complex.

(*b*) The common feature appears in consequence of the experience which each process has of the other processes in the complex (in so far as those processes precede the one under consideration).

(*c*) The reappearance of the feature in each new process of the complex is ascertained by the continuity of subjective form (see § 17) combined with the mutual reinforcement of prehensions resulting from facts of similar character (see § 16).

(*d*) There is a positive prehension of the common feature in the conception of each process of the complex, which prehension also contains an anticipation of its transmission (see § 23, second paragraph).

It follows from these conditions that a society provides a special environment for each of its members, characterized by a *definite element of order*. This element is persistent in consequence of the genetic relations between the members of the society.

A society is the cause of its own persistence. It continually reproduces itself. This can be expressed by saying that a society contains the basis for its persistence within itself.[33] Hence, a society is more than a mere collection of things having some kind of similarity. It follows that the notion of a society is more specific than the mathematical notion of a "class of similar objects." The members of a society belong to a class as a result of the circumstance that their similarity furnishes a condition producing similar characteristics in further members of the society.

The description given in the preceding lines has been intentionally formulated in such a way that it is illustrated by features found in human societies. To make the comparison effective, one must not think primarily of the persons forming a human society but rather of the activities exhibited by the members. A human society serving a particular aim has an existence which need not be connected with the time of life or with the time of membership of the individual persons belonging to it; its objects and its functions are borne by a succession of people, each one taking part in it for a certain period. We have to consider the society as the institution which guarantees the performance of these objects and functions. This analogy between human societies and the more general societies of processes defined earlier may sometimes serve as a guiding line in the following discussion.

Human societies form only a small group in the multitude of societies contained in the universe. All enduring things are societies as long as they endure: atoms, molecules, crystals, radiation fields, and everything that is built up from them.[34] Living beings are societies of much more complex character than atoms or molecules. The existence of societies forms the basis for the laws of physics as well as for all biological phenomena. This will be considered in Chapters 4 and 5. In the present chapter we are concerned only with the general features characterizing societies.

§ 28.

There are no isolated societies.[35] Each society must be seen in connection with its background, formed by a more extensive collection of processes. Experience derived from these processes is prehended likewise in the conceptions of the processes belonging to the society under consideration, but these prehensions will have a character differing from that which is peculiar for the society. They must, nevertheless, satisfy the condition that the experience derived from the background is compatible with the persistence of the society. When the experience derived from the background contains incompatible elements, the possibility arises that conceptions originating from them may cause a deterioration of the society. Whether this shall occur or not is dependent upon the intensity of the prehension of the common characteristic in the conceptions of the members of the society.

A society together with its background, in so far as the background is favorable to the persistence of the society, forms a wider but less specialized society. Extending this notion, we are able to imagine *hierarchies of societies.*

From the point of view of any society the universe can be considered as forming a background in layers of various types of *social order,* the characteristic features of any such order becoming wider and more general when the background is moved further away. The processes of the distant layers of this widened background will have their own characteristic features and may belong to types of order entirely different from that of the society under consideration. But these features are insignificant for the members of this society: as a result of their mutually discordant natures they are weakened and eliminated in the integration which leads to the formation of the conception in each particular process of the society.

§ 29.

Within a society of sufficient extension one may find subordinate complexes of processes which, along with the general features characterizing the society, possess certain features peculiar to the complex alone. In such a case the society exhibits a certain structure. It can then be termed a *compound* or *structured* society.[36]

Some of the subordinate complexes of the compound society may be able to persist amidst the general background without needing the particular type of surroundings presented by the society to which they belong. In such a case the complex itself has the character of a society; it may be called a "subordinate society."

Other complexes within a structured society may lack the property of being able to reproduce themselves. Such complexes cannot exist outside the society of which they are a part, and the society functions as the necessary carrier of these complexes. Such complexes cannot be termed societies.

§ 30.

While a society is determined by a set of essential characteristics, it may also present accidental features which are common to all or most of its members but which may change during the development of the society. Changes of such accidental features may occur for instance, as a consequence of changes in the environment. It follows that a *society has a history* which exhibits the society's reactions to changing circumstances.

Societies can interact with one another. This occurs when processes of a society obtain important experience from the processes not only of that society but also of another society. The influence can but need not be reciprocal. The resulting effect can be small, if only a small group of processes of the society has experience from processes of the other society. The influence, however, can also be far reaching. It is even possible that during a certain period the situation can be better described by saying that there is a "combined" society instead of two separate societies. The "combined" society can have a persistence of long duration, but it may also occur that after a certain period the "combined" society resolves itself again into two (or more) societies. A special case is when two societies reappear with the characteristic features of the original societies before the interaction started. In this case it will not always be possible to consider each of the emerging societies as the "resurrection" of a particular one of the original societies: their sequences of processes may not be prolongations of the original sequences. It is of interest to note that a comparable doctrine holds for the interaction of atoms, electrons, and other elementary particles in physics.[37]

§ 31.

As long as there is no strong interaction between various societies, a society will remain more or less identical with itself. This self-identity is the consequence of the identity of the characteristic features determining the society, and in its turn this identity is a consequence of the mutual immanence of the processes constituting the society. In view of the conceptual autonomy of every process, which is limited by the continuity of subjective form (§ 17) but *which is never lost*, the transmission of the relevant features is never absolutely guaranteed. The identity of a society with itself is therefore never absolute: it is possible for the society to perish.

It is never possible to attain a perfect type of order which would guarantee the unlimited persistence of a particular society. The favorable background will disappear in the long run or will become unfavorable for the persistence of the society. This may be the result of the emergence of new forms of valuation obtaining such an intensity of feeling that they can break through the massive effects of the experience dominating the society. Under such circumstances the society will cease to reproduce its membership and will disappear.

The doctrine of this section is the basis for freedom in the world.

The converse of the disappearance of societies is the *emergence of new societies.* This subject is of importance in connection with the problem of life and will be considered in § 62.

§ 32.

The circumstances that a society has a history, that its character can change, and that the society finally will disappear preclude the possibility of defining the character of the society in an absolute way so long as the society itself persists. It is only when a society has become a thing of the past that one may succeed in formulating a complex of facts representing everything that resulted from the society and containing all its features as unchangeable elements.

The consequence of this doctrine is that we can analyze the history of any collection of occurrences and find definite lines in it only *post factum, by looking backward.* Whosoever speaks of a "historic line" with reference to a society still progressing into the future expresses not a fact but a hope, an expectation, the realization of which is uncertain. One may attempt to influence future events by pointing to such a line, but to say that the society necessarily must follow the line is a form of dogmatism which can stifle genuine development.

So long as the society is in existence, the complex of processes which carries the characteristic features of the society can only be described as far as it is realized at the instant the description is made. Since we accept the doctrine of conceptual autonomy and that of the creative advance of the universe, we must be prepared to recognize that the valuations appearing in the conceptions of new processes can acquire new features in consequence of which the society will change.

Considering human societies once again, we recognize the importance of this doctrine. All societies, including those which we call nations, churches, and all social institutions must develop: none of them can be restricted to one particular pattern.

§ 33.

A society which is formed by an uninterrupted purely progressive complex of processes (as defined in §§ 25 and 26) at each instance of its existence is a society with *personal order*.[38] Personal order has a meaning in consequence of the subjective form in which it is prehended in the conceptions of the processes belonging to the society.

When a society possessing personal order is considered as a datum for the experience of other processes, it will be termed a *persistent object*. A society of more general character often can be analyzed into a number of persistent objects. Such societies will be called *corpuscular societies* (the name will be applied even when there is only one persistent object). All persistent things found in nature must be considered as corpuscular societies, which may be either simple or complex.

A purely coordinative complex of processes (as defined in § 25, subsection *b*) can never form a society since a complex of this type does not exhibit the genetic relationship. A coordinative complex, however, can be a part of a society.

§ 34. *Societies as carriers of extensive causal relationship*

At the end of § 17 it was stated that the primary ground for causal relationship in the universe is contained in the doctrine that each process arises out of the experience of past facts. The particular way in which this relationship comes to effect is influenced by the continuity of subjective form.

From the definition of a society it follows that, so long as it exists, a society imposes certain conditions on its members in consequence of the mutual reinforcement of prehensions resulting from a large number of facts of similar nature. *These conditions determine an intensified causal relationship reigning within that society.* The causal relationship which is meant here can be considered as a transmission of experience with a definite subjective form, reinforced by the dominant character of experience in that society. The causal relationship which becomes effective within a society is thus an intensification of the primary relationship between single processes. It will therefore be termed *"social causality."*

The laws of physics, which express features concerning the behavior of persistent objects (atoms, electrons, matter built up from them, light waves, etc.), describe properties exhibited by societies of processes. Hence *physical causality is a form of social causality.*

It is of interest to note that the introduction of the notion of social causality points to a certain similarity between the notion of "laws of nature" and the notion of laws in a human society: in both types of laws the effectiveness of the law results from the positive awareness of the existence of a society within which the law holds, which awareness appears in each conception arising in the society.

§ 35.

Since the persistence of each society is limited, it follows that the type of social causality characteristic for the society (in other words, the laws reigning in that society) will have only a limited persistence. This must hold for the laws of nature in the same way as for laws of human societies although the persistence of what we call laws of nature will be far longer. It also follows that the laws of nature as recognized at present have features which were derived from some history. In so far as the previous history is unknown to us these features may be termed accidental.

The presence of accidental features makes us aware that we find ourselves in a particular "cosmic epoch," this term being used to indicate the most extensive society whose features have direct importance for us. Our epoch must be considered as the society which ensures the validity of the laws formulated in physical theory, e.g., the three-dimensionality of space, the measurability of space and time, the theory of relativity, quantum theory, etc.[39]

The reader should not feel disturbed that fundamental laws of physics are ascribed here to a particular cosmic epoch. One should not be dogmatic about those relations which we suppose to be "laws of nature." It must be kept in mind that our "laws of physics" are relations formulated in human terms, conceived by us upon the basis of a discussion of observational data, guided at the same time by a sense of harmony which appears to be innate in us. On many occasions, however, we have found that new observations and new conceptions of harmony induce us to change former concepts and to state new types of relationship. Several principles of physics once considered as fundamental were later rejected or altered in major features.

Astronomical observation combined with the analysis of various physical data has led to the idea that on the present physical time scale there apparently was a "beginning" of the world at an epoch some 20,000 million years ago. This means that our present description of the stellar universe and its development, as summarized in the laws of physics now in use, does not hold beyond a certain limit in the past. This is equivalent to saying that the present laws of physics do not hold beyond that limit. A new form must be sought which will give a meaning to the words "before that limit," which now seem to be senseless. The new form must be more general than our present formulations and should enable us to see the laws known at present as a specialization of the more general scheme.

This is simply a restatement of what has been said above concerning a possible change of the laws of physics. We merely have pointed out that the change may affect even such features as the three-dimensionality of space or the measurability of space and time. Changes of this nature would be far-reaching, but in themselves they are not more strange than the introduction of "antimatter." With each such change we extend the picture we construct of the universe, and each change makes us understand that the present picture was of limited application only. In this way the philosophy developed here interprets and expands the old dictum *"panta rhei, ouden menei"*: all things change, nothing is permanent.

In Chapter 2 we have assumed that the relations of arrangement, formulated in §§ 20 and 21, are more fundamental than the present laws of physics, but the possibility cannot be excluded that even the relations formulated there might change.

§ 36. *The doctrine of evolution*

The realization of values in a conception becomes more rich and the satisfaction attained more intense when the conception has at its disposition prehensions of certain forms of order already recognized in the experienced data. This is an obvious generalization of what we observe in the conceptions arising in the human mind. The required prehensions can be obtained if the process in which the conception arises belongs to a structured society.

We therefore amplify the picture of the universe as a never ending complex of processes by adding the following doctrine: *The creative urge in the universe promotes the emergence of structured societies of manifold types and of great complexity in order to reach more intense satisfactions.*

This doctrine is the ground for evolution in the world of which we are a part. Hence we state: *Values are realized in the universe by the grouping of processes into societies and of societies into more extensive societies of elaborate structure. These societies must have a certain persistence and possess a sufficient measure of stability against changes of their environment since otherwise the values would be lost with each such change. There will never be an end to the emergence of new societies.*

In so far as we see the emergence of a society as the result of an urge to realize certain values, we can say that the creative advance of the universe sets itself certain aims. The word "aim" is used here in a restricted sense (one may say "in a local sense"): it means an aim conceived at a certain instant and considered as important in a certain period of activity; it does not mean an aim directed at eternity.

It should be remembered that absolute stability can never be attained. Neither are there valuations or aims which can hold forever. There is no absolute continuity of subjective form, and there is always room for new initiative.

§ 37.

We summarize the preceding considerations as follows.

The creative urge active in the universe leads to the formation of persistent points of support in order not to lose itself in chaotic variability. Persistence is obtained by a recurrent repetition of certain patterns. The repetition is made possible by the continuity of the subjective form of each new process, a continuity which is reinforced by the mutual immanence of processes which together form a society. Thus the creative advance of the universe has two poles: initiative and repetition.

Patterns of repetition or rhythms can persist independently of the initiative which brought them into existence. Once established they obtain the character of a *tradition* and become carriers of causal relationship. The amount of conceptual work needed for the repetition in each successive period becomes vanishingly small. We shall denote the carriers of causal relationship as *"material apparatus"* or simply as "matter." The term "matter" is used here intentionally in a much wider sense than usual: it embraces everything that is a carrier of traditions.

When the traditions are sufficiently persistent, the behavior of matter can be described on the basis of an analysis of the relations found in the strands of facts which are the results of processes belonging to the societies ensuring the repetitive patterns. It follows that this behavior can be described in the form of objective laws.

Patterns of repetition are never absolute; they will deteriorate and perish. They can always be interrupted by the emergence of new patterns of repetition, that is, by the creation of new forms of matter.

In the world known to us two types of societies stand out conspicuously: those which primarily are carriers of traditions and sometimes retain these traditions without change for billions of years; and societies which carry life in which new initiatives occur repeatedly. We shall discuss these types in Chapters 4 and 5.[40]

4

MATTER

§ 38.

In the preceding chapters a picture has been set forth of our basic assumptions concerning the functioning of the universe. This has provided us with a canvas against which we can project particular aspects of the world surrounding us. In the present chapter we start with *matter.*

That societies of processes can possess a very high degree of stability is a well recognized fact. The stability must be the result of massive unified objectifications of complexes of experiences, in which the differences between the individual members of each complex are eliminated. The elimination of unwelcome detail occurs through the mutual reinforcement of prehensions of what is analogous in the experiences.

Repeating earlier considerations, we state that the following conditions must be fulfilled in order to arrive at a society of stable character: (a) the experiences which a process derives from several processes in its past must be prehended with the same conceptual form; (b) in some phase of the integration leading to the satisfaction of the conception the manifold data must be prehended as a single datum. Their totality is interpreted as a new entity; it is objectified and acquires a status typical of a physical law.

Since all forms of matter which are considered in physics and related sciences appear to be subjected to a system of interconnected laws of high persistence, we conclude: *In matter we have before us the historic routes of societies which are focused on persistence as a result of a high degree of conformity between the processes belonging to these societies.*

This confirms the doctrines stated in §§ 16, 17, 27, and 34. It also gives an answer to the question raised in § 4: how far the regularities observed in the physical world are compatible with the doctrine that in each process experience is clad in a form peculiar to that process and to no other process. The answer is that in massive societies the peculiarity, although present in principle, can be reduced to almost nothing.

§ 39. *Inorganic (nonliving) matter is the carrier of causal relationship*

In stating this doctrine we do not restrict the term matter to those physical objects which possess mass, e.g., protons, electrons, and what is built up from them; but we include electromagnetic fields, wave motions, photons, etc., that is, all things which are studied in physics and are characterized by a measurable (and often very high) degree of persistence. For our present purpose there is no point in distinguishing between "matter" and "field."

As mentioned in the preceding chapter, we may find it useful to take the term matter in a still wider sense so that we can include in it everything that is transmitted by tradition, e.g., human societies, nations, churches, etc., and also every form of tradition in the more restricted sense of the word. The term "matter" thus will include all that which forms the material apparatus of life. Quite generally we can say: *Matter is a habit, is any form of habit.* However, in the present chapter this extension of the term matter is not needed, and we restrict the discussion to matter in the sense of physics, including both fields and particles whether with or without mass.

§ 40.

Matter is everything that is reproduced during long periods. To repeat once more: protons, electrons, atoms, molecules, light waves, etc. are entities which represent the historic routes of certain societies, each society containing many processes of more elementary character united by a certain pattern of order.

In none of these cases is persistence eternal. *It cannot be said that matter "is"* if the verb "to be" is intended in an absolute sense to indicate a fundamental category. In the philosophy presented here all "being" (for which we prefer to use the term "existing") is derived from ever new becoming which binds it to the progress of the universe and limits it at the same time.

To look at the concept of matter from this point of view is of fundamental importance for many aspects of our thinking. In the present picture matter has ceased to represent something static since it is conceived as the historic route of a chain of processes which repeat a certain pattern very many times. When this insight is gained, matter as such loses much of its refractoriness, and it will be recognized that the antithesis between matter and mind, which has haunted large parts of human thinking, has lost its seemingly irreconcilable character.[41]

There are forms of matter which can persist for thousands of millions of years: atoms, crystals, rocks, stars, for instance. In contrast with atoms molecules are societies which are stable only in particular types of surroundings; when the environment of a molecule changes, the molecule can be decomposed or taken up in a new compound. Modern research has acquainted us with forms of matter presenting very short life times, as exhibited by some types of the "new particles." It can be expected that no particle or wave system will persist forever as such, and the concept of matter as the historic route of a pattern of processes makes it acceptable that matter can be created and that it can be annihilated. Such happenings will have their roots in other happenings: there is no creation from nothing nor disappearance into nothing. In several cases it has been found that conservation laws which apply to such happenings can be formulated.

§ *41.*

We shall review some of the results of modern physics and discuss how far they fit in with the philosophical scheme developed. Our main points will refer (*a*) to quantum theory, (*b*) to phenomena of dispersion, (*c*) to the appearance of order in nature. We shall not enter into either the newest results or the latest problems of physics and thus omit the new particles, the concepts of anti-matter, strangeness, parity, etc.

As is well known, atoms are described by a pattern of motions manifest in their electronic structure as well as within the atomic nucleus. The particle picture has been supplemented by a wave picture, and it is understood that both pictures are needed to describe the various aspects of the phenomena which physicists, for convenience, call an "atom" or an "electron," etc. Neither picture is fully adequate in itself. These ideas support the assumption that the properties of elementary forms of matter are dependent upon the unceasing repetition of certain patterns of motion. However, we cannot consider periods of oscillation, of orbital motion of electrons, or of wave motions of light as equivalent to a succession of individual processes. We postpone until § 56 the question whether and where we may recognize individual processes in the sense of our philosophic picture. First it is necessary to attain some general insight into the description of physical phenomena given by quantum theory.

Quantum theory can be considered as a systematic elaboration of the idea of stages in the development of a system. It is the mathematical formulation of a principle of discreteness in both the temporal and the spatial aspects. Quantum relations determine the rhythms in time as well as the spatial dimensions of atomic systems.[42] Pauli's principle, for instance, which asserts that two electrons never can be in the same quantum state, furnishes the ground for the ultimate impenetrability of atoms and sets a limit to the smallest distances between them. Other principles in quantum theory, considered in the theory of field quantization, provide the basis for the fact that one can work with separate "particles" of identical properties in such a way that no fractions of particles will appear in the descriptions and calculations.

The mathematical formulation of the theory cannot be rendered in simple words. In the usual presentation it is connected with the theory of eigensolutions and eigenvalues of linear partial differential equations, in many cases of great complexity. The simplest analogy is found in the theory which accounts for the fact that a string stretched between fixed endpoints can vibrate in a series of definite forms, the first one giving the ground mode, the second one the octave, the third one the perfect fifth above the octave, and so on. Thus the theory imparts a fundamental role to integral numbers in nature. It is therefore also the foundation for the appearance of geometric patterns in crystals and for the structure of matter in general.

§ 42.

Quantum theory has further introduced a dualism between two complementary aspects in the behavior of atomic systems, which one in a certain sense may call the "subjective" and "objective" aspects of any happening.

The *"subjective"* aspect is then described by the development of an abstract mathematical function, introduced in order to arrive at an algorithm for the calculation of the potentialities for future happenings. We come back to this function in § 46.

The *"objective"* aspect of a physical phenomenon is the result which can be observed in the outcome of an experiment. Again there is a point of contact with the philosophy presented here: to obtain factual information about atomic systems it is necessary that these systems be subjected to interaction with something else.

All statements that can be made about the behavior of a physical entity are based upon the outcome of experiments. The performance of an experiment requires that the phenomenon under consideration, for instance, certain aspects of the society of processes which features an electron, be brought into connection with other societies of processes featuring a material apparatus, which we may term an "observational apparatus." The society of processes featuring this apparatus must be of sufficent complexity to be a carrier of relations referring to time, space, and other physical entities that may interest us in the experiment. A result can only be obtained when some process, which combines experience derived from the processes featuring the electron with experience from the processes featuring the apparatus, reaches its satisfaction and becomes a fact. In certain circumstances the fact may induce us to say, "an electron was found within this region of space between such and such limits of time"; in other circumstances it may induce us to say, "somewhere there was an electron having a certain velocity"; or it may be that the result refers to the charge of the electron, etc. We add that the terms used here, such as "electron," "to be found at some place," "velocity," "charge," are no more than pictures in the guide books which physicists have made to trace roads between results of observations and their applications.

Physical observation thus always gives the results of processes which have passed into facts, that is, which have been brought to completion. Here we see the individualization which pervades all our knowledge about physical phenomena. Physical observation never shows us the interior (subjective) development of any process: the subjective aspects remain completely out of sight.[43]

§ 43.

The necessity of introducing physical contact between the phenomenon to be observed and some physical apparatus in order to perform an observation has the consequence that an influence is exerted upon the society of processes featuring the phenomenon. In other words: *Each observation produces a disturbance in the object under observation.* The influence may be small if the phenomenon is featured by a society of processes of sufficiently large dimensions to make it relatively insensitive, but in the case where the phenomenon observed refers to objects of atomic dimensions the disturbance cannot be made small in comparison with the data we wish to obtain. This makes it impossible to find the magnitude of the disturbance: it is uncontrollable. Indeed, to find the magnitude of the disturbance it would be necessary to carry out some measurement before the experiment and another one after the experiment; however, both additional measurements would themselves be observations producing uncontrollable perturbations. Hence no exact comparison between the situation "before" and the situation "after" is ever possible.

§ 44.

Physical investigation has led to the formulation of two important laws governing these perturbations.

In the first place there is a mathematical complementarity or duality. Most physical entities which can be observed and measured (the so-called observables) can be grouped into pairs of such nature that measurement of one member of the pair produces an uncontrollable change in the other member of the pair. Such pairs are, for instance, position on a coordinate scale and momentum (for a simple particle this is the product of mass into velocity), angular position and angular momentum, energy and instant of time. The members of these pairs are related to each other by formulas derived from the so-called Hamiltonian function, a mathematical expression connected with the energy involved in the situation. Although experiments are possible in which various observables are measured at the same time, it is never possible to measure two "complementary" observables simultaneously in a single experiment with exactness.

When a certain measurement is repeated many times, starting always from a similar initial situation, the value obtained for any particular observable will usually present some fluctuation, showing that there is some uncertainty as regards its value. The second point recognized through physical investigation is that the product of the uncertainties in the values of two complementary observables can never decrease below a definite minimum, given by a constant of nature called "*Planck's constant.*" For instance, when the experiment is set up so that the value of one member of the pair can be obtained with great precision (meaning that practically the same value appears in numerous repeated experiments), there is no limit to the magnitude of the disturbance and hence of the uncertainty produced in the other member of the pair. In some cases one can devise experiments which will give both members of the pair with margins of uncertainty of about the same order of magnitude, but the rule about the product of the uncertainties will always hold. The mathematical expression of this relation is called "*Heisenberg's principle of uncertainty.*"

In these two points physical investigation has led to results conformable with but at the same time far more definite than those reached in our general considerations about systems of processes and the experience which one process can have of another one.

The existence of a limit for the accuracy which can be reached in physical observation has the consequence that situations differing by less than this limit *cannot be distinguished by physical means.* This again is a statement about the fundamental individualization: there are limitations in nature, determined by the relations formulated in quantum theory, which must be exceeded in order that we can arrive at a situation which is distinguishable from a neighboring situation.

§ 45.

There is a further consequence to the result that each observation disturbs the phenomenon observed, viz., *there is an unpredictable element in the outcome of every experiment.* As mentioned in the preceding section, if an experiment is repeated a number of times, starting each time from as similar an initial situation as possible, we can never be certain that we really have the same initial situation. Every step taken in the preparation of the initial state, for instance, in order to give a certain value to one of the observables, is of the nature of an observation and produces an uncontrollable disturbance in the complementary variable. Hence, all our initial states contain unknown quantities in their make-up.

Thus, we are compelled to say that every objectification of an elementary happening, that is, every method which brings it to an observed fact describable in terms of space and time and other physical entities, introduces features for which we cannot give a causal ground. It introduces an element of *non-causality*. The result is that physical investigation never can give a complete answer to the question: "Why is the outcome of this instance of this happening just so?" To account for a number of aspects of the happening we must accept the term "random chance."

In other words, the results which are given by physical observation can never be brought into a completely deterministic scheme. It is not possible to predict exactly what will happen in any experiment even upon the basis of the most complete data which physical observation can provide about the state of the system prior to the experiment.[44]

§ 46.

What we may call the "subjective aspect" of an atomic system is represented in quantum theory by the development in time of a particular mathematical function, called the "wave function" or "probability amplitude." It does not in itself constitute an observable quantity, but it can provide the following information:

1. It can take the form of a member of a set of functions which are connected with the mathematical equation characteristic of the effect of the interaction of the atomic system with some piece of apparatus. These functions are called the

"eigenfunctions" of the observable which is measured in an experiment performed upon the system with this apparatus. In general each observable has its own set of eigenfunctions. The equation also determines the various values which can be obtained for the observable in that experiment; these values are called the "*eigenvalues*" of the observable, and in general there corresponds an eigenvalue to each eigenfunction. With certain observables, such as, for instance, position on a coordinate scale in unbounded space or momentum in unbounded space, all values are possible; the scale of eigenvalues is then the continuous system of all numbers, integers and nonintegers. With other observables, e.g., with the energy of an atomic system in a stationary state, there may be a discrete set of eigenvalues that can appear as the outcome of an experiment; values other than these cannot appear. There are even certain observables of abstract nature, such as the "spin" of an electron, which can have only two values, for example (in a certain system of units), either $\frac{1}{2}$ or $-\frac{1}{2}$.

2. While it is not possible to predict beforehand which one of the various eigenvalues will be obtained from a particular experiment, the wave function can give the means to calculate the *statistical frequencies* with which the various eigenvalues will appear in a series of many experiments all starting from as similar an initial situation as possible. Thus, while there is indeterminacy in the individual results (cf. § 45), there exist statistical laws which can be calculated from the data we have about the wave function, giving information concerning the average outcome of a large number of identical experiments.[45]

§ 47.

We recapitulate the conclusions reached in physical theory concerning the behavior of atomic systems and compare them again with some of the doctrines developed in Chapters 1 through 3. This gives an opportunity to bring forward some further features.

We have seen that in the conception active in each process there are aspects which are peculiar to *that* process and not to other processes. A process expresses its reaction to experience in certain forms of definiteness characteristic for that process. We can say: "A process projects its experience against a set of forms of definiteness characteristic for that process" (evidently, the forms of definiteness of a process may be vague, but this is of no concern here).

The "objects" of physical observation are constituted by societies of processes strongly dominated by traditions which give persistence to them. An observation of an "object" requires interaction between the society of processes carrying this object and another society carrying the observational apparatus. The interaction itself is a set of processes emerging from the contact between the two societies which influences both the object and the apparatus. Its effect upon the apparatus marks the feature which the observer considers as the result of the observation (say, a spot on a photographic plate). As to its influence upon the object we say that the observation "projects the object against a reference system" determined by the observational arrangement. This notion of a projection upon a reference system can be applied to any kind of observation, even in realms other than physics. The projection gives a new "state" to the object, the "state" which is the result of the interaction that has taken place. In certain cases the interaction can be very weak with little influence upon the "state," but in such a case it may be that the information gained from the observation is correspondingly small. When observations are made sharper and more comprehensive by increasing the interaction in order to attain greater definiteness, care must be taken that the object shall not be destroyed (a possibility which is not to be excluded) and that there is continuity in the character of the society carrying the object beyond the observation. Consequently, it is understandable that there exists a limit to the sharpness which can be reached. On the other hand, there is no limit to unsharpness and lack of precision when only a vague observation is made.

The interaction occurring in the observational process(es) cannot be fully predicted from the results of previous observations since it involves a certain amount of subjectivity in these processes. This has the consequence that it usually is impossible to predict beforehand which precise projection will appear, and that at most a statistical prediction can be made concerning the frequencies of the various possible results. Thus, the idea that physical observations primarily lead to statistical data concerning the behavior of "objects" is a natural outcome of our picture. Exact fulfillment of the statistical rules at the same time indicates that the societies of processes which we are studying have lost every trace of initiative in conceptual activity and are "nonliving." If more than one observation is carried out upon a persistent object, the order of the observations is of importance, since observations which are penetrating enough to give meaningful results influence the state of the object to a nonnegligible degree and consequently interfere with one another's results. Hence, we must say that physically meaningful observations in general do not form a commuting set.

In the case of certain observations carried out on particular classes of objects such as are studied in physics it is possible to devise a "complementary" observation which directs attention to the nature and the intensity of the interaction. It is not possible, however, to arrange a single observation which simultaneously gives the result of the original observation and that of the complementary observation with arbitrary sharpness for both. It has been found that the product of the uncertainties of the two results cannot be made smaller than a certain minimum value; this outcome must be accepted as indicating a characteristic feature of the universe in the present epoch. The possibility of such complementary observations is the basis for the fact (mentioned in § 44) that many physical observables can be paired into canonically conjugated sets and that two conjugated observables can never be measured precisely in a single observation. When an observation is arranged so as to give one of them with great precision, it produces an uncontrollable perturbation in the conjugated observable.

When the result of the observation has a quantitative aspect, the resulting quantity is termed an eigenvalue connected with the observational procedure and its reference system; as mentioned in § 46, the commonly used expression is *"an eigenvalue of the observable"* measured in this procedure. Each reference system (and thus each observable) has a certain set of eigenvalues; their number can be finite or infinite, and also a continuous range of eigenvalues is possible. As noted already, the observation produces one of the eigenvalues according to some statistical rule.

In the case of observations of sufficient precision and completeness carried out on those classes of objects to which physics gives attention, the hypothesis is introduced that each reference system can be compared with a generalized coordinate system in what is called a (multidimensional) Hilbert space and that a particular mathematical function corresponds to each "axis" of such a generalized coordinate system. Each generalized coordinate system, that is, each reference system and thus each type of observation, has its own set of functions, the eigenfunctions of the observation or, as usually said, the "eigenfunctions of the observable." To define these functions, a mathematical equation is adjoined to each observable (as was mentioned in § 46); this equation makes it possible to calculate the eigenfunctions and the corresponding eigenvalues. In general the eigenfunctions are complex functions; the eigenvalues are real numbers.

When the result of an observation is a particular eigenvalue, this eigenvalue characterizes a particular axis of the reference system connected with the observation and determines the corresponding eigenfunction. It is then said that the observation has projected the observed system upon that axis, and the corresponding eigenfunction is taken as the "wave function" or "probability amplitude" characteristic of the state of the object immediately after the observation. This extends what has been said in § 46, subsection 1. An imme-

74

diate repetition of the same observation does not change this state and again gives the eigenvalue belonging to that state. Another observation, however, projects the object upon an eigenfunction belonging to a different set of eigenfunctions, viz., upon a member of the set of eigenfunctions belonging to that other observation.

The mathematical theory introduces linear relations between the sets of eigenfunctions for different reference systems. It is assumed that the coefficients occurring in these relations give information concerning the probability that an object projected by an observation A upon one of A's eigenfunctions shall be projected by a subsequent observation B upon a definite member of B's set of eigenfunctions. Comparison of calculated probabilities with observed probabilities provides a check upon the correctness of the theory.

In this way it is possible to arrive at some of the principles of quantum theory directly from observational results, interpreting them in the light of our philosophy. Several rules then acquire a more natural aspect than when the theory is derived from the classical equations of physics by means of certain substitutions. So far the discussion here does not provide information concerning the "dynamical" problem which refers to the development of the state of an object and its wave function during the interval when it is not subjected to deliberate observation, an interval in which it still can have interaction with other (specified or nonspecified) objects or can change as a result of internal effects in the society of processes which carries the object. Quantum theory uses the Schrödinger (or an equivalent) equation to describe this development, but the way often followed in textbooks to introduce this equation is rather dogmatic. It would be valuable if a method could be formulated to arrive at such an equation by means of a suitable set of assumptions framed in direct connection with observational results. This might enable us to arrive at an extension of the philosophical scheme which undoubtedly would prove to be of great interest.

It will have been noticed that some of the statements in this section have been given in such a form that they also hold outside the domain of physics. This was done to emphasize their connection with fundamental features of the universe; it is inappropriate to consider them exclusively as results of the mathematical formalism of quantum theory. The recognition that the precision of observations is limited by effects of complementary uncertainty is of importance everywhere; from a human point of view it can even be interpreted as the assertion that strong action to settle one aspect of an issue may entail that other aspects of the issue become totally unrecognizable. The mystery of physics is not the uncertainty principle: the wonder is that so much sharpness can be reached in observation from the outside alone.

Finally, it must be observed that those entities which are called "elementary particles" in physics are not simple systems from the point of view of our philosophy. They are highly complicated societies of processes constituted so as to provide appropriate persistence amidst the general background of processes carrying the space-time relations discussed in Chapter 2 (there is no "empty" space in the philosophical picture). Their intricate properties revealed by physical research are a warning that many relations involved in our picture of the universe as a developing complex of processes require highly abstract methods for their description.

§ 48. Macroscopic phenomena

After this discussion of features which are encountered on the atomic scale (often termed the "microscopic" scale), we now turn to some features which appear when physical phenomena are due to the combined result of large numbers of atomic or molecular happenings (phenomena on the "macroscopic" scale).

The important point to be noted here is that the relative spread in the combined results is much smaller than the relative spread in the separate results of the elementary happenings out of which a combined result arises. This is a general feature found in all cases where elementary phenomena are governed by statistical laws; it is not confined to physical phenomena alone. The simplest case occurs when a result is obtained by the addition of a great number of values, each value being given by a phenomenon subjected to fluctuations. When the fluctuations in the elementary phenomena are random in such a way that the fluctuation of each single phenomenon is independent of those of the other phenomena, the fluctuations in the various elementary phenomena will balance one another to a certain and often considerable extent.[46]

Ordinary matter is composed of immensely large numbers of atoms; the number in a gram of water, for instance, is of the order 10^{23} (hydrogen and oxygen atoms together). The consequence of these large numbers is that the fluctuations which quantum theory predicts for the behavior of the individual atoms are usually not observable in the behavior of matter in ordinary experiments. Thus the statistical character of the laws expressing the behavior of atoms is hidden from sight by the massive cooperative effects found in ordinary matter.

In classical physics and mechanics, as developed in the previous century before the advent of quantum theory, it was assumed that the behavior of matter always followed exact laws which left no room for any fundamental uncertainty. The importance of the disturbance brought about in any atomic system by the act of observation was not known. It was supposed that the disturbance due to the observation could be continually diminished by improving the technique of experimentation, and there was no suspicion that a limit might exist such as is now given by Heisenberg's uncertainty principle. It was assumed that exact knowledge could be obtained concerning all relevant data pertaining to any physical system. In connection with the form of the physical and mechanical laws then considered to present a true picture of nature, it was believed that in principle it would always be possible to predict future occurrences completely by starting from a set of data giving the location and the velocities of all particles concerned at the present instant.

The laws of classical mechanics can be applied equally well with increasing time and with decreasing time. Given the present situation, it is also possible to calculate all previous situations. The most striking example of the application of these laws is found in the theory of planetary motion where the precision of observational technique is extremely high and the disturbance produced by looking through a telescope at any planet is completely negligible. It is well known that positions of planets and eclipses of the sun or the moon can be just as precisely calculated for the past as predicted for the future.

The success of the theory in these cases was so impressive that it led to the formulation of the classical law of causality and to the concept of determinism, which together were raised to a fundamental principle of nature that has had great influence in science as well as in other realms of thought. The principle expressed the following notions: (a) that everything has a definite cause (an old philosophical idea); (b) that we can find these causes by studying nature according to the methods of science, that is, with the exclusion of any valuation in terms of good or bad, beautiful or ugly, etc.; (c) that the causes were always found in the past; (d) that the determining initial data for the operation of these causes could be found completely by means of physical observation; and during an important period in the development of classical science it was held that (e) knowledge of the present positions and the present velocities of all the masses in the universe together with the laws governing their interactions (e.g., gravitational attraction) would make it possible to predict completely all future states (and also to find out all previous states) without the need for other data.

From our present point of view we consider this law as an abstraction, an approximation deduced from what can be observed in large scale experiments but losing its sway when we descend to smaller and smaller objects and arrive at atomic systems. As stated, the assumption that absolute causality and determinism would hold on the atomic scale is not supported by experimental evidence.

The large scale causality, which is sufficient for the prediction of the behavior of most of our technical applications, is a secondary and not a fundamental feature. We can express this by denoting it as *statistical causality*. It is a form of social causality, as defined in § 34.

§ 49. Observations on the notion of time

The idea of time as an independent entity emerged in classical mechanics when it was found that a large number of periodic phenomena, including the rotation of the earth about its axis, the oscillations of a pendulum, the rotation of a freely revolving body, the oscillations of a spring, etc., bear constant ratios of great accuracy to one another. This led to Newton's idea of time as progressing uniformly throughout eternity independently of all material phenomena. The construction found its usefulness both in physics and in common life.[47] Nevertheless, it had a meaning only in virtue of the existence of phenomena exhibiting regular periodicity. The notions of a "definite instant of time" and of an "interval of time" lack real content when one deals only with a single event. They cannot even be made precise when one deals with a few events. The localization of some event on a physical time scale requires that this event be brought into relation with the many processes of a reliable periodic system.

The mathematical equations describing the motion of mechanical systems, as given by Newton and elaborated by later scientists, had the peculiarity that they exhibited a complete symmetry between the positive and negative directions of time. Not only could the past be calculated from the present, as mentioned before, but all phenomena could happen equally well in the reverse direction provided that at a certain instant of time all directions of motion were reversed. The equations did not provide any ground for a difference between increasing time and decreasing time, just as there is no ground for a difference between forward and backward, upward and downward, left and right if there is no material system which makes it useful to introduce such distinctions with reference to that system. Many physicists have assumed that this symmetry in time is a basic fact of nature.

The theory of relativity, in the first form which Einstein gave to it (1905), did not destroy the doctrine of symmetry in the direction of time. It did destroy, however, another notion connected with Newton's concept of time as an independent aspect of nature, viz., the notion of *absolute simultaneity*, which was conceived to be present throughout the entire universe independently of material phenomena. Einstein showed that this notion of simultaneity cannot be supported by any possible experiment and that it must be considered as a fiction. Any attempt to define simultaneity with reference to observers at a certain distance from each other involves a margin of uncertainty equal to the time interval needed by light (or electromagnetic waves) to go from one observer to the other or to return from the second to the first observer. For distances on the earth this time interval is very small; if an observer could operate on the sun, the uncertainty relative to the time on earth would be eight minutes; if observers could operate on stars, there would be uncertainties of many years or of centuries. The notion of an undubitable "now" valid here and everywhere at the same time is thus lost.[48]

The development of the more general theory of relativity, known as the theory of gravitation, gives an account of the way in which the structure of space and time in so far as it is amenable to physical measurement is related to the presence of matter. It has also raised problems referring to the structure of the universe as a whole (in so far as it is observable with our instruments) and to the question of whether there may have been a beginning of time. Various mathematical models are under consideration, and thus far there is no *communis opinio* concerning the most satisfactory model.

The idea that there may have been a beginning of time breaks away from the old idea of symmetry in time. Other grounds for abandoning the notion of symmetry in time have been furnished by the development of quantum theory.

Quantum theory moreover has led to the conviction that the idea of an "infinitesimal instant of time" is an abstraction without real basis since the measurement of time, like that of coordinates in space, is subjected to Heisenberg's principle of uncertainty. As indicated in note 10, certain speculations on the behavior of electrically charged particles and the fields produced by them have led to tentative formulations of new concepts concerning physical time. So far no definite opinion has found acceptance. Any progress in this direction evidently will have important philosophical interest.

§ 50. Phenomena of dispersion

We must next give attention to a class of well-known and commonly occurring phenomena which indicate that there are many features in nature *progressing in one direction only.* Such "irreversible" phenomena are, for instance: the *flow of heat,* which always passes from a body of higher temperature to one of lower temperature; the *diffusion of matter* in a mixture where the constituents are not evenly distributed, for this is a process leading to uniformization, ending only when uniform distribution has been attained (occurring, for instance, in solutions and in mixtures of gases); the *internal friction* in a liquid or in a gas, which appears when there are differences in velocity between the various elements of volume and which leads to an equalization of the speed over the whole mass.

These phenomena have in common what we may call dispersion, spreading, mixing, a blurring of the boundaries between domains with different properties, a loss of sharpness, of definiteness. They never "by themselves" occur in the reverse direction: a mixture of gases does not automatically unmix, nor does heat by itself go from a body of lower temperature to one of higher temperature. It is true that this can be obtained by means of special arrangements which an experimenter can set up in his laboratory, but this is a case of human intervention, to which we shall return in § 55.

The mathematical equations by which these processes are described have a form different from the equations of classical mechanics: they are not symmetric with respect to the two directions of time. On the contrary, there appears a difference between time going forward and time going backward. While it is possible to calculate a future state from data specifying any present state (thus following the progress toward greater dispersion, greater uniformization), it is in general not possible to calculate previous states from an arbitrarily given present state. For instance, take a case of diffusion: when the present state shows considerable nonuniformity (for example, one constituent concentrated in a small part of the total volume), calculation forward will show how this constituent will spread through the volume, but calculation backward can lead to impossible results, such as finding negative concentrations at certain places. In such a case we must conclude that the state chosen as a starting point could not have appeared as a natural consequence of some previous state without the interference of circumstances not accounted for in the equations: for instance, it should have been prepared initially by some experimenter.

Since classical physics kept to the Newtonian assumption of symmetry in time and of reversibility of all elementary phenomena, including molecular motions, the observed irreversibility of heat flow, diffusion, and internal friction required a particular explanation. This was sought in the presence of the extremely large number of molecules, each of which behaves regularly but which cannot be observed individually. Nor is it possible to operate upon them individually, so that the notion that all directions of motion could be reversed at some instant, although imaginable, is inapplicable.

When Maxwell and Boltzmann and other physicists developed a method for the mathematical treatment of the behavior of such large assemblies of molecules, they introduced statistical assumptions concerning the probability of certain classes of events (e.g., concerning the frequency of the collisions between the molecules). These statistical assumptions by their very nature entail the character of irreversibility. At times it has been thought that there was some contradiction between the statistical theory and the underlying classical equations; after thoroughgoing analysis it has been recognized that the apparent contradiction was connected with a lack of clarity in definitions regarding initial data, and the origin of the former difficulties has been explained.

It is not necessary for our purpose to go into the details of these investigations, which continued into the twentieth century and which still are the subject of study. However, we must be aware of the fact that all physical happenings on the macroscopic scale (that is, depending upon the collective effect of many happenings on a molecular scale) are subject to a certain degree of dispersion. The dispersion will never automatically decrease. In general it increases with each further step.

There are phenomena in nature which give the impression of an opposite tendency. In reality the contradiction is only apparent, but sometimes extensive analysis is necessary before the true relations come forth. We shall return to this problem in §§ 52 (*Order in anorganic nature*) and 54 (*Apparent individualization in anorganic nature*).

§ 51.

To illustrate some of the features of the statistical theory which has been constructed to explain the general tendency toward dispersion, we consider the following example. Suppose that a certain quantity of a gas (a given number of molecules, which for simplicity we suppose to be all of the same kind) is enclosed in a container of known volume. Assume also that the total kinetic energy (energy of motion) of the system of molecules is given, and that the walls of the container are of such type that they reflect the molecules colliding with them without loss of energy. Then there is no exchange of energy between the gas and either these walls or the further environment. The data, which are the number of molecules, available volume, and total kinetic energy, admit a large number of different positions for the individual molecules and a great variety of different velocities for each molecule. This is expressed by saying that the three "external" data are compatible with a large number of internal *configurations* differing from one another on the molecular scale. To distinguish between "different" configurations, the rule of § 44 must be observed: as stated, there is a limit which must be exceeded before two configurations can be considered as physically different. The precise formulation of the way in which internal configurations are defined and can be counted belongs to quantum theory.[49]

The interplay of the forces between the molecules and their collisions with one another and with the walls of the container have the result that there is an incessant change from one configuration of the system to another configuration. The statistical rules of quantum theory predict that in the long run each configuration compatible with the three external data has the same chance of appearance. Actually the number of possible configurations is so immense that there is not enough time for all of them to appear. Nevertheless, the never ending alternation of configurations leads to the appearance of a state of equilibrium, the properties of which can be calculated by taking an average over all possible configurations, giving the same weight to each of them. For a gas in a given volume as considered here this equilibrium state is that state in which the density of the gas (the average number of molecules per unit volume) and its temperature (determined by the mean kinetic energy of the molecules) have the same values in every element of volume occupied by the gas, while there should nowhere be a mean flow of the gas if the container enclosing it is at rest.

The number of configurations compatible with the equilibrium state for the given external data is a quantity of great importance in physical theory. Although immense, it can be calculated with sufficient precision. Its (Napierian) logarithm multiplied by a certain physical constant (*"Boltzmann's constant"*) is called the *entropy* of the equilibrium state.

One may consider other states of the gas, such as a state in which the density of the gas in one half of the container is larger in a given ratio than the density in the other half, or a state in which the temperature in one part of the volume is different from that in the rest. Such states are also compatible with the external data concerning number of molecules, total volume, and total energy. Each such state again has in itself the possibility of a large number of different internal configurations which can be counted; thus it is possible to assign an entropy to each such state. The total number of internal configurations for such a state, however, is always less than the total number compatible with the equilibrium state. Thus: *The equilibrium state is the state having the largest value of the entropy.* Hence, the fact that the gas reaches an equilibrium state can be described by saying: *The gas assumes the state with the largest value of the entropy.*[50]

What has been described for a simple gas can be extended to systems of more general character, which may contain a variety of substances, liquids, solid bodies, gases, etc. In every case it is possible to define internal configurations and to calculate their number for a state which has been specified in macroscopic terms. In this way the value of the entropy can be determined for every case.

The entropy can be considered, on one hand, as expressing the potentiality of a system to realize itself in various configurations all satisfying the same macroscopic specification. On the other hand, we can say that the entropy is a measure for the coarseness of our macroscopic specification in comparison with the degree of distinguishability of internal configurations theoretically possible on the basis of quantum theory. In other words: *The entropy is a measure for our lack of information concerning the precise internal state of the system.* This relation between entropy and lack of information is widely utilized by authors of studies on information theory. The term "neg-entropy" is sometimes introduced as equivalent with information, as "increase of definiteness."

It is evident that a subjective element is present in the formulation of the notion of entropy, referring to the point of view of the observer who in certain cases can bring more or less definiteness in the macroscopic specification. This does not lead to difficulties in the usual applications of the notion of entropy to ordinary systems treated in thermodynamics. But the concept becomes more elusive when we deal with systems of atomic dimensions. The notion of entropy cannot be applied to a single atom in a fully specified state (or we must say that such an atom has zero entropy). Molecules which consist of long chains of atoms can be subject to various kinds of distortions and wave motions which need not be specified in detail in order to describe the properties of such molecules: then an entropy can be assigned to such a molecule in so far as its precise configuration is not specified, by calculating the number of configurations compatible with the data which are specified. In any case, entropy refers to what is not specified in the state of a system and is left open to random fluctuations, each possible configuration (in the sense of quantum theory) being considered to have the same weight.

§ 52. *Order in anorganic nature*

Having given attention to the phenomena of dispersion and the statistical character of the laws of nature, we must now consider how *order* can arise in inorganic systems. As a conspicuous example we take the phenomenon of *crystallization.*

The order in atomic or molecular arrangement which appears in crystals is the outcome of two fundamental properties of matter: (*a*) the existence of attractive forces which bring atomic nuclei and electrons together to form atoms, and atoms to form molecules and the lattices which are the foundation of crystal structure; (*b*) the existence of minimum distances which prevent too close an approach of the various particles. These minimum distances are guaranteed by repulsive forces coming into play when there is a very close approach; they are connected with Pauli's principle, mentioned in § 41. The attractive forces together with the minimum distances bring the atoms into regular patterns. There is the further circumstance that space has three dimensions; this is an important geometric fact when lattice structures are built up. Together these data determine the manifold symmetry relations possible in crystal lattices.

In the application of these ideas account must be taken of what has been said about maximum entropy in the preceding section. This requires the following consideration. Attractive forces are connected with potential energy. In investigating the various possible configurations in the sense of § 51 one must take into account the distribution of the total energy between kinetic energy (energy of motion) and potential energy connected with the attraction. Two extreme cases may be mentioned, between which there is a long series of intermediate cases. The potential energy has a high value when attracting atoms are far apart from one another. Large distances make possible a great variety of positions, so that we obtain many different configurations because of the various positions of the atoms. The high value of the potential energy, however, leaves only a small amount available as kinetic energy; this reduces the possibility for a large diversity in the velocities of the atoms, so that on this side of the picture there is a decrease in the number of possible configurations. On the other hand, a low value of the potential energy in a system of attracting particles means that many of the particles must have come close together; this forces them into a more or less definite pattern of positions with a greatly reduced possibility for variation in positional configurations. But now energy becomes available as kinetic energy, leading to a large number of configurations on the velocity side of the picture. This holds both for the atoms which have not been brought into a definite pattern and are moving around, and for the atoms which are close together, since the latter can have oscillatory motions in great variety.[51]

Elaborate mathematical calculations are necessary to find which distribution of the energy gives the largest number of possible configurations with regard to both variety in position and variety in speed. It appears that when the total energy is large, the greatest number of configurations and thus the largest value of the entropy is obtained when the atoms or molecules for most of the time are so far apart that the whole system is in a gaseous state. On the other hand, when the total energy is small, the greatest possible number of configurations (much smaller than in the case of large total energy) is obtained by decreasing the potential energy and giving most of the available energy to motions of the atoms.

Thus it follows that when a system of atoms or molecules loses energy (which can be the consequence of transferring energy to surrounding matter or radiating it away in the form of heat and light waves), there is a tendency toward *condensation.* Since loss of energy brings a fall of the temperature of the system, we obtain the result that with decrease of temperature there will occur a transition from the gaseous state to a liquid or to a solid state. An ordered pattern of atoms, as is found in crystallized solid matter, has the lowest potential energy (lower than the less ordered state which is found in a liquid); hence, the crystallized state in general appears when the temperature is decreased more and more.[52]

The conclusion to be derived from the preceding considerations is that order is attained in the atomic system when energy can be disposed of. The order in positions appears together with more dispersion in velocities or with greater dispersion in the configurations of surrounding matter to which energy has been transferred; or it is the result of the emission of energy in the form of radiation which itself is a form of dispersion. *The production of order in nature is always a local phenomenon and is accompanied by increase of configurational variability, that is, by increase of dispersion elsewhere, which more than compensates the local gain in order.*

That such processes can take place is due to the presence around us of large-scale nonuniformities. For instance, the earth receives heat from the sun and radiates energy into the almost empty surrounding space from where radiation practically never will return. Everywhere in the universe there are regions of concentrated matter and concentrated sources of energy amidst empty vastnesses. These facts are in the background of what happens when galaxies are formed or when a solar system is born; it is upon their presence that the panorama of anorganic nature depends. We come back to this point in § 54.

§ 53. *Additional observations on crystallization*

It is convenient to give a wide latitude to the notion of crystallization so that it can embrace not only the formation of solid crystals of the various types found in minerals and in chemical products, but also filamentary and plate-like structures which are observed in colloidal solutions and in substances of high molecular weight (rubber, plastics, etc.). Certain chemical compounds can present "liquid crystals" in which there is a partial ordering of molecules combined with the possibility of sliding alongside one another in certain directions.

Various solid crystals, such as those presented by the minerals quartz, beryl, spodumene, feldspars, mica, and others, can be of large size with dimensions of several meters. Since the basic pattern of these crystals, the so-called elementary cell which is repeated again and again to produce the full lattice, has dimensions of about 10^{-7} cm, we see that the pattern can be repeated in a more or less regularly ordered array for more than a 100 or a 1000 million times.

Closer investigation has revealed that the periodic repetition of the pattern in a crystal is never perfect. There are various kinds of imperfections or "errors" in the structure, such as: empty places, atoms in wrong positions, atoms foreign to the material, and also defects in the succession of the layers out of which the crystal is built up, so-called dislocations. For instance, a lattice plane may end with a sudden edge instead of continuing as it should; in that case the planes on both sides must accommodate themselves beyond the edge in such a way that the normal type of structure is reestablished with one lattice plane less. A structural defect of this type is called an edge dislocation. Another type of defect is the spiral dislocation; this appears when there is a line through the lattice around which the lattice planes are connected in the same way as in a spiral staircase.

These structural defects, which play an important part in many physical properties of crystallized matter,[53] originate by chance as a result of random processes operative during the growth of the crystal. Whether the crystal grows from a melt or from a solution or a vapor, the procedure by which atoms or groups of atoms come together to constitute a regular pattern is influenced by the heat motion in which the atoms partake. The heat motion can interfere with the play of the attractive forces between the atoms. The coming together consequently is subjected to statistical fluctuations, and errors can occur when the energy of the heat motion is of the same order as the differences in potential energy upon which the proper arrangement depends. An atom may have excessive kinetic energy which drives it beyond the proper position so that it arrives in a wrong position; a vacancy may appear in this way, or a row of vacancies, etc.

We have given attention here mainly to the interior or lattice structure of crystals. No less important are their exterior appearances, the individual crystals themselves, which are bounded by plane faces making definite angles with one another and which strike us by the beauty of their forms. The exterior form of a crystal is dependent primarily upon the lattice structure and secondarily upon interaction with the surrounding matter, usually the liquid from which crystallization took place. In particular, so-called surface energy plays

a part, which is dependent upon differences between the inter-
atomic attractive forces of the crystal and the forces acting
between these atoms and the surrounding matter.
Crystals start from nuclei, which can be formed by chance
at various places within the liquid or at points of the walls
containing the liquid. Growth from these nuclei is a matter
of competition which can lead either to the appearance of a
compact crystallized mass or to the formation of separate
crystals. The latter case occurs when the number of nuclei is
small so that they are relatively far apart; a further condition
is that the crystallization must occur slowly. Crystals growing
close together do not grow completely independently: there
can be transfer of matter from one crystal to another depending upon the nature and the size of faces (there can be solution at certain crystal planes and deposition on other planes
or on planes of another crystal). Thus, in the formation of
crystals we sometimes witness a complicated process of mutual adjustment.

§ 54. *Apparent individualization in anorganic nature*

As mentioned in the preceding section, processes of crystallization often lead to the formation of separate crystals.
In this way there is a kind of individualization in nonliving
matter. It is, however, appropriate to speak of *"apparent individualization"* since the separate crystals are not organisms
comparable with the organisms of the living world. It should
be noted that the formation of crystals is a result of attractions between atoms and is characterized by phenomena of
ordering on the atomic (or molecular) scale.

Along with physical processes driven by atomic attractions
there are others, more mechanical in character in so far as
flow phenomena play the main part, that can lead to the
production of local fields of motion or local assemblies of
matter. These fields or assemblies usually do not have sharp
boundaries; nor do they present an ordering descending to the
molecular scale. Nevertheless, they can become sufficiently

conspicuous to stand out against the background and to be recognized as more or less definite entities. As instances we mention the following: waves on the surface of water, wave propagation in gases or in the atmosphere, vortices, which can sometimes be very strong and form whirlpools or tornadoes, atmospheric and oceanic currents, storm fronts, clouds, etc. Outside the solar system we find clouds of interstellar gas; and still further away, galaxies consisting of enormous masses of stars, interstellar gas, and dust.

The motions which lead to the appearance of these formations are themselves called forth by pre-existing large-scale nonuniformities either in cosmic space or more locally in our surroundings on the earth. The peculiar point is that the motions engendered, although subjected to effects of dispersion which in the long run tend to produce uniformity, do not immediately proceed in that direction: very often they initially enhance small inequalities to such an extent that these may develop into well marked individual fields of motion. In a later phase of their history these fields may be broken down again; they may perhaps reappear on a smaller scale and again be broken down; ultimately they will disappear through diffusion or friction, but it is the intermediate history which is significant here. A general term for these phenomena is *"turbulence."* Mathematically their cause is to be found in complicated relations between speed and forces, which cannot be easily explained in mere words (in general they depend upon nonlinear terms in the equations of motion). A related case, which can occur when solid bodies slide over one another, is that of "self-locking" motions in which friction increases to such a degree that further motion becomes impossible.

These phenomena are of the utmost importance in the shaping of the world in which we live. Even the surface of the earth has never been smooth and at rest: continents and oceans, mountain ranges and basins have been formed by tectonic processes; rivers and glaciers have eroded the surface and have transported the debris over immense distances, and new mountains have been formed out of the material of previous mountains. The totality of physical processes in the universe has sometimes been described as the "running down" of an immense store of potential energy originally given in the primeval nonuniformity. The point I am bringing forward is that the breaking down of the stores of potential energy *never has been and never is a smooth running down:* local nonuniformities are enhanced on a variety of scales, and through these local nonuniformities a host of other physical phenomena originate.

The nonuniformities upon the earth, the existence of oceans and continents, of mountain ranges and valleys, the variety of climates, and the constant reshuffling through the ages have had great influence on the evolution of living beings. I am convinced that they also have provided stimuli which played a part in the appearance of life upon the earth. Among the basic features of inorganic nature, along with quantum phenomena, the properties of atoms and molecules, and the general tendency for dispersion, it is the turbulence of nature, the continuous re-formation and reshuffling of nonuniformities before they are ultimately broken down, which has been of decisive importance in providing a cradle for life (see a remark in § 70).

§ 55. *Influence of man's technical achievements*

The preceding sections considered phenomena of ordering occurring in the nonliving world. While the present chapter does not consider life as such, it is nevertheless important to insert a few remarks concerning the production of order by man in the objects surrounding him.

Man can locally change the direction of what we have called "irreversible" phenomena: man can combat dispersion; man can unmix things or species of matter which have been mixed; man can transfer heat from cold bodies to warmer bodies; man can bring heavy masses from a lower to a higher level against the action of gravity; man can produce patterns of order which are not based upon energy relations but are defined by relations conceived by himself.

At this moment it is not our intention to discuss the part played by conceptions and creativity in these processes; on the contrary, we wish to point out that the activities mentioned are very often performed by specially designed apparatus and machinery. Once made, these machines function by themselves,. They even can be designed in such a way that they correct errors. Industry for a large part is based on such machinery.

When machinery is in operation, it follows the laws of physics. Hence, the rules for increase of dispersion stated before still apply. As in the case of crystallization, order is produced *locally* by machinery at the expense of dispersion appearing elsewhere. Taking into account apparatus, product, and environment, thermodynamic description always finds that there is an over-all increase of entropy.

What is important, nevertheless, is that some direction is given to the phenomena. *Man can make entropy decrease in certain spots chosen by him or in certain amounts of matter of particular interest to him, at the expense of entropy increase in waste products which he considers to be uninteresting.*

This can be put into a somewhat different form. All the achievements mentioned, when produced by machinery, have in common that they operate between a store of energy found in nature and a sink of energy present elsewhere in nature. The existence of the nonuniformities in our environment considered in the preceding section provides the necessary background for these processes. Now consider a particular case, for instance, the combustion of oil (itself a product of processes which took place in nature long ago). Oil can be burned at the head of a well and then simply produces transfer of energy from the system "oil + oxygen" to the environment (the atmosphere for the main part in this case) with an immediate enormous increase of entropy. Or the combustion can take place in a more or less guided way within the cylinder of a motor, and the rise of temperature and pressure in the gas resulting from the combustion can be used to drive a piston. The latter can serve to produce motion for some useful purpose, for instance, for the production of electricity. The electricity can be made to pump up water, or it can serve to call forward valuable chemical reactions or unmix isotopes, etc. Although the ultimate increase of entropy cannot be avoided, *the increase of entropy is retarded.* The entropy increase is divided over a certain number of steps, and products with a reduced entropy content are obtained in some of the intermediate steps.

The notion of retardation of entropy increase is equivalent to the notion that man can increase order locally at the expense of more dispersion elsewhere. Most of the things made by man ultimately become dust and are mercilessly subjected to the law of increasing dispersion. But temporarily, be it for hours or be it for centuries, there can be a slowing down of the increase. Retardation of entropy increase is a main feature of the biological aspect of life upon the earth.

§ 56. *The problem of the distinction between successive processes in the history of a physical system*

In § 41 the question was raised whether we can find evidence for the occurrence of individual processes in the development of physical systems of atomic dimensions, the word process being taken in the sense of the philosophy here presented. This is a difficult problem, and it seems as if no unequivocal answer can be given. It is true that in *Process and Reality* Whitehead attempts to give some hints in this direction when he speaks of the origination of "reversions in the mental pole" of a process, which according to him are the basis for the dominating influence of vibration and rhythm in the physical world. But I do not consider these hints satisfactory.[54]

Direct physical observation cannot give evidence for conceptual activity. It is true that there will be conceptual activity when the result of an observation reaches the mind of a human observer and is evaluated by this mind. In such a case we can say that a process has been terminated in the sense of our philosophy, a process which embraced experience derived from the physical system, from the observational apparatus, and from all that which pertained to the activity of the human mind.

Such a reference to human conceptual activity, however, cannot be a final one since it would bring in human activity everywhere, whereas the original question referred to physical systems not influenced by human activity. Moreover, in many cases observations are made by means of apparatus which produce *records* of their interactions with the physical system under observation. These records can be stored away for a long period of time, and their scrutiny by a human mind can be postponed indefinitely. What has happened to the system under observation was a matter between that system and the observational apparatus; human judgment was not involved in the physical interaction. Can we say that this physical interaction terminated a process independently of what may occur later in a human mind? To this question quantum theory replies: One may do so in a certain sense if for "conceptual activity" one substitutes the chance which has led to a selection between the various possible eigenvalues that can be the result of the interaction.

As an example, imagine two physical systems which at first evolve independently of each other. During a certain interval of time, say from t_1 until t_2, they are so close together that some form of interaction takes place. After the instant t_2 the systems separate again, each one carrying with it some results of influences exerted by the other system. According to quantum theory such a case can be treated in two ways. Starting with one of the two systems, one can treat the interaction which it suffers from the other system in the same way as when the second system is considered as an observational apparatus. One must then apply the formalism for observations, as indicated in the rules mentioned in §§ 44 ff. On the other hand, one can consider the combination of the two systems as a single system and follow its subjective course from beginning to end, describing it with a single wave function for its entire history, starting from the period before t_1, continuing through the interval from t_1 until t_2, and finally through the period following t_2.

In comparing the results of these two descriptions, we must keep in mind that the only results that can be checked by experimental observation are predictions concerning the behavior either of the original first system or of the combined system if interaction is arranged with some other apparatus at an instant later than t_2. Without such a further observation nothing can be decided. The theory maintains that the outcome of such a further observation, that is, the eigenvalues which the observation can disclose and the statistical frequency with which these eigenvalues will be obtained, *can be calculated upon the basis of either of the two modes of description*. In both systems of description the outcome of the calculations leads to the same prediction.[55]

In this way we arrive at the conclusion that interactions between physical systems can be considered as terminating a process, if this point of view appears useful in connection with the further context, provided we keep in mind the statistical rules which hold for the type of interaction.

§ 57. *Observational apparatus that can store data*

Before we leave the subject of nonliving matter it is important to introduce one more point of view connected with observation.

In the preceding section we mentioned apparatus which can produce records of their interactions with other physical systems. These other systems were the "systems under observation." Until thus far it was these other systems which held our attention in the discussion: we were interested in their history, and the observations were made in order to have data about the state of these systems.

For future purposes, however, we now propose to *concen-*

trate attention upon the observational apparatus. We assume that the apparatus is so designed that it will collect records of the outcomes of its interactions with other physical systems, interactions occurring either in succession or simultaneously to some degree. We consider the apparatus with its record which is growing in time as the more important item before us and relegate the collection of "systems under observation" to the status of the "environment of the apparatus," an environment with which the apparatus has to cope as it were. The apparatus can be made so that simultaneously with each interaction it records the instant of time at which the result was obtained. An apparatus can even be designed so that it processes its records and produces new records presenting the outcomes of calculations based upon the results of the primary interactions. The apparatus can also make predictions deduced from such calculations and determine its future reactions according to these predictions. Thus the apparatus can become a kind of "robot" that adapts itself to its environment.

In view of the recording and the processing, the apparatus can be thought to be a sufficiently massive piece of machinery so that the processing, etc., will be governed by the laws of classical mechanics and physics in a completely deterministic way. The primary interactions with the environment, however, can be interactions with systems of atomic dimensions, and for our present purpose this is the more interesting case. The primary interactions are then subject to quantum laws, and the outcome of these interactions is not fully predictable. The consequence is that the record and the final outcome of the processing will also present unpredictable features. As an example, one may think of an apparatus to photograph the track of a heavy particle through a gas or some other medium. The result obtained will depend upon the chances for the interactions of the particle with atoms or molecules of the medium, interactions which are governed by the statistical rules of quantum theory. It follows that to a certain extent the ultimate behavior of the robot will also depend upon these chances.

In the next chapter we shall discuss the notions which enter into the concept of life and the features which are characteristic of the behavior of living beings. In § 74 we shall compare a living being to an observational apparatus making records of its interactions with its environment and processing those records. Again the principal interest will be directed toward primary interactions taking place on the atomic scale. Although there is an important analogy, we shall be concerned principally with the point of view that in living organisms there is conceptual activity which on occasion can exert influence upon the outcome of the primary interactions. This constitutes a far-reaching difference between the machine and the living being.

The potentialities of automatic machinery have been expanded so enormously in recent years that in the literature concerning these machines the problem is turning up again and again whether they can be considered as models or substitutes for living organisms. Such an idea is in opposition to the point of view adopted above. Some of the questions which present themselves in this connection will be discussed in the Appendix to Chapter 5.

APPENDIX TO CHAPTER 4

It has been mentioned that the assumption of perpetual validity of the laws of physics is a hypothesis. One may venture beyond this hypothesis and speculate upon a possible history which may lie behind some of these laws. When one enters upon such a course, it is necessary to look for principles which are more fundamental than the physical laws in their present formulation, principles from which the latter may have developed. Attempts in this direction are involved in various theories concerning the origin of the physical universe. Such theories are extrapolations from the mathematical equations which purport to describe the behavior of matter and fields as presently observed. Consequently, they depend upon what is supposed to hold more persistently in distinction from what may be considered as variable. For instance, consideration has been given to the possibility that the so-called constant of gravitation actually may not be a constant but a quantity decreasing with time and related to what is called the age of the universe.

Once we begin this speculation, other questions may turn up. For instance, Planck's constant might be a function of time and perhaps be gradually decreasing. One may also ask: Why is it that all electrons seem to carry the same charge? Can it be that the presently observed uniformity of this charge has a history behind it, and that in a distant past electrons may have carried unequal charges?

In the following lines I will sketch some speculations of this kind to which we are led by the philosophical ideas set forth in the preceding chapters. They will remain tentative and vague, and a source of difficulty is that notions concerning a starting point in a chain of reasoning are often confused with ideas concerning a "beginning" in time. This seems to be unavoidable, but it does not make all speculation useless. Here it will give us an opportunity to discuss some of the ideas embodied in Whitehead's philosophy from a slightly different point of view.

A primary feature which we must assume to be effective in the universe is a tendency for individualization. There must be a property which is at the basis of the fact that "things" manifest themselves more or less as distinguishable entities. "Manifestation" here means to appear as an object that can be experienced. A feature of this nature must have been at the origin of the phenomena which led to the appearance of particles and the quantum laws, two basic and intimately related aspects of the physical world.

"Matter," "forces," "energy" are not considered to be primary features of the universe and are supposed to be secondary (derived) aspects. Among these, energy is the most important notion. We suppose that the existence of "relations involving energy" has resulted from relations between situations which more or less presented a similar pattern. In other words, relations involving energy have arisen from a kind of conformity between situations. It is assumed that conformity has gradually become a physically influential effect. This is an idea which had been advanced in various schools of philosophy. The circumstance that even in modern physics "resonance" between configurations in atomic systems has been found to play an important part in energetical relations may be an indication that some fundamental principle of conformity still can have theoretical interest.

We need a principle which can make effective the ideas of pattern and of similarity versus difference in pattern. For this we introduce an activity which will be called "conceptual."[56] This activity must form the basis for the recognition of similarity in pattern, and it is presented as an ultimate notion which we do not relate to anything more fundamental. One of the reasons for the introduction of this metaphysical notion is that without the assumption of something that can serve as a repository for recognition there can be no feature through which "similar" situations could exert any influence upon one another. In considering the need for this principle it should be noticed that there is an essential incompleteness in current physical theory. In physical theory we are taught (as mentioned earlier) that an electron reacts in one way to an electric force and in quite a different way to a magnetic force. Physics gives us equations expressing the rules governing the two types of behavior, but it does not consider the question what it is that enables an electron to distinguish between an electric and a magnetic force. Although all physical relationship is formulated in such a way that one can handle the equations without insight into the nature of electricity or mass, this does not mean that the question itself is meaningless. Physics disregards the question and consequently must introduce a large number of prescriptions postulated ad hoc.

A certain analogy with the principle just enunciated may be seen in the opening words of the Gospel according to John: "In the beginning was the Word, and the Word was with God, and the Word was God." If we take the "Word" (*logos*) as denoting the medium to create or to conceive and express forms of order, the thought with which the author of these lines is struggling may be the same as the one considered here: the belief that an ordering principle is at the basis of all things, a principle which is not a mere mechanical or physical rule of succession but is something which embodies conceptions and gives sense to all that happens. The words occurring somewhat further in the Gospel text, "all things were made by it," can then be seen as expressing the belief that this principle resides in the functioning of the entire universe and is not a mere static principle. Thus I would read, "In the beginning — meaning, as an ultimate principle which we can reach with our present forms of thinking — there is conceptual activity, and conceptual activity is the essential manifestation of the universe."[57]

Coming back to physics, we repeat that differences of energy and forces derived from energy relations are not primitive features of the universe but have evolved from more fundamental features. They have emerged and have developed.

At the level of the relations considered here there do not yet exist clear notions concerning time, or concerning dimensions in space, or concerning mass. Nevertheless, I would presume that in the possibility of recognizing similarity and its counterpart of recognizing differences of pattern a certain quantity is involved which has a "dimension" in the sense in which this notion is applied in physics. The notion of difference is thus not merely something qualitative but involves an aspect which refers to a scale, so that terms such as "more similar" and "less similar" are applicable. The scale factor should have the dimension of what is called "action" in physics (the product of energy and time). We return to this point later.

As a necessary feature in this train of thought we assume a tendency toward repeated conceptual activity. Once relations of similarity had become effective, they were recognized repeatedly. We postulate that the process of recognition has developed in such a way that it furnished the possibility for successions of decisions as to whether or not situations would conform to certain standard patterns. Conceptual activity must therefore be endowed with some persistence, some continuity of subjective form such as is at the basis of memory. In other words, there must be a continuity of the effects evolving from the recognition of a pattern, leading to a preferential recognition of similar patterns. We shall say that repeated acts of recognition lead to appreciation either of degree of similarity or of degree of contrast.

The possibility of repetition together with some persistence of the effect of each step must be the origin of a time scale, which now appears as a second quantity having a dimension. When this had taken shape, there arose the possibility of a resolution of the basic quantity involved in recognizing differences of pattern into a time factor and another factor. It is the latter factor which must have been essential for the development of energetical relations. The possibility of repetition of similar situations must have afforded a basis for the development of more and more precise energetical relations. Thus two points are involved: the appreciation of a difference between dissimilar situations has given meaning to a difference of energy by isolating a factor of the nature of a time (recognition of differences could become effective in a shorter interval of time if the difference of energy was larger); and the possibility for manifold repetition of acts of recognition introduced a sense of tradition in the magnitudes involved which more and more became subject to standardized conditions.

This must have been the origin of the emergence of laws of physics. The tendency toward repetition is also the origin of matter, and the most appropriate definition of matter is that it presents the historic routes of patterns which repeat themselves with great regularity. Thus physical laws on the one hand and matter as the collection of objects to which the physical laws apply on the other hand have developed together. In the sequences of processes there may have been accidental elements which have resulted in the fixation of the laws of physics. Different results might have evolved from the same metaphysical background. However, we consider a gradual increase of precision and an approach toward fixed laws as necessary and important features.

This assumption entails that the constancy of basic physical quantities, such as the charge and the mass of the electron, Planck's constant, etc., has evolved gradually. Their precision is an achievement resulting from a long history. The uniformity of all electrons, of all protons, etc. is not something which was given once for all at the very beginning of things: it has taken shape only after numerous repetitions. It may be that there still is a secular change or that perhaps there are slight fluctuations in some or in all of these quantities. Their present values were not directly given in the fundamental data of the universe and are more or less fortuitous.

We now add another item to the description of conceptual

activity and postulate that its essence is the formation of a conception based upon data received from past situations integrated with expectations concerning future situations. The notion of "conception of a pattern" can have a sense only if it is related to something else. There must be a basis for comparison, and it seems appropriate to look for this basis in the relation between existing and expected situations. Conceptual activity is the juxtaposition of what has already become and what may become. Emphasis can be more on what has become or more on what may become, but it always must combine elements of both. There is not a passive reaction to data received: the data are grasped or are taken in under aspects of definiteness involving notions concerning that which may become.

As conceptual activity is the attempt to make a unified projection based upon data concerning the past and expectations concerning a future, it never does give us the past "without more" (i.e., "objectively") since it views the past under aspects connected with the future. It can emphasize more and more data of the past by taking more expectations for granted; but there is always the subjective aspect under which the past is viewed and experienced. Neither does it ever give a full set of arbitrary expectations concerning the future since expectations are always bound up with data concerning that which has gone before. This feature must also be basic for the fact that physical observation can never give us all the data on which the development of the universe seems to depend: a physical observation is a projection, and at most it can give definite aspects only to one half of all the features involved. In quantum theory this finds expression in the circumstance that many observable results are determined by the absolute values of certain coefficients which the theory itself must consider as complex variables having dual intrinsic natures.

It has been mentioned that something quantitative is involved in the recognition of differences. With this as basis a limit can be introduced for the difference between two patterns that can be experienced as unequal. Two situations which differ by less than this limit cannot be distinguished and are experienced as identical. There exists, consequently, an unavoidable minimum of indefiniteness which can never be completely eliminated; in other words, there is an ultimate limit to precision in any observation. This limit extends itself over an interval of time as well as over another quantity, for which we have used the term energy. It follows that there is always a brief interval between that which is experienced as past and the future about which expectations arise.

In physical measurements the limit of precision is at the basis of the uncertainty relations; it involves Planck's constant and is often expressed mathematically with the aid of the "commutation equations" for conjugated observables. As suggested before, Planck's constant may have obtained its present value as a result of a long history. It may be appropriate to suppose that originally this quantity has been large and variable, while during the development of the universe, with its ceaseless repetitions, it has become definite and probably at the same time smaller. If it would continue to decrease, this would bring about that in the long run higher precision could be reached in measurements, but at the same time it might bring about a shrinking of the minimum distances between atoms and consequently lead to a decrease in size of all objects built up from them.

We next draw attention to the multiplicity of conceptual activity. There is in the universe not a single instance of activity, not one single act of creation, nor even a single ordered sequence of instances. Instances or, as we have called them before, "processes" occur everywhere. Each instance (each process) has experience from a past in which other instances of activity have taken place, and each has expectations concerning a future in which new processes will arise. We must here refer to the notions discussed in Chapter 2 concerning the forms of coordination in the developing complex of processes.

According to the description given there, each instance (each process) has its own "past," "future," and "coexistent world." We shall not repeat the relevant considerations, but we observe that the introduction of this distinction, as developed in §§ 21 through 23, gives rise to the appearance of a further important quantity, viz., the notion of speed or velocity. This notion arises from the fact that the past of a process becomes wider in extent when we recede further backwards in time, just as the future, considered as a collection of possibilities, becomes wider when we project further forward in time. Speed is a third quantity having a physical dimension along with "action" and "time." Again, the speed involved here originally may not have been a quantity with a definite magnitude but may have had a value peculiar for each process, a value which even may have been dependent upon the direction into the past or future to which the conception is referring. Definiteness and precision in the magnitude of the speed involved in the distinction between "coexistent world" on one hand and "past" or "future" on the other hand may have been a gradual result of endless repetition in certain series of processes, viz., in those which constitute the world of matter together with the physical laws. It may be that here the value has resulted which we now denote as the speed of light (which is that of the propagation of electromagnetic phenomena). It may be that there still are processes for which the distinction between "coexistent world" and "past" or "future" is different from that which holds for the phenomena of matter. This might perhaps involve transmission of effects with an apparent speed much greater than the velocity of light.

Coming back to the material or physical world, we note that once we have three quantities with dimensions (action, time, speed), other quantities with dimensions can be based upon relations between the three fundamental ones. For instance, the notion of "mass" may have arisen from a relation between energy and the square of a speed.

We now stress a further point of the picture. We have stated that conceptual activity is the recognition of patterns and the evaluation of similarity or contrast between patterns. We add that there are infinite possibilities for patterns, and we postulate that continually new relations of similarity and contrast are finding recognition. This postulate will be called the principle of creativity. The principle states that the universe in its evolution did not limit itself to the appreciation of a finite number of relations between patterns, which then gradually became fixed in physical laws: on the contrary, it continues to evolve new relations. Out of these relations, through endless repetitions definite forms of physical relationship have evolved. However, the appreciation of new relations has never stopped. The recognition of new relations has continually initiated new developments which until the instant of their appearance could not have been predicted from the already existing relations. Because of the continually added relations the world is not merely repetitive: there is a never ending emergence of novelty, and in essence each happening is unique.

It will be evident that with these considerations we are giving a new expression to the principle of causality. We have started from conceptual activity, which recognizes and appreciates similarities and contrasts in patterns. The tendency toward repetition, which is a fundamental feature of the universe, has led to the evolution of more or less fixed chains of patterns; this is the basis for the appearance of physical laws and of matter. The regularity of succession in these chains is the basis for a law of causality which looks backward to past situations in order to predict what aspects will be presented by later situations. This is the law of causality accepted in physics; it holds in a very wide but nevertheless limited domain, for it presupposes regularity. There is a complementary side to the picture: the appreciation of new similarities and of new contrasts in patterns. The universe does not stop progressing after certain patterns are established; creativity, meaning the appreciation of new patterns, continues. From this have evolved stress upon expectations concerning future situations and forms of conceptual activity directed toward the promotion of newly appreciated patterns. Thus, along with sequences coming up from the past along more or less definite lines, there has evolved the notion of preparing for a future and of purpose. This embodies another notion of causality. Both aspects of causality essentially go together. The realization of purposes requires attention to the chains which already have been established. On the other hand, no happening in the universe is exclusively governed by relations coming from the past; there is always involved a measure of decision directed toward a future.

In connection with physics the following comment is necessary. We know from physical theory as well as from observation that there remains an essential indeterminacy in the description of sequences of events, which is expressed by the statistical interpretation basic to quantum theory. The acceptance of the statistical interpretation means that in the physical events there is no recognizable bias leading to what we have called "preparation for a future" or purpose. The statistical interpretation accepts this idea through the assumption that all possibilities that are left open have equal weight and make their appearance in a completely random way (as explained before in § 51, this involves the correct distinction of situations or configurations differing from one another, which is possible in connection with the rules expressing the uncertainty relations). As a method of calculation the assumption of equal weight is sufficient, and statistical predictions based upon this rule are the essence of physics.

The realm of physical relations, however, is not the only line of development. There is a line in which purposes have gained ascendancy. There are chains of events in which certain patterns have been realized as a result of a particular bias in preparing for the future, a bias dispelling the equality of weights. This may have occurred first intermittently and on a limited scale as a form of "play". At a further stage a kind of continuity has become effective, leading to play in a more elaborate form and ultimately to the purpose of not letting the play come to a stop. It is here that we must look for the origin of life, as will be discussed in the next chapter (see § 70 in connection with the notion of play). For the essence of life is not repetition and reproduction — these had already appeared earlier. But life is a way for more effective preparation for a future in ever new forms.

When we look back over the discussion presented in this Appendix, we see that we have repeated in a different order much of what was examined in Chapters 1 through 4. The discussion also has suggested the following ideas:

(*a*) At least three definite, dimensioned, physical entities may be connected with Whitehead's picture, although the numerical values of these quantities may once have been variable and different from the values of the corresponding physical quantities at present.

(*b*) Physical laws and the properties of matter have gained their present regularity in the course of a historical process, that is, in the course of time in a distant past when even the time scale itself was not yet fixed.

(*c*) A quantity like Planck's constant may perhaps still be changing and decreasing.[58]

5

LIFE AS COORDINATION OF INITIATIVES

§ 58.

The question "what is life?" haunts many thinkers. Within our usual environment we feel pretty certain that we can distinguish between living beings and nonliving matter. However, when it is attempted to frame a precise definition of life, many difficulties confront us. Various definitions have been proposed by biologists, but on inspection it appears that life has something elusive which escapes description in finite terms. Much weight is given to the stability of life, to the way in which its continuity is guaranteed, and to its reproduction — features which undoubtedly are of great importance. As examples of definitions based upon these features we mention:[59]

"Life is a potentially self-perpetuating open system of linked organic reactions, catalysed stepwise and almost isothermally by complex and specific organic catalysts which are themselves produced by the system."

"Life is a collective term for 'living objects'; and a 'living object' is an object which will absorb substances from some environment and synthesize from them a replication of each of the substances which comprise that object."

Some further definitions are collected in note 60. The features enumerated can be exhibited also by nonliving systems. With the present techniques of automatic machinery it is to be expected that any form of behavior which can be described in a finite set of terms can be reproduced by an appropriately constructed automatic machine or robot.[61] Even the reproduction of robots by robots taking materials from their environment is already conceivable.[62]

What is wrong with such definitions based upon the points of view holding in physics and chemistry is that they do not give us a clue toward the understanding of the emergence of anything really new. It is here that the central problem lies. Several scientists therefore invoke the term *"complexity"* as a carrier of possibilities for the explanation of the peculiar features of life. They intimate that highly complex molecules may have properties which perhaps cannot be inferred from what we know about simpler molecules; they speak about the information content of complex molecules, vaguely surmising that information can be obtained from the environment and that this may lead to the appearance of still more complex systems. However, none of the notions brought forward in these surmises is clearly defined; and when considering the complexity of living beings, it is again their stability and reproduction which are the main issues to be explained.[63]

For complexity other authors substitute *"organization"* and *"organism."* I believe that when the latter term is used, *a borderline is crossed.* The fact that this often is not noticed is a source of confusion. The use of the term "organism" implies the idea that there is effectiveness in being an organism. It suggests that there is a relatedness between the notion of organism as a whole and the parts into which it can be analyzed, which relatedness refers to more than can be expressed by a physical description, however detailed it may be. The word *"more"* as used here is substantiated by the conviction that there is a set of efficient relations connected with the persistence of the organism. But the efficiency of the relations can have a sense only when the persistence of the organism is seen as a goal, as a purpose.

When the notion of *purpose* is accepted and when it is recognized that this is a notion outside the picture of physics, we can bring greater clarity into the issues to be considered. It is only by reference to the metaphysical notions of purpose and value that terms such as information and organization obtain a meaning. Without such reference these terms, like "programming," are empty words. On the other hand, in accepting these notions and in following up the consequences attached to them, we obtain ways for framing new problems and eventually may find new ways for ordering the mass of data which present day biological research puts before us. It is my conviction that the explicit introduction of these metaphysical notions will be of great help in the understanding of life, even if later research may make it preferable to substitute other notions for them. At the present juncture they should be accepted in order to bring sense into what otherwise is unintelligible.

It is therefore that this point of view will be taken up in the present chapter. We consider life as a result of the creativity which we have assumed as a fundamental feature of the universe. In order to distinguish the notion of life from creativity in general, we say that life is a coordinated and sustained form of creativity, the coordination and the persistence serving to enhance the extent of the creativity. As creativity involves an amount of freedom, life can be seen as the *persistent struggle to retain freedom.*

Thus, we invert the customary picture of present day science. Instead of starting with ideas derived from physics and looking to phenomena of metabolism and reproduction as expressing the primary character of life, asking whether the increasing complexity of living beings is a result of properties of molecules, and hoping that human values and human belief in freedom will come out at the end as a kind of ornamentation, we relate values and freedom to fundamental features of the universe and consider metabolism, reproduction, the appearance of definite living bodies, and their evolution during the ages as their consequences.

We shall discuss this point of view from various sides, beginning with some general notions based upon the ideas expressed by Whitehead (§§ 59 through 65).

§ 59. *Spontaneous reactions or initiatives*

The basic point of the philosophy expressed in § 1 and onward was that each newly developing process of the universe contains a germ of initiative. This germ finds support for its appearance and its growth in a new vision on experience, which vision is stimulated but never fully determined by new elements in this experience. A new conception is a new way of prehending some contrast which is felt in a way different from the way in which it was felt before.

From what has been explained in § 36 we expect that certain forms of environment, such as are provided by particular structured societies, can be favorable for the attainment of intensive feelings with respect to some contrast prehended in a process belonging to that society. The intensity can be such that the emerging conception will exert its influence on a protracted series of subsequent processes. Certain subjective features connected with the experience, until that instant not partaking in the group of features dominating the society, may then emerge from the background and obtain the rank of a positive prehension of great intensity. In consequence of this, a more or less extensive complex of processes can appear within the society, which complex supports a new form of prehending the experience out of which the processes of the society arise. The emergence of a conception with such consequences will be called a *spontaneous reaction* of the society. When looking from the outside, we may say the society gives evidence of initiative in its reactions.

It is impossible, however, to recognize initiative when one has access to the outcome of a single process only or even when one has data about no more than a few processes. Initiative can be recognized only when there is an observable change in the outcome of a longer series of processes in such a way that a statistical rule which seemed to be prevalent until some instant has clearly given way to a different rule.

It is impossible to describe completely in objective terms what is involved in the emergence of initiative. When a series of facts in which one believes to find evidence for initiative is afterwards subjected to analysis, one may find indications for influences coming from the environment and in hindsight may consider these influences as a "cause" of the initiative. Sometimes no clear indications are found, and one describes the new course which has appeared as a result of mere chance. Both points of view are unsatisfactory since they cannot take account of the subjective aspect.

A spontaneous reaction may embrace only a few processes and then lose its influence. Or spontaneous reactions may appear from time to time within a certain society without any recognizable connection between them. In such cases an observer looking at the facts which are the outcome of these processes cannot decide whether there has been initiative or whether there was only randomness due to chance. Uncoordinated initiative fades out in the general dispersion to which physical processes are subjected.

These considerations stress the difficulty of recognizing initiative when one must rely exclusively upon objective analysis of facts. We add, as a complementary observation, that it is just as difficult to decide in which cases one has to deal with complete randomness. Randomness, for all the simplicity of its mathematical definition (which requires a statistical frequency law and rules for the calculation of mean values based upon this law), is a queer notion in its practical application in view of the impossibility of collecting the "infinite number of cases" which is presupposed in the abstract mathematical notion. The idea of "no correlation" is as elusive as the concept of randomness: whenever we make a choice, there can never be complete absence of correlation (positive or negative) with what we did before. What we can do is to repeat the making of choices as often as possible under such reversions of correlation that we may believe that ultimately the correlation becomes negligible.[64]

The idea that there is no aim in physical occurrences, that there is nothing revealing conceptual activity, that frequency distributions amidst eigenvalues are the expression of complete randomness of those features which are not fixed by the relations of quantum theory is a matter of tradition in theorizing. It is supported by its practical results when applied to systems which we consider to be nonliving. But no physical experiment can give a decision concerning presence or absence of something subjective in any process, for physical theory and physical method of observation are built upon the idea that one must not look for such a thing.[65]

When we look at what happens in the universe from the inside point of view which we find within ourselves and extrapolate from there, the more natural notion is that there is always some subjective feature, with the consequence that there can always be some correlation between successive happenings. It is then possible to assume that there are means for intensifying correlation as well as for obscuring or destroying it. The randomness which we believe to find in the physical behavior of nonliving matter appears as a result of a number of contrasting subjective features leading to the loss of correlation. Subjective features, aims, conceptual activity, and correlation are primary features; absence of aim and randomness are secondary features developed in large but limited classes of happenings. They reveal an important set of traditions, not a basic principle of the universe. The fact that aims become noticeable in living beings is a direct consequence of the fundamental structure of the universe and cannot be considered as a feature to be deduced from physical principles, which have eliminated all possibilities for its recognition.

§ 60. The notion of purpose

Creative work can be recognized as such only after it has been completed or after at least an important part of it has been completed. We can understand its meaning when we recognize that it is directed toward a purpose, even if the purpose itself cannot be explicitly stated in words, as is the case with many works of art. Still we recognize that there has been a purpose and that this purpose has given direction to the form of the work, to its growth, to the selection of the materials in which it is realized, and to their arrangement. The coordination of the elements which have been brought together and combined can only be understood in terms of a whole; this whole is the purpose of the work created.

It is true that a purpose may be but dimly visualized at the beginning of the creative process, and it can develop as well as change during the execution of the work. Nevertheless, purposes are in essence wholes. Each purpose embodies something for itself. Purposes are separate entities, each having its own individuality.

Purposes can be transmitted, and a single purpose can lead to the creation of a number of works. In the course of its transmission the purpose can show variations, but these variations follow from some underlying theme, even if this is only dimly felt. Purposes also can develop: they can engender new purposes. There is an evolutionary process in many cases. The evolution may present a series of steps of small extent which seem to be transitional forms between one purpose and another, as may occur in the case of inventions. Nevertheless, each invention is a separate step.

Important in the evolution of purposes is that *the change of one element in the plan or in the material needed for its realization requires coordinated changes in a number of other elements.* Indeed, we are not just interested in what would be the consequence of a change in some single element: we wish to realize something that shall fulfill a purpose we have in mind, and each step therefore is directed toward some goal. Hence the development in time is essentially different from the progress of the motion of nonliving matter, as for instance a river, in which each new position of the water follows from former positions by the summation of steps determined by causal laws.

For examples of the relations considered here, one may think of the creation of a musical composition, of a painting, or of the conception of a personality needed for a novel. But similar relations hold for every form of artistic creation as well as for creative work in mathematics.

The evolution of purposes or of the works created in consequence of them can sometimes "overshoot" the mark: there
may be a development toward something grotesque, something that is a caricature of what was aimed at in the original
conception. There is an unpredictable element in the emergence of purposes. A conception of a purpose may arise; or
sometimes it may not arise — an opportunity can be lost.

§ 61.

The logic of purposes is of a nature complementary to the
logic which is applied in science.

In science one attempts to understand any phenomenon by
comparing it to what has gone before; an ultimate ideal — in
all probability never to be reached — would be to find one
master principle from which all should follow. One who thinks
exclusively in terms of purposes compares each happening or
each object with an aim to which it should conform. Sometimes one is inclined to imagine a single master purpose to
which all other purposes would be subordinated. This may be
a subject of theology, but the ideal is as unattainable as is the
other one.

In science the proper course is to proceed from what is
known and to search for more and more embracing principles,
constantly correcting each formulation as knowledge advances.
Similarly in life, in our thoughts on morals, on ethics, and on
religion, we must start from what we find within ourselves
and around us: we must formulate purposes, stretching to
the utmost what we can understand and mutually adjusting
the various expressions of these purposes; we must restate
again and again what we consider to be the most valuable
goals.

While the methods of science are based upon analysis, we
find something like "quantum effects" in the logic of purposes.
The analogy should not be pushed too far: purposes cannot
be measured on the scales applied in physics. Nevertheless, in
the logic of purposes we find an expression of what Smuts has

called *"holism"*: the tendency to produce things which have a completeness in themselves.[66] Again works of art form a supreme example, but it holds for every purpose: the purpose sets a goal toward which all relevant elements are directed. The conception of purposes as a regular phenomenon of nature originates within ourselves since we experience the creative principle from the inside. The most primitive way of thinking was to look for purposes everywhere—this is a basic expression of our instincts. The development of religious thinking is an effort to bring the notions of purpose into a connected scheme. While this thinking has been of immense importance in the entire history of mankind, it has often concentrated on two extremes: (1) rules for human behavior and adaptation in view of such nearby aims as honesty, love, etc.; (2) the contemplation of an ultimate destination, such as heaven is imagined to be. There is a wide domain which needs attention: the elaboration of purposes for the activities and forms of organization which bind the whole of mankind together. The powers that have been obtained from science and technology require a new formulation of goals to serve as guiding principles for the life of our communities.

§ 62.

We return to the line of thought of § 59.

The emergence of a new intensive way of prehending certain contrasts can be promoted by the order existing in a society since the processes arising within this society can avail themselves of decisions already current in the society. Their power for conceptual activity can thus be concentrated on some special point. Thoroughly structured societies seem to be particularly favorable in this respect. We must assume that the order existing in the society also will promote the *fixation of the new way of prehending*, its "encoding" in a form which is easily transmitted. This is necessary in view of the persistence without which the spontaneous reaction would be lost. Thus the society must have a "memory apparatus."

On the other hand, the preexistence of a society or the presence of a certain set of traditions is not sufficient, for traditions in themselves oppose the appearance of new forms. There must be a measure of conceptual sensitivity in certain processes of the society or in groups of processes. The society should guarantee this sensitivity and the corresponding freedom of reaction for some of its members. This statement expresses the never ceasing drama which faces us in the conflict between tradition and evolution. Evolution from chaos to chaos has no sense: the support which tradition brings cannot be dispensed with, but the only way in which a spontaneous reaction can bring progress of some permanence is by breaking an existing tradition to introduce a new one.

The new tradition embodies a new mode of reaction with reference to certain elements of the experience. Its object is to expand the set of contrasts which finds expression in the conceptions of the society in such a way that a new adaptation is brought about, intensifying certain values in these conceptions. When this has occurred, we can say: *The society has undergone a mutation.*

A mutation may lead to the emergence of two (or more) separate societies in the place of the old one as a result of the circumstance that perhaps not all processes of the society accept the new conceptual form or that not all processes accept the same new form. A group of processes which accept the new conceptual form may perhaps accept experience of other processes of the society with negative prehensions; this may lead to a loss of contact with them and to a dissolution of the old society. Other cases may present themselves: for instance, a coalescence of two (or more) societies is possible. The phenomenon of mutation with its various possible consequences is the source for the appearance of new societies. Hence, it is the basis for the evolution of societies (compare § 36).

Since there are no societies in complete isolation nor processes without connection with some society, we conclude: *Societies emerge from societies as a result of mutations intro-*

duced by spontaneous reactions with regard to changing fea-
tures of the environment and of such nature that a new
pattern of valuation appears in the conceptions of the new
society.

§ 63.

A society can have spontaneous reactions repeatedly, in a
form which gives evidence of a connection between these
reactions. This will occur when the spontaneous reactions
extend the conceptual content of the society in such a way
that its sensitivity and the chance for initiative is increased.
The society then has a more or less persistent tendency toward initiative, and its sensitivity is sustained by the reactions arising out of the initiative. *A society which is endowed*
with such sensitivity and with this persistent tendency for
initiative will be called a "living society."[67]
A necessary condition for the persistence of a living society
is that the spontaneous reactions shall not endanger its persistence: they must be favorable for the appearance of further
spontaneous reactions. When a society possesses these characteristics, we may term it a *"living organism."* The terms
"living society" and "living organism" are almost identical, but
the latter one stresses the necessity for a certain order which
must be present to retain and protect the life which comes
to appearance in the society.

Thus, *a living organism is a structured society which has*
room for initiative, that is, for the repeated appearance of
spontaneous reactions of a certain effectiveness. The initiative
must accept changing elements in the experience in such a
way that the new features are prehended in the form of contrasts which extend the conceptions already present in the
society; moreover, the extended conceptions must promote
the persistence of the society and its tendency to initiative.[68]
This brings us to the conclusion that *life is coordination of*
extensive spontaneity.[69]
Since life refers to originality, it contains features which

121

are *not* susceptible to regular transmission by traditions. Traditions form points of support for the manifestation of life, but in themselves they do not represent the essence of life. In so far as a society can be called a living organism, its reactions exhibit something which cannot be predicted from tradition. This entails that *a causal explanation of life in the sense in which such explanations are accepted in physics is not possible.*

§ 64.

We stress again that the doctrine of life as coordination of spontaneity is not at variance with the fact that spontaneous reactions lead to the appearance of new traditions. On the contrary, the introduction of traditions must be considered as a central characteristic of the forms of life known to us on earth and of their evolution. The formation of traditions out of initiatives is a feature in the development of the universe just as fundamental as the concretization of a fact out of a process starting with a conception. The formation of traditions is a way of realizing values in the universe (compare § 36).

In all living societies known to us the complexes of processes leading to initiatives are only a small group amidst the whole system of complexes. We might call these special complexes "completely living." The society can be termed living only when the completely living complexes are dominant.

Along with the completely living complexes there are more or less "inorganic" complexes. It is the inorganic complexes which ensure the persistence of the society in virtue of their traditions. *The living complexes cannot persist without their presence.* Many of the inorganic complexes on the other hand can persist outside of the society. This holds in the first place for all separate atoms and further for many compound substances present in living bodies, e.g., the skeleton.

The living complexes in which the spontaneous reactions make their appearance thus need the protection of the inorganic complexes embodying an extensive system of traditions. These inorganic complexes form the *material apparatus* of the living organism. The properties of this apparatus in many respects are open to physical (and chemical) investigation. In so far as they are, the behavior of the material apparatus exhibits the operation of the laws of physics and chemistry, and thus can be explained on the basis of causal laws or of statistical laws when one has to do with systems of atomic dimensions. *Hence, whereas the essence of life is outside causality, a very important part of its manifestations exhibits causal relations.* The fact that all forms of life known to us need the protection of matter leads to the statement: *Life creates matter* for this purpose.[70]

§ 65.

From the preceding discussion it follows that *the complexes of processes which together form a living organism contain more than those processes which are apparent in the material apparatus of the organism.* When we fix our attention upon the complexes which form the material apparatus (the atoms, molecules, membranes, tissues, etc. together with their physical and chemical interactions), we do *not* see all that which is functioning in the living organism. Along with the complexes of processes carrying the properties of molecules known to us from the anorganic world, there are complexes of processes which are carriers of the sensitivity leading to conceptual activity.

The distinction between complexes which are carriers of the inorganic (physical and chemical) properties of the molecules and complexes which are the carriers of life, however, must not be taken too literally. All processes are coupled with one another, and the manifestation of life needs the coupling. A better way to express this is as follows: a complex of processes which features the behavior of a certain atom or molecule within a living organism, although in many aspects analogous to the complex which features the history of a similar atom or molecule outside the living organism, *is not completely identical with the latter:* there is a difference which makes itself felt just as the fact that the organism is living.[71]

When scientific observation considers the properties of the material societies to which life is bound and concentrates on the regularities exhibited in the behavior of these societies, the essential problem of "what is life?" evaporates before it. Such observation can never prove or disprove that there have been valuations or intentions. It eliminates the problem.

The following quotation from Niels Bohr may be appropriate at this place:

"Thus, we should doubtless kill an animal if we tried to carry the investigation of its organs so far that we could describe the role played by single atoms in vital functions. In every experiment on living organisms, there must remain an uncertainty as regards the physical conditions to which they are subjected, and the idea suggests itself that the minimal freedom we must allow the organism in this respect is just large enough to permit it, so to say, to hide its ultimate secrets from us."[72]

§ 66.

We shall now take up a second line of thought and attempt to confront our notions concerning life with our knowledge of the behavior of physical systems. Evidently, the point where we should look for effects of conceptual activity must be at the atomic or quantum level. This assumption is based upon the fact that all intimate chemical processes in the living body operate on the atomic level, while some organs of perception can react to single quanta. The eye is sensitive to a few quanta of light; the ear can perceive acoustic energies of a similar order of magnitude; thus, there must be amplifying systems which are triggered by single quanta or at most a few quanta.

It is not attractive to suppose that conceptual activity should have the effect of a force and might contribute directly to energy or momentum. Effects of conceptual activity must be sought elsewhere. The way which is open starts from the observation that the equality of statistical weights, which physical theory assigns to the various configurations compatible with a given over-all specification of a physicochemical system, is no more than a hypothesis. As a working assumption it is supported by the elegance of its simplicity and by the success of its applications in the study of nonliving matter. But there is no background from whence this assumption comes forward as a necessary consequence. It is merely the statement that physical theory thus far has found no need to give attention to the specific features of each configuration as a reason for assigning unequal weights to them. Thus it is a limitation to a subset within a wider domain of possibilities.

Here the metaphysical picture presented in Whitehead's philosophy introduces a new point of view, or rather restores what is natural. *Configurations are different*; conceptual activity distinguishes them from one another and appreciates differences prehended as having some importance in view of future possibilities. When this is the case, conceptual activity may sometimes attach a particular value to certain configurations, a value connected with an anticipation of what may happen. It is a basic assumption of Chapter 1 that such a subjective feature exerts an effective influence upon the outcome of a process. This means that conceptual activity can introduce a bias for the appearance of certain results of a reaction.

When a reaction can lead to any member of a set of configurations all belonging to the same energy level, physical theory may give the same weight to each configuration of the set. This means it makes us expect that each configuration has the same chance of appearance, so that, when the reaction can be repeated many times, each configuration will come out with the same frequency.[73] When this indeed is observed, we shall be convinced that there is no effect from conceptual activity. It may be, however, that sometimes we observe another frequency distribution without being able to find a physical reason which could explain its appearance. For instance, there might be noted a preference for reactions leading to the persistence or the elaboration of a certain structure, the pattern of the reactions being such that the conclusion emerges that we have before us an organism giving evidence of having some purpose. To account for the effectiveness of a purpose, we must go outside physics, and we are forced to recognize that conceptual activity has given an increased weight to the particular configurations which are favorable for that purpose. Then there has taken place an evaluation in view of future possibilities, and this has led to a "break through" away from the randomness which is found when there is no indication of organization or purposiveness.[74]

We do not introduce conceptual activity as an "epiphenomenon" setting itself to disturb the "natural" behavior of matter. The point of view, as stressed repeatedly, is that *conceptual activity is the natural feature.* Sometimes it seems to be absent or to work without any correlation from process to process, so that no tendency for a particular bias comes to effect. It is then that the physical type of behavior appears. In other cases there appears a bias and we find life. In this train of thought the physical type of behavior is not a primary form but a secondary one, a system of habits into which a great deal of the phenomena of the universe seems to have fallen.

§ 67. *A model for certain aspects of life.* (I) *Introduction*

In §§ 67 through 73 we attempt to illustrate these ideas by discussing a model which may give some light upon primitive stages of life.[75]

It is generally assumed that in an early period of the history of the earth atomic groups of the amino acid type were formed in large amounts under the influence of powerful ultraviolet radiation from the sun acting upon a particular composition of the atmosphere supposed to have existed at that time.[76] It is possible that these amino acids (or amino acid residues) arranged themselves into larger associations, and the presence of flakes of crystallized clay minerals may have promoted the growth of these associations. Ever since the erosion of mountains started, tiny flakes of such minerals must have been present in great quantities in the silt which rivers bring to the ocean; and the idea that they have served as catalysts and as a substratum for the formation of biologically important structures has been expressed more than once.[77] The lattice structure of the clay minerals, which consist of two-dimensional networks of silicon-oxygen groups alternating with layers of metal ions, would seem to make them very suitable for this process; and it is quite possible that the earliest structures formed from amino acid residues may have been two-dimensional networks with some regular pattern.[78] At various locations the network may carry groups of atoms endowed with a particular sensitivity for reactions with ambiant material or with light. These reactions may bring energy into the structure, leading to processes of energy transfer and of "random motion of energy" through the network.

Suppose that we can fix attention upon a system with a structure of this kind, and assume that as a result of processes within the system, as well as through interactions with its environment, the system can pass from an initial state *a* to another state *b,* and from there to a state *c*, etc. To take account of quantum indeterminacy we suppose that each of these states may present a number of different configurations. While it may be possible to foresee when a transition shall occur, the objective data concerning the state and configuration of the physical system plus its environment at any instant do not permit us to predict which of the various configurations of the next state will occur. The "objective data" as meant here are the data which can be obtained by means of physical observation; as explained before in Chapter 4, the only feature which can be predicted from them is the statistical frequency with which the various configurations will appear, and this is possible only if we can work with a large number of identical systems, all originally brought into the same state *a* with the same configuration of that state.

The distinction between the "system" and its "environment" at this moment is a distinction made by the observer, who decides which "system" interests him. We make use of this distinction in the following way: in describing the configurations we shall henceworth *give attention only to the aspects of the system*, and we leave aside all features of the environment. In some of the states a, b, . . . , it may be that the aspect of the system is the same for all configurations of that state, while the variety involved in the laws of quantum theory is found entirely in the aspects of the surroundings corresponding to this state, aspects in which we are not interested when making our description. Other states, say state c, may have a few different aspects c_1, c_2, c_3 in so far as the system is involved, which aspects then are of importance for our description; each one of these aspects may still be accompanied by a variety of aspects of the surroundings which are not counted. The omission of the aspects of the environment brings a considerable simplification in the description of the history of the system.

We construct a diagram of the various states with their aspects a, b, c_1, c_2, c_3, d_1, d_2, . . . , e_1, . . . , etc., which the system can assume when it starts from a given state a, which for convenience we assume always to be taken in a single aspect only. The diagram will have the form of a branching tree;[79] it presents the possible histories for the development of the system when the corresponding configurations of the environment are taken for granted. For simplicity we assume that the number of histories which can be realized in a finite number of steps is finite.

Having mapped the various histories upon the branching tree, we make a distinction between those histories which at most transition points (and also at the last juncture in the finite number of steps which we are considering) have a number of different branches before them, and those histories which from a certain juncture onward have only a single path before them. These latter histories are those which either terminate at some juncture or which from a certain juncture onward continue in a fully determinate way for which no alternatives are open within the system. We denote histories of this type as *"dead ends."* A history which is a "dead end" leads to a fully deterministic development of the system. This is not in contradiction with statistical theory: the statistics then apply to the aspects of the environment. Evidently, a history leading to a dead end cannot be used as a model for life. We may think, for instance, of a process of crystallization in which hard solid crystals are formed which, once formed, remain forever.

The histories which admit various alternatives as long as they continue will be called *"open ends."* They are the more important ones for our purpose.

At any juncture where a number of branches are available the course of the system cannot be predicted beforehand and is a matter of chance. When the nature of the system and its environment is known, and the histories are properly mapped on the tree, it is possible to count how many "open ends" and how many "dead ends" the tree contains. If we have to do with a number of identical systems all starting from state a, we can calculate (or observe) the frequency or probability of the various histories.

§ 68.

Still keeping to physical systems, we extend the picture by supposing that one, or perhaps more, of the configurations reached after, say, step n is the same as state a with its original aspect from which the system started. We assume that when state a happens to be reached by the system in its development, the history starts over again. The system then is endowed with a possibility for periodicity. The repetition, however, is a fresh experiment, and the course which it will take is independent of what has occurred before. It is again ruled by the same distribution of probabilities: there is no way to predict beforehand which branch will be chosen. The same applies if the outcome once more should be state *a*, after which a new repetition will follow.

When initially we have before us a large number of cases all starting from state *a*, only a certain fraction of them will come again to state *a* after completing a cycle; from this fraction a smaller fraction will complete a second cycle; and ultimately all cases will have run into dead ends from which there is no return. Thus, there is no ultimate "survival."

We obtain a more interesting case if we add the further assumption that, when step *n* brings the system back to state *a*, there appears a certain number of systems all in the same state *a*. This requires that at or before step *n* there occurs a *multiplication of systems*. We assume that this multiplication is a normal consequence of the interactions between the system and its environment, and that the environment supplies the necessary material and energy. This is still completely possible in the physical realm, and various instances are known of such "self-multiplicative" systems (sometimes also called "cascading" or "avalanching" systems).

The multiplication increases the chance for recurrence of the cycles; and if the multiplication factor is sufficiently high, it becomes possible that there will always be systems completing new cycles, so that there is unending "survival," perhaps even with an increase in numbers.

However, we do *not* consider this multiplicative scheme to be a model for life. It might be argued that the weeding out of "dead ends" which occurs in each cycle is something like "natural selection" since the open-enders are the only ones that "survive." But the scheme lacks a feature which will predispose the "surviving" cases to having a higher probability of further survival. Each time state *a* has been reached in our model, we start with the same probabilities and the same chance for either "survival" or running into a dead end. There is not a selection which sifts out material that is better prepared than the material which we had at the start; there is nothing suggesting heredity. To come closer to life, a feature must be found which introduces a memory able to counteract quantum dispersion.[80]

§ 69. *A model for certain aspects of life.* (II) *Systems endowed with conceptual activity*

In view of the considerations of § 66, we now introduce the assumption that in systems which must serve as a model for life there is *conceptual activity* which gives a subjective form to each aspect. This subjective form shall be the feature introducing that form of relatedness which characterizes the system as an individual and as a subject, so that we no longer need make an arbitrary distinction between system and environment from the point of view of an observer.

The notion of "subjective form" is inseparably connected with that of a "subjective aim." Conceptual activity evaluates the aspects which the next step can bring, and selects which one of these aspects offers greater possibilities for further transitions and thus should obtain greater weight in view of this subjective aim. We express the effect of conceptual activity upon the behavior of the system in the following terms:

(*a*) It is focused upon a certain region and thereby distinguishes this region as the "system" (at higher levels, as the "organism") from the background or environment (the distinction may not always be sharp and will often have a more or less gradual character).

(*b*) It involves a conception of what is important for the system in the next transition and thus is endowed with anticipation.

(*c*) *The notion of "importance" is directed toward the avoidance of dead ends.*

The subjective form active at some instant cannot be known from objective observations carried out before that instant. Objective physical data (the data that can be obtained by an outside observer as a result of observations and experiments involving interactions with the system) are insufficient to permit predictions of the precise aspect which will come to appearance in the next transition or reaction. We cannot say that the subjective form is something that can be observed; nor can it be connected with definite atoms. We may say that it operates in the "field," but it has no definite location (see also the quotations from Whitehead in note 71). The subjective form is something that in a certain sense prevents the appearance of a definite, physically describable, and stable state: *it is directed toward keeping open a variety of possibilities.*[81]

When a particular outcome is obtained in some transition, one may be inclined to say that the system apparently had been in a subjective form favorable for that outcome; however, before that outcome appeared, no prediction could be made and the subjective form was unknown. The effectiveness of a subjective form in driving reactions toward particular configurations or aspects can be inferred only in hindsight from a series of results. The situation in which the results appear must predispose the observer to recognize that he is dealing with an organism having an appetite for some freedom.

§ 70. *The notion of play*

We have assumed that the subjective form involves a power which can evaluate in one sense or another the possibilities connected with the various outcomes to which a reaction may lead. This power of evaluation may at first extend only to a single step. It must involve the ability to recognize something of the effect of the environment so that a decision can be reached adapted to a guess concerning the expected effect. The vagueness of the words used here is intentional: conceptual activity is not a physical measuring and calculating apparatus of which we can postulate that it works with certainty. It can waver, and it can make errors. We must ascribe a certain amount of freedom to the activity of the subjective form, and the best description that we can give of its activity involves the notion of *play* with all its elusiveness. It "experiments," and this is influenced by some conception of purpose in view of which possible courses are evaluated.

Appropriate occasions to start playing may have been furnished by the turbulence of nature mentioned at the end of § 54.[82] It is difficult to recognize effects of play in its first stages. The play may peter out, and it may take some time before a new occasion of play can be surmised. However, once started and repeating itself, the playing can lead to the emergence of more coordinated results which extend the scope and the sense of the play. Gradually the purpose may evolve to obviate that the play shall come to an end. We suggest that this is the root of the urge to stay alive. The play is then turned into a more earnest game, a game against the effect of the environment with the object that the play shall not come to an end. In this sense life may have evolved from occasional play.[83]

To give substance to this idea, we must incorporate the feature of *learning*. We therefore introduce the additional assumptions:

(*d*) The subjective form is transmitted from state to state, and the connection between the subjective forms of successive states is ensured by more intimate features than the data which can be obtained by physical observation carried out by an outside observer (this is the continuity of subjective form, considered as a basic feature in the connection of successive processes, as stated in § 17).

(*e*) The subjective form is influenced by the sequence of states through which the system has passed; in other words, it is influenced by experience.

The fullest use of the last assumption comes when it is assumed that, just like the physical system considered in § 68, a system endowed with a subjective form can also hit in its development upon the original state *a* and *enter upon a new cycle of transitions*. We then have repetitive experience, and we assume the following:

(*f*) *The influence derived from experience can grow and become more effective with repetitive experience.*

Assumptions (*d*) through (*f*) express the idea that conceptual activity involves *memory*. It follows that in returning to state *a* our system comes to this state with a subjective form influenced by the experience of the history that has led to this state. *We assume that this experience has enriched the subjective form in such a way that it can make its next decisions with greater chance for success.* Where this is the case, we have arrived at a form of *learning*. The learning can become more effective when the system can repeatedly pass through the same or similar cycles.

To make the scheme complete, we still need the following important assumption concerning multiplication:

(*g*) When multiplication occurs as a result of a cycle of transitions, something of the memory is communicated to *all* systems which appear through the multiplication.

§ 71.

We postulated that the power involved in the subjective form of a living system in the presence of an environment with a certain amount of turbulence or fluctuation attempts to steer a course which at each juncture hopes to find a possibility for a number of choices. This occurs so long as the environment does not become too refractive and drive the system into a dead end.

The preference for transitions to states which leave openings for further influence of the subjective form can show itself as a preference for reactions which, having regard to the ever present fluctuations in the environment, are reversible. The arrival of atoms into situations where they will be "trapped" must be avoided. There must be a tendency to avoid reactions which involve a great release of energy that cannot be regained from the environment. This is in agreement with the findings of biochemistry: reactions in living

134

cells are generally coupled in such a way that energy released by a certain step is stored, at least to some important amount, in a chemical bond which keeps it available.[84] It can be described as a tendency to retard the increase of entropy.

We must not suppose that the course followed by the system will always be a single definite line, not even when cycles have been repeated many times. We must expect that the course will show deviations depending upon changes in the aspects of the environment and perhaps also upon what we might call "whims" of the subjective form. We expand our set of assumptions by a further supposition:

(*h*) The experimenting can go so far that the subjective form, when it has sufficient experience concerning the possibilities involved in various sequences of states and aspects, *can adopt a new evaluation of the possibilities connected with these sequences.*

As a result of such a new evaluation, preference may be shifted to an alternate line of development which likewise avoids dead ends but which in its first stages has a smaller margin for variation (that is, offers a smaller number of open branches in the earlier stages), while *giving a wider margin for decisions at a later stage.* There is then chosen a more deterministic path from stage *a*, say to a stage *m*, from which stage a wide field of possibilities is reached. Such a procedure can have certain advantages when it is expected that the more deterministic path in the beginning can be entered without danger of harmful influence from the environment, and when the ultimate field of possibilities is wider than that which could be reached by the line of development previously followed. In game theory this corresponds to a change of strategy. It is the basis for the evolution toward new forms.

It is possible that the special path which ultimately is selected is one which has only a single form of realization over a certain number of steps, so that for these steps it is fully deterministic. We can then say that the sequence followed, say from state *a* to state *m*, is ensured as a result determined by the physical situation (quantum alternatives are realized in the environment). The choice of such a deterministic path may involve the appearance of particular fixed atomic arrangements or other structures. These arrangements then represent physical constraints for the system which formerly were not there. In such a case we say *that this part of the development of the system has become codified in that structure* (compare § 62).

In the scheme presented here, codification appears for certain sets of reactions, while choice is left open at junctures between these sets where the uncodified and still flexible memory must be effective. This corresponds to the statement made by Elsasser in his book *The Physical Foundation of Biology* that organisms on the whole do not store information by mechanistic means.[85] In our scheme "information" is a notion which has its seat in the activity of the subjective form, and we have postulated that the subjective form by its nature is endowed with memory. Now we have arrived at the possibility that part of the information content can be codified physically (or chemically) and becomes physically retrievable. This is a progress in the evolution of life, an "invention." Life did not start from codified information but had to develop it. Moreover, we must constantly keep in mind that the aim of life is freedom, and that codification is a means to greater freedom in what is felt to be of ultimate importance. Hence, not all can be codified.

The freedom of choice at the later stage may be so great that the development of the system is continued along a new path. Various cases can be imagined. For instance, instead of coming back to state *a* with the same aspect as originally assumed, the system may now come to another aspect which perhaps may directly lead into the deterministic path. Or a different state may be reached which leads to the new deterministic path with bypassing state *a*. Or a fully new domain of development may be entered, leading to new types of cycles. Thus we see the possibility of the occurrence of what in biology is called *mutation.*

§ 72.

The point of view presented here concerning mutation does not give less influence to chance than does the usual point of view since in general the choice of a new path will be induced by some chance effect in the environment (sometimes perhaps it may be a whim of the conceptual activity). The specific point made is that the *reaction to the chance* is not a purely physical process, and that the chance is met or is accepted with some concept and some anticipation of its possible consequences for the subjective form already present.

It is not necessary that all systems make the same choice, and with the appearance of a mutation there will be a number of systems still following the old line. Also, many of the experimental lines of development will come to dead ends. Hence, we can say that there appears a *"natural selection"* which eliminates ill-conceived lines of development and thus performs that function which evolutionary theory in biology has ascribed to it. But in order to arrive at this point of view, we found it necessary first to assume a principle which made possible the existence of organisms directing their reactions to the environment in such a way that lines of development could appear which did not lead to dead ends. There must be subjective forms with conceptual activity, and cyclic lines of development must be established together with the consolidation of memory *before the notion of natural selection can be applied.*

The idea that natural selection operates in a domain of purely random events has no sense. Natural selection is not a notion which has meaning in the frame of description of physics. In physics it is not even possible to make a distinction between life and death.

In order to arrive at the possibility of living beings as we know them on the earth, still further assumptions must be introduced. We suppose that (1) the multiplication process need not necessarily lead to separate cycles but may bring about the appearance of connected groups of cycles matched to one another, each cycle playing around on its own and at the same time being in contact with the others; and that (2) in such groups a new form of conceptual activity can develop which exerts upon the original cycles constraints conceived in view of a subjective aim in the higher form of conceptual activity.[86] Organisms which have developed in such a way may show a hierarchy of structures corresponding to the levels of conceptual activity.

The cyclical nature of the paths of development which we have considered as a model for reproduction refers to the state of the system or organism. Each step of the system is accompanied by a spectrum of possible configurations in the environment and consequently by dispersion and irreversible processes in the environment as a result of the randomness in quantum reactions. When every step in the cycle is analyzed with reference to the notions of statistical theory, it is found that each step is accompanied by an increase of entropy for the system plus its environment. However, in so far as an entropy can be defined for the system alone (which is possible only for systems of sufficient size to allow a large number of configurations in their structure), entropy must decrease in certain steps since it must periodically return to the same value. The increase of entropy is in the environment. *When a mutation occurs, there is no definite way for comparing entropy* since here unique phenomena are involved. (We refer to note 74 concerning the possibility of entropy decrease as a result of conceptual activity.)

Cyclic sets of processes of the kind considered are possible only when there is available a source of free energy, as is furnished by the constant flux of sunlight. Moreover, there must be available a dump of energy (say, in the space around the earth), although some energy can be dumped into particular forms of matter produced by the cyclic set of processes as a side product (for instance, the energy stored in the coal deposits).

Conceptual activity as found in living systems needs energy flow through the system; apparently it cannot lead to an observable result when the system is in equilibrium in the thermodynamic sense. Although in a system in equilibrium there is always heat motion accompanied by Brownian motion of particles composed of many molecules, life cannot thrive upon equilibrium heat motion and needs a directed energy flow for the maintenance of its activities.[87]

§ 73.

The discussions of the preceding sections have brought several points of interest.

In the first place, it has become clear that we may consider various steps in the series of reactions as "processes" in the sense of the philosophy presented before, and that conceptual activity can be effective in them.

In the second place, the discovery of cyclic sets of processes made possible the strengthening of conceptual activity and the development of a flexible memory. In the chapter on matter it was pointed out that the massive transmission of facts in societies where there is a certain conformity between all processes can lead (and does lead) to suppression of the awareness of possibilities for the selection of new forms of relatedness. In such societies there is no longer awareness of anything which would mean freedom, and tradition develops into more and more rigid laws. *Certain cyclic sets of processes, on the contrary, have led to the evolution of types of societies in which conceptual activity remains awake.* These are the societies which repeatedly can have spontaneous reactions, as discussed in § 63. Thus, we are facing here the origin of the important bifurcation between the two lines of development which characterize our world. The distinction between these two lines may have evolved gradually, and for a long time it may have been subject to oscillations from one type to the other. It is here that we must look for the origin of life in the biological sense.

In the third place, it has appeared that the assumption of one directive principle, viz., assumption (c) of § 69 concerning *the tendency to avoid "dead ends,"* introduces an aim wide enough to reach a large number of biological phenomena. Combined with the invention of multiplicative processes as elements of cycles, it led to the reproductive process. We found the accumulation of memory and reached the notion of learning. We came across mutations in the choice of paths as a result of new evaluations of possibilities; often these lead to dead ends, but occasionally new cycles are able to persist. We also discussed that mutations can lead to a partial codification of the data collected in the memory. Apparently this is realized through the production of special types of molecules which guide reactions in a desired direction.

At the same time, we have come to the picture that all physicochemical reactions in living organisms are arranged in complexes of interlocking cycles.[88] Each cycle is involved in reactions with other cycles and exchanges matter and energy with them, while certain cyles are in contact with the exterior environment. As a result of these exchanges, each cycle can be seen as a consuming and producing agency. Some cycles can lead to the continued production of special types of molecules. It seems probable that the first cycles originated in systems attached to a solid substratum with crystal or lattice structure and that the origin of life must not be sought in liquid systems. The appearance of fluids as a part of living bodies must have been a later invention.

The picture of interlocking cycles of reactions will have a counterpart in the *modus operandi* (or, as we may say, in the "structure") of conceptual activity. As we hinted in the preceding section, we assume that some form of conceptual activity is connected with each cycle. It is involved in each cycle in such a way that the cycle is prehended as a unit, although it remains a unit analyzable into separate steps. Each cycle has a certain amount of autonomy, but it is also under constraints exerted by neighboring cycles. These constraints can give rise to the effectiveness of a higher level of conceptual activity springing up from the already existing forms and exerting further constraints. This is an instance of what is called the "holistic" tendency (compare § 61). There is no way of describing what happens here, but we experience examples of it in what happens in structured human societies.[89]

The picture of interlocking cycles, moreover, brings to evidence that so long as an organism is living, it does not seek a form of equilibrium in the static sense. It is in persistent transition. While in our previous description we spoke of the attainment of successive states, we must put stress on the *transience* as the important feature. In so far as we speak of an "equilibrium" between an organism and its environment, this means that cycles will remain operating with appropriate changes when the aspects of the environment are changing. So long as these changes of the environment are not too large, conceptual activity can make new evaluations and counteract damaging effects. In so far as there is stability, this is stability in movement. Part of this stability is ensured by structures or "mechanisms," including feedback, operating without conceptual activity through physical relations. But however impressive the protective effect of all feedback mechanisms may be, we must not leave out of sight that they owe their existence to former conceptual activity, and that their aim is to open wider possibilities for other conceptual activity. Merely retaining the status quo (although this may occur in various organisms) is a regression from the aim toward greater creativity.

All living organisms known on earth exhibit an immense complexity in their structure, a complexity which becomes continually more impressive with every advance made in observational methods. Evidently, this complexity must be an important feature in making possible the persistence of life. It is sometimes brought forward as a basic principle and a ground for explanation. Against this I defend the idea that complexity and complication must be a result of conceptual activity. Apparently a certain high level of complexity had to be reached before life could become persistent in the form of organisms as we see them on earth.

Complexity is a feature which cannot be grasped in its full meaning by making a description in physical and mathematical terms alone. Order in the make-up of a living organism is not a simple notion. To describe a living organism, we must intuitively recognize the presence of patterns, and this requires the recognition that they have a function and a purpose.[90] All biological description and explanation must face this fact and the difficulties involved in it. It cannot solve its problems by merely taking into account causal relations with the past (whether statistical or deterministic): it must give attention to conceptions concerning possibilities as active agents.

The "order" recognized in a living organism can be described as a set of traditions which have grown up and have been elaborated and for a part have been codified in mechanisms, such as feedback, etc. We may try to obtain a measure of order by attempting to find the number of traditions embodied in the organism. But even when this is done, we must keep in mind the conflict that exists between tradition and evolution: the essence of life is in the freedom which is obtained amidst, through, and beyond the traditions.

§ 74.   Additional remarks

(a) *A living organism as an instrument of observation.* It is useful to bring forward an aspect of a living organism which introduces a connection with the discussion of an observational apparatus in § 57. This can be framed as follows: *A living organism can be considered as an observational apparatus which makes a record of its interactions with its environment and is endowed with conceptual activity that evaluates the record; this conceptual activity influences the outcome of further interactions between the organism and its surroundings in such a way that the record is extended according to a pattern which has subjective value for the organism.*

The words "this conceptual activity influences the outcome of further interactions" are needed since conceptual activity not having effect in the physical world would be meaningless. The influence can include adjustment of the apparatus and extension of the apparatus by building new parts into it. For instance, it may refer to what happens in the synthesis of biologically active molecules and their combination into complicated structures.

The words "that the record is extended according to a pattern having subjective value for the organism" indicate that there is purpose in the conceptual activity.

The statements "conceptual activity evaluates the record" and "conceptual activity influences the outcome of further interactions" must be considered as describing two complementary aspects of what essentially is a single activity. There is not first an evaluation and second a decision to influence subsequent interactions: these two occur together (compare § 11).

We add (again) that conceptual activity is the "individualizing" agency: it is that which makes it possible for an organism to be a subject, i.e., an "I," however vague this notion may be, in opposition to what the "I" experiences as its surroundings. Thus, it is that which is responsible for the existence of biological units, i.e., organisms. It can assert itself only when it has a certain minimum effectiveness and when it can occur repeatedly. It acts rhythmically and is quantifying with respect to time, as it is with respect to space.

Conceptual activity can induce similar activity in other systems, as occurs, for instance, in the multiplication of living cells by division. Each cell division is accompanied by the formation of (one or more) new centers of conceptual activity.

The conceptual activities of several systems can be integrated into an activity operating on a higher level (compare note 86). Perhaps it is better to say that conceptual activities existing in one another's neighborhoods can induce the appearance of a new form of conceptual activity constraining and dominating the previously existing ones. This occurs in all processes of growth, for instance, when cells combine to form a structure with extended activity. In so far as we speak of "integration," we must be aware of the fact that the integration is only partial: the conceptual activity of the higher unit in the hierarchy mainly refers to what this unit stands for and is not aware (or at least not fully aware) of all that which can occur in the activities of the lower levels. The most conspicuous example is the way in which our own mental consciousness bypasses all the manifold processes which are going on in the subconscious and in the body in general.

(b) *Death.* In the discussion of the behavior of sets of processes in §§ 67 through 69 we spoke of the possibility of running into a "dead end" and of the tendency of conceptual activity to avoid this. Nevertheless, dead ends do occur, and they even have obtained an appropriate place and function in the evolution of life. This refers, in the first place, to the formation of material structures which become nonliving, such as shells, scales, hair, etc. (sometimes parts can be resorbed again into the living part of the organism, as may occur with parts of shells). In the second place, there are the parts which are dropped, such as leaves from trees and exudates or excrements. Finally, with those organisms which in the process of multiplication separate the progeny from a parent organism it usually is a regular feature that the parent structure or even the parent generation is destined to die at some time; there can be a gradual preparation for this event through a kind of "aging" of various cycles of processes.

Sometimes the dominating conceptual activity of a higher organism can run into a dead end which takes away the freedom for extending the subjective pattern of the organism and thus becomes a cause of death. Physical damage to important cycles of processes can also be a cause of death. The problems involved in aging and deterioration of cycles are still awaiting investigation.

§ 75. *The problem of the first appearance of life on the earth*

As far as is known to us, life on earth has evolved from other instances of life, and all known forms of conceptual activity which we can recognize are connected with living beings possessing material structures. All known forms of life involve growth and multiplication, and the metabolic processes taking place in living beings lead to a continuous incorporation into their structure of atoms which first existed outside living bodies. We must conclude that as soon as these atoms have obtained a function in the community of processes carrying the life of the organism, they are influenced by the forms of conceptual activity reigning within that society, which forms include initiative. The behavior of these atoms then must present aspects which differ from the aspects which they manifested before they were incorporated (see § 65). This seems to demonstrate that all atoms still are endowed with some peculiar sensitivity which permits conceptual activity to involve them in its play. It is to be noted that most atoms are incorporated only for a limited time; in the human body, for instance, atoms apparently are eliminated after a period of a few months, while others must take their place. It thus looks as if the incorporated atoms are subject to some process of "aging" which makes them unfit for indefinitely prolonged cooperation. As mentioned in § 74, subsection *b*, there are also atoms which are retained for indefinite periods in the solid parts of the structure (skeleton, etc.), but these are the atoms that have run into (useful) dead ends. The fact that life involves multiplication has had the consequence that more and more atoms on the earth are now taking part in forms of life. While their amount may be called small in comparison with the mass of the earth, the total mass of all living beings existing on the earth is not a negligible quantity.

There is a theory which asserts that forms of living beings have always been in existence somewhere in the universe, and that some of them accidentally reached the earth in a period of its history in which conditions were favorable for the existence and the evolution of these forms on the earth. The original living beings sometimes have been thought to be a kind of germs or spores, possibly resembling primitive algae or bacteria. However, algae and bacteria are organisms of considerable complexity, and the assumption that they can disperse through interstellar space does not eliminate the problem of their origin. What role can be played by viruses in this connection is uncertain since there is no indication that viruses can become living organisms when no such organisms are already in existence.

In the philosophy presented here we assume that forms of life have resulted from particular forms of conceptual activity. These forms of conceptual activity must have led to the appearance of societies of processes which gave occasion for forms of play involving initiatives. In so far as these societies are endowed with persistence, we can say that they represent forms of matter, so that we may keep to the statement that there has been no life without some material structure (see § 64). This structure, however, need not have been a system of atoms or molecules such as we see in the living beings now around us. It may perhaps have been more like a wave field, and it may have extended over distances which would seem very large in comparison with the dimensions of ordinary living organisms. Such systems, societies of processes with sufficient traditions to be self-supporting but with room for initiatives, may have evolved along with other societies much more strongly bound by their traditions. While the latter societies developed into forms of matter carrying the physical laws and leading to the appearance of galaxies and stars with planetary systems, the other, more flexible societies likewise evolved and thus remained in existence, perhaps in parts of space where atomic matter was rare.[91]

That forms of conceptual activity may be effective in systems of very large dimensions and on occasion may concentrate this effectiveness into systems of much smaller dimensions should not be considered as impossible. Conceptual activity is more fundamental than the forms of space and time which now exist around us. Even in physical theory we accept the idea that a wave front of light coming from a distant star will have a very large transverse extent when it reaches the earth, and nevertheless can concentrate its power in the form of a single photon hitting a rod of our retina or a silver atom in a photographic emulsion. What is occurring here baffles geometric description in simple terms and warns us that there are relations in nature reaching far beyond our imagination. Thus, the assumption that conceptual activity, though not having a definite location itself, sometimes binds together phenomena occurring at large distances from one another and on other occasions concentrates itself within a narrow domain seems acceptable. Forms of conceptual activity connected with something of the nature of wave fields extending over immense distances may perhaps be resistant against effects of atoms with high velocities and thus be resistant to high temperatures.

We therefore propose the idea that forms of conceptual activity playing around in societies of processes resembling wave fields more than systems of particles have existed throughout the entire period of evolution of the universe in which galaxies and stars were formed and on occasion have induced (or "kindled") forms of play in systems of the nature suggested in §§ 67 through 73. These systems probably contained both wave fields and sets of atoms, as we have discussed above that life can make use of existing atoms and can incorporate them as temporary carriers. The idea thus is that there may have been (and that there still may be) forms of what we perhaps should call "proto-life," carried by entities different from the material systems now around us (organic molecules and structures built up from them); and that the conceptual activity effective in these entities can induce new conceptual activity in systems containing atoms.

The picture raises the question: "Why do we not now have evidence of comparable manifestations of conceptual activity calling forth new forms of life where no life was before? Why has there never been a new start of life in the geologic periods since the Precambrian?" Perhaps we are too blind to recognize other manifestations, and it may be that our customary point of view that nonliving matter is not affected by values is wrong.[92]

Speculations concerning such possibilities are not meaningless. It is alleged that scientists at some time in the future may actually succeed in creating something resembling life in the course of laboratory experiments. In itself it will be a difficult matter to assess whether real life has appeared, that is, life which manifests itself as a creative potentiality. If no more can be demonstrated than a possibility for perpetuating itself and for growing in mass, including dividing and multiplying, so long as adequate "food" is supplied, I would hesitate to recognize it as life. It might better be denoted as a refined process of crystallization. The property of being able to multiply when adequate food is available is also exhibited by a fire.

But let us suppose that there would be convincing indications of creativeness. Then *I would presume that the experiment in some way has opened contact with carriers of conceptual activity of which we had not been aware.* These might be carriers of such nature as suggested above.

In this case the outcome of the experiment will require discussion from a point of view much wider than that of physics and chemistry, a point of view which must have *room for the consideration of values and of other metaphysical concepts, including that of our responsibility.*

The creation of life is not a subject for mere physical experimentation without due attention to philosophical, moral, and religious concepts. With the present structure of our society and its haphazard way of spreading news and commenting upon it, there is the greatest danger that any such discovery would stir up a mess and would soon be directed to unholy ends. Great concern would be needed, for which we are little prepared.

This holds, by the way, also for the possibility of making trips to the moon and to other planets. We have no idea of the forms of life which may be encountered there nor of the experiences which their discovery may involve. Neither do we have any idea of ambitions, hopes, convictions, or moral ideas which might be carried by the unknown forms of life. The

148

record of the destructions which have followed upon the discovery of new forms of life on the earth, both human life and other, has been extensive, and history leaves little hope for modesty and respect.

The new developments of the biological sciences and of their allies which probably are before us *call for an awareness of a deep responsibility for the ways in which we handle our discoveries.* This should be a point of prime importance in all forms of education.

APPENDIX TO CHAPTER 5

The construction and application of modern automatic computers of great capacity, together with the theoretical analysis of their manifold powers of combination and decision, have raised issues that seem to have a bearing upon the role assigned to conceptual activity. The idea is brought forward that the possibilities of "programming" computers are so far-reaching that the notion of conceptual activity as something fundamental can be abandoned. I believe, on the contrary, that a clear discussion of what "programming" means will confirm our philosophical point of view.

What can be done by automatic computers is stupendous. They have evolved to such a degree of perfection that extensive and complicated calculations can be carried out extremely rapidly. This has opened possibilities for applying mathematical calculation to domains where formerly it did not play a part. It has also extended the notion of calculation itself, and processes of mathematical reasoning, of logical deduction, and of decision making can be formalized to such extent that they can become a subject for machine computation.

Taking, for instance, the "model" developed in §§ 67 through 71, we can classify the various possible histories (open-enders and dead-enders) if a sufficiently complete description of the branching tree of states and aspects of a system is available with data concerning the reactions of the environment. A mathematical evaluation of moves can then be worked out, more or less corresponding to the evaluation which we assumed to be performed by the conceptual activity of the subjective form, an evaluation which takes account of the possible reactions of the environment. It will be devised so as to give greatest weight to strategies which are directed toward unending continuation of the game. If these strategies have been worked out in detail, it becomes possible to programme a computing machine so that it can "play the game." Up to a certain point the behavior of the computing machine can be considered as a model for life. But we should not forget that by setting the aim of unending continuation of the game *we* have programmed the computer. The program is a result of our conceptual activity.

A case which has received much attention is that of the construction of a chess playing machine. When put before a chessboard with any distribution of pieces, the machine can observe the situation and work out within itself — with the speed now characteristic of electronic computers — all possibilities for a first move; then work out the possible moves of the adversary; work out the moves that it can make next; and perhaps consider what the adversary can do after that move. On the basis of the possible consequences the machine can calculate a figure of merit expressing the gain that can be obtained from each move which was open to it. If the machine then carries out the move for which the figure of merit is highest, it can perhaps make a better choice than many a human player would be able to do. In its mode of operation and evaluation it can have stored the accumulated "know-how" of the expert chess players, and it might be feasible to make machines which could perform calculations over longer chains of possible moves and which gradually could improve their modes of play.[93]

Automata have been constructed which guide a vehicle in such a way that it will come out of a maze. For this purpose the machine must be sensitive to a variety of signals, derived from contact with surrounding objects, electric potentials, light emission, etc., which would furnish information concerning the situation surrounding the vehicle. In response to these signals the machine can work out a possible path; it must be able to influence the direction of its motion, and it should do this until an unobstructed way is found.[94]

Machines can also be arranged so that they can make a

selection between various programs for action, the selection being based upon the outcome of test calculations. Machines sometimes are built so that they can have a series of different internal states, each state having a particular way of responding to signals. If there is no suitable response to the signals when the machine is in state number 1, for instance, an inbuilt selecting device after some time may put the machine in state number 2; if again there is no response, after some time the selector will bring the machine into state number 3, and so on until an efficient response is forthcoming. Either the selection of states can follow a prescribed way, or there can be a mechanism which makes selections "at random."[95]

Von Neumann has discussed the question of whether or not machines can be designed which can reproduce themselves.[96]

Much thought is given to what are called *"self-organizing"* systems.[97] An important class of such systems is being investigated by F. Rosenblatt and co-workers.[98] Rosenblatt has developed systems which are called *"perceptrons,"* consisting of a set of "sensory units" connected through the intermediary of various layers of "associators" to a set of "response units." In these systems not all connections are arranged a priori; on the contrary, there is a large degree of arbitrariness or randomness in the original layout (which puts less requirements upon the construction). In the initial state the response reaction to a stimulus may come out without any apparent sense. However, sets of connections between successive layers of associators or between associators and response units can be adjusted or reinforced according to a certain program, depending upon the way the receptors react to stimuli patterns presented successively to the sensory units. Systems have been developed which can "learn" by this procedure to classify sets of stimuli according to certain characteristics, e.g., according to the geometric pattern of the stimulus independently of the position, orientation, or size in which it is presented. The "learning" can result either from the action of a "teacher" or from inbuilt reactions of "reward" and "punishment." A memory for the recognition of patterns is obtained by the system itself through the gradual reinforcement or adjustment of certain connections.

A point of great importance in the study and the construction of machines for transmitting data and for deducing results from them is the problem of how errors can be prevented and eliminated. This is also a point of interest in the comparison between the activity of machines and the activity of nervous systems. When "messages" are translated into elementary signals, the transmission of the signal can introduce errors. The ultimate effect of errors can be greatly reduced when a large number of channels is used, all of which must transmit the same elementary signal so that a "majority" effect, so to say, can be introduced. An elaborate theoretical literature is developing in connection with these problems, and one of the intriguing points is to find the minimum of "complication" or "duplication" which is needed to ensure correct results in sufficient cases. We shall not go into these questions.

After this excursion one may be inclined to ask: *"Does it make sense to appeal to conceptual activity and to creativity as metaphysical principles in the phenomena of life when so much can be done by machines? Can perhaps all phenomena of life be explained as activities of sufficiently complicated machines?"*

When a reply is sought to this question, the point that must be noted is that all systems considered are built up from construction units which have been prepared beforehand. The construction has only been possible through human conceptual activity which has introduced a large number of essential arrangements. When properly planned, certain systems are able to develop and to refine themselves so as to produce better responses and organized responses. This is of great importance for the understanding of the ways along which certain biological structures and reaction systems may have evolved. But there is no vision of a machine building itself from scratch when there is no previous machine. *Machines may be considered as an extension of human life, but they do not constitute life that has sprung up by itself.*

This holds for all mathematical or physical models of intelligent behavior. Apparatus for sensing, mechanisms for positive or negative feedback, memory, computation, deductive logic, ability to discern patterns and to derive abstractions, all these devices can be built into machines, and the results which are obtained will far surpass our imagination. But the underlying construction and the arrangement of all connections has been made by man, and man has programmed the machines.

While it is true that computing machines work according to principles and rules which are purely mathematical and which make use of the properties of inorganic, "dead" matter, we must recognize that *it is a form of mathematics in which, through the technique of programming, aims and purposes have received a place.* Mathematical reasoning makes it possible to analyze the consequences which these purposes can bring with them and to formulate the rules according to which new forms of activity can develop out of seemingly simple beginnings. That those developments often show similarity with purposeful behavior of living beings is remarkable, but it is not strange when one realizes that purposiveness has been infused into the programming.

To those who maintain that most phenomena of life can be explained as the activities of sufficiently complicated machines, our answer could be: "Yes, *provided suitable programming has been taken care of.*"

To those who assert that life is a property of matter which can be explained on a physicochemical basis, our reply would be: "This can only be the case *if physics is extended in such a way that the notion of programmed systems is incorporated into its formalism.*"

This would be an extension reaching far beyond the dominant conceptions of physics which are held now. It does not belong to the present structure of physics and it is preferable to denote it as a metaphysical extension. Metaphysics here does not refer to esthetics or to ethics, but it does refer to some form of purposiveness. This may be an inbuilt purpose of maintaining a certain freedom of activity and of avoiding "dead ends." This is equivalent to saying that a concept of value has been introduced and is built into the program of the machine.

We must add that such an extended form of physics would need still further extension if it were to aim toward an explanation of human behavior and even of a lot of forms of behavior of other living beings. When the only values built into the machine are such as refer to the maintenance of its persistence and of its powers, we shall not reach the domain of esthetics and of ethics. While machines can simulate features of life, features which many biologists seem to consider as the only important ones, they never will be able to present life in its full reality. If life were no more than the performance of programmed computers, it would not have the depths we recognize in it.

Granted that machines can be constructed which in the presence of an extremely large set of possibilities and contingencies can do much more in analyzing and making decisions or reaching conclusions than the most powerful human brain at present can do, we still face the implication that their number of alternatives is *finite*, and that it is impossible to build into machines the infinite possibilities which can be reached by our feelings of responsibility. I am certain that there are always openings for man's conceptual activity beyond the set of possibilities put into a machine or found out by a machine, however large the latter may be.

This is an article of faith based upon the conviction that life is worthwhile and is not a programmed automaton. Given the most powerful computer to work out a suitable economic system adapted to the needs of all men, it still would require a human decision to make out what needs should be looked after; and even then there still can rise in some human mind a thought of charity, of religious faith, or of reverence for all life on earth leading to attitudes completely outside the domain in which the machine operates. This is the divine element in man's potentialities. We must not lose this element by submitting to machine-ridden traditions: we must keep faith in the possibilities as well as in the responsibilities of our own conceptual activity.[99]

Since the discussion of what machines can do is based upon the notion of programming, the earliest beginnings of life cannot have been "programmed machines" unless one admits the activity of still earlier living beings or of spirits. If somebody says that perhaps all matter has been programmed, then he himself is adding to physics metaphysical ideas which are approaching those which we have in mind when introducing conceptual activity as an efficient agent in the universe.

On every side we face the conclusion that, if life is to be explained as a property of matter, the properties of matter must be extended so as to embrace programming and values, while the full evolution of life cannot be reached unless the value system is wide enough to attain esthetic and ethical values.

6

PROBLEMS OF ORGANIC EVOLUTION
AND NATURAL SELECTION

§ 76.

As a continuation of the analysis of the meaning of life in the preceding chapter, it appears useful to discuss various findings and concepts presented in the literature on the theory of organic evolution. This will enable us once more to consider the problem of whether the phenomena of life can be fully explained on the basis of the principles of the present day physical sciences, or whether there is evidence that some other principle must be added to them. As the main characteristic of the physical sciences we take the assumption that values cannot play a part in the description of natural phenomena, and that there is nothing else than "rules of succession," as analyzed in the laws of physics (which rules in many cases are expressed in statistical form). The contrasting principle is the assertion that evaluation of possibilities counts along with experience from previous situations, and that in the phenomena of life an effective part is played by conceptual activity, that is, by some form of anticipation which provides a bias through aiming at qualities not recognized as effective in physics. The assumption of the effectiveness of values does not mean that we believe in "supernatural" influences: the recognition of values is as much a part of nature as are the physical relations.

There are many authors who defend the first mentioned point of view (some opinions have been collected in note 60). It has been noted that their explanations sometimes are clad in a vagueness which gives rise to uncertainty concerning what is meant. This is particularly the case with applications of the notion of *natural selection,* which is often hailed as a principle completely explaining biological evolution as a result of the interplay of "blind forces" operating without direction and nevertheless leading to a directed result. It is curious to observe that the three-volume book on *Evolution after Darwin,* published in connection with the Darwin Centennial meeting in Chicago, November 1959,[100] does not start with a clear definition of the principle of natural selection either in the form in which Darwin conceived it or in the form in which it is accepted today. It is left to the reader to guess the implications of the principle from what is presented in various chapters throughout the first volume. The circumstance that some authors (H. J. Muller, for instance[101]) continually use the term "Darwinian natural selection" almost suggests that a certain qualification is considered to be indispensable. There is, of course, no objection against using a concept which is based upon the results of biological observation, and which attempts to summarize a trend recognized in these results. But when it is derived from biological data, the principle cannot be used as a proof that the whole of organic evolution is a result of blind physical forces, for the influence of life is then tacitly accepted. It should be remembered in this connection that death itself is a phenomenon which requires more than a physical explanation.

§ 77.

To facilitate the discussion, I propose the following definition of natural selection: Natural selection, *sensu stricto,* is the effect of differences in birth and death rates between various types of living beings which find themselves in a certain environment, upon the ultimate composition of the total living population.

This formulation contains the essence of the ideas expressed by most biologists. It summarizes that which is contained in the principle when one attempts to make the closest approach to physical notions. The principle in the form chosen here does not state what gives survival value. Nor does it equate greater survival value with progress in organization of such kind as we believe to see in the usual arrangement of the animal kingdom from protozoa, through simple metazoa, up to vertebrates, mammals, and man. Observational data may point to development in such a sense, but when this is postulated as an instance of a specific trend, it forms a separate thesis.

Even with this simple form of the principle it is necessary to consider the suppositions which are involved in its formulation. I will not be concerned with the word "type," which is used merely as a convenient expression to denote forms which are sufficiently stable and recognizably different, so that it makes sense to say: this type is increasing in numbers, and that type is dwindling out. Whether the "types" shall be species in the accepted biological sense or varieties within a species is not of immediate importance here.

In the usual application of the statement in evolution theory it is supposed that during some period of time in a certain region there exist several types of not too distant character which are considered as being in competition with one another for their persistence, and which have different survival rates. It can then be expected that in the long run (that is, after the passing of a sufficiently large number of generations) the differences in survival rate will lead to a more or less complete elimination of some types, to be considered as the "weaker" types, so that ultimately only the "strongest" type(s) will survive. The longer the chain of generations that can be taken in view, the more effective the selection will become.[102] When data are assumed for the survival rates, it is possible to construct mathematical examples illustrating the efficiency of the selection.

The phrases "there exist differences in birth and death rates" and "there is a certain environment" are both vague. They can only be defined as statistical notions obtained by averaging over large numbers of individuals on one hand and averaging in some way over areas and periods of time on the other hand. It will be recognized that difficulties are involved in such averaging, in particular with reference to areas and to periods of time. Leaving aside the ordinary seasonal variation of the climate (since the individual life of the larger animals and plants usually extends at least over a full year), we must be aware of the possibility of slow changes occurring almost everywhere which can become quite conspicuous and influential after time intervals of some centuries or of the order of a few thousand years. Examples are alterations in the course of rivers, changes from lakes to swamps and to forests or from forest to prairie and desert, persistent climatic changes such as have occurred repeatedly in the last 20,000 years, changes of sea level. Major tectonic movements and erosion phenomena may need longer stretches of time to become effective, but they can be accompanied by biologically important changes of habitat appearing within a few millennia. Such phenomena interfere with the birth and death rates of animals and plants.

In studies on evolution these effects are clearly recognized. But from a quantitative point of view they make it extremely difficult to define the samples which must be considered in order to form adequate averages. Varieties which have a lower survival rate in one set of conditions may appear to have a higher rate in changed conditions. Moreover, many animals and plants seem to show some adaptation to changing surroundings. Theoretically, one may consider this as a property of a species or type to be included in a full description of that type when one has a sufficiently large sample to work upon, but again the practical realization is more an ideal than a possibility. Even the results of selection itself produce changes of the environment for the remaining types since the less favorable types have gradually disappeared. This can be of importance with regard to mutual interaction between groups of animals and plants which feed upon one another.

160

§ 78.

These considerations bring into evidence that the principle of natural selection, although highly illuminating as a line of thought, is hardly a law which can be used for prediction. In practically all cases we can only conclude *post factum* that certain types have survived better than others. We can then form an opinion concerning features which apparently have been important in this connection, but a proper analysis is handicapped by the circumstance that many factors are active simultaneously and interfere with one another in a complicated way. The only exception is the investigation of survival differences for a limited group of types under artificial conditions in a laboratory or upon agricultural experimental plots, but also here the survival rate is found only at the end as a result of counting the individuals that have survived. There are perhaps a few cases in which one has information beforehand, derived from properties of the type or from data concerning the gene system. The other predictions that can be made are from small scale experiments toward situations on a larger scale with similar characteristics. Thus far predictions cannot be based upon knowledge of bodily structure or chemical constitution.

In the theory of organic evolution natural selection is considered in connection with the occurrence of mutations. Many animals and plants produce offspring in which certain percentages of new forms occur. Apparently this arises only within particular periods of the presence of the species upon the earth. If such a period of mutation is in progress, the principle of natural selection can be invoked to explain why not all new forms will persist, and why new forms sometimes can supplant the parent type. Evidently the mutation phenomenon introduces two time factors: the interval between two successive periods of high mutation rate, which perhaps may be of the order of 100,000 years; and the mutation rate itself (the rate at which new types are produced), which must be considered in connection with the period of reproduction and

161

with the rate of change of the environment. If a certain sturdy species with a favorable mutation rate at the same time has the property of persistently producing some mutations of unfavorable type amongst its offspring, these unfavorable types can remain a permanent part of the total population, notwithstanding a high death rate, as a result of their constant production rate (mathematical examples can be constructed to illustrate such a possibility). It is further possible that a mutation unfavorable in the original surroundings may appear to have a higher survival value when changes in the surroundings have arisen.

These effects are discussed in many biological investigations. What I have attempted to point out is that the explanation can handle data only *post factum,* and even then it remains difficult to obtain precise results.

§ 79.

This lack of definiteness must be kept in mind when we turn attention to one of the major problems in evolution theory, the *problem of the direction of organic evolution.* There is a general consensus that evolution has led from "lower" to "higher" forms of organisms, and, while there is some difficulty in applying these notions to flowering plants, there is rather convincing evidence in the animal world, the main point being the appearance one after the other of the major classes of vertebrates in the geological record, while detailed sequences have been recognized also within certain families or genera. However, beyond this very little is known with definiteness. G. A. Kerkut in his book *Implications of Evolution* extensively discusses the problems and the unsolved difficulties involved in any attempt to arrange the invertebrate phyla in an evolutionary sequence. So far there is no reliable evidence for any scheme.[103] C. E. Bremekamp in a paper "Comments on the Doctrine of Evolution" points out that genetic research thus far has given information only concerning mutations within the limits of a species or at most within those of a genus.[104] No data are available concerning mutations which could lead to new families or higher divisions. Nothing is known about the origin of the major phyla.[105] Neither do we know whether all possibilities have been exhausted. It might be thinkable that a new phylum could appear if the earth exists for another billion years at its present temperature.

When we look at the basic definition framed in § 77, the only efficient factor which has been accepted in the concept of natural selection is survival rate. It is not evident that selection according to survival rate will automatically lead to more and more complicated organisms and to the production of more "advanced" types, although this seems to be tacitly supposed by many authors. If survival rate alone were to count, then we might be forced to consider certain species of bacteria or certain species of insects and of weeds as the most successful living beings, to say nothing of the fact that rocks are also products of nature's "blind forces" and usually have shown a much higher survival rate than any kind of living being. There are various cases in which organisms have made their appearance in which faculties have been lost and the organization has become more simple; this holds for nearly all parasites, while Cirripedia among the Crustaceans can be taken as an example. Thus, one can say at most that natural selection has not prevented better organized living beings from getting a foothold, while no one knows what hard times they may have had to cope with.

The problem of direction in evolution is usually discussed in relation to adaptation. This, however, requires a definition of what is meant by "adaptation." If it is taken in the sense that the type with the largest survival rate is considered as the type which is best adapted, the term does not convey a new point of view. I shall come back to this matter in § 89, where another notion concerning adaptation is presented.

In this connection it may be of interest to mention a passage from a paper by Dobzhansky on "Evolution and Environment."[106] Dobzhansky starts by making a distinction between "evolution from within" and "evolution from without." After quoting some authors who have expressed the idea that "evolution is to a considerable degree predetermined . . . an unfolding or manifestation of preexisting rudiments," Dobzhansky points out that there is no sufficient support for such a hypothesis, and that nothing in the history of life on earth compels us to believe that evolution is predetermined, or that organisms are able to change in just one direction. Next he considers Darwin's opinion on this subject, stating that "interaction between the organism and its environment in the process of natural selection is the principal driving force of evolution."

Both statements need comments. Natural selection is essentially selection. Hence, there must be something to select between. The property of living beings to produce offspring with mutations, a process which involves many internal adjustments, points to the presence of a basic mechanism "within." This cannot be denied. It does not imply that all mutations are predetermined, or that they will always proceed in the same direction. The available evidence indicates that there is a large amount of randomness in the mutations. Among these there may be some that present an elaboration of organization, a form of progress; others may not do so. So far we do not have a case where all the observed mutations have been classified according to their value for evolutionary progress; thus, on the species level we have no sure data as yet to conclude whether there is a bias in a certain direction, or whether every bias is absent.

Natural selection operates on the mutations and is effective in determining what ultimately will survive. This is an influence coming "from without." Moreover, natural selection is operating in history, and its effects themselves contribute to the history of life upon the earth. It brings about that new generations find themselves in changed conditions, and this will be of importance in the further evolutionary process (along with geological changes). The phrase "interaction between the organism and its environment," however, is vague, and, when it is not precisely specified, it leaves open the question of whether it should refer exclusively to the effect of differential rates of death, or whether there can be other, more direct effects of the environment influencing the appearance and direction of mutations through forcing the individual living beings to adopt a certain way of life. It often looks as if those who speak of "Darwinian evolution" or "Darwinian natural selection" and use this as an explanatory principle for the direction of the evolution of life are counting on effects which embody something more than mere differences in survival rates, although they themselves may often not be aware of this.

The expression used by Dobzhansky is: "Environment does not impose specific changes on the organism, either directly, . . . or via natural selection, . . . Nor is the role of the environment reduced to an *ex post facto* judgement of what is fit or unfit to survive, ... The role of the environment in evolution is more subtle. I know of no better way to describe it than to borrow Toynbee's phrase: — challenge and response."[107] In my opinion the words used here have uncertain meanings. I would except only the last one, "response": in my interpretation (which may be different from Dobzhansky's intention) this term can only express a form of conceptual activity in the responding living being. I come back to this point in § 89.

§ 80.   The regulation of cellular activity

In §§ 69 through 73 of the preceding chapter we considered certain concepts entering into the evolution of a primitive living system. As the discussion was based upon the analysis of a very simple model, it may be useful to summarize some of the recent findings concerning processes occurring in living cells. The summary can touch upon a few basic points only, and, as the entire subject is developing rapidly in many directions, it is not possible here to bring the latest views concerning any point.

Within each cell there occur a large number of interlocking

cycles of processes bearing upon a host of chemical transformations. The cycles involve carbohydrates (sugars), which play an important part in the metabolic reactions furnishing energy; they involve substances in which energy can be stored, substances which have the necessary mechanical strength to support the cell structure, enzymes, and nucleic acids.[108] Almost every biochemical process is catalyzed by a special enzyme; hence, enzymes (which are proteins) play a key part as "tools" in the complicated factory with which a cell sometimes is compared. It is understandable that such a complicated system needs an apparatus for the regulation of its activities and for the proper extension of these activities into each new cell. For this purpose one must look to the nucleic acids, in particular, to the so-called deoxyribonucleic acid molecules (DNA molecules), which are found in the chromosomes of the cell nucleus and are supposed to contain the "codified information" necessary to direct the synthesis of enzymes. This information must be kept available during the life of the organism, while it also must be transmitted to the offspring. The way in which it codified is therefore of the greatest interest.

The DNA molecules are long chains made up of alternating groups of the nature of a sugar and of a phosphate. To each sugarlike group is attached a basic nitrogenous group, one out of four types (adenine, guanine, thymine, cytosine). There are two parallel chains in each molecule, and the units or "nucleotides" (each unit consisting of a sugarlike group, a phosphate, and a nitrogenous group) occur in pairs, usually with adenine in one chain paired with thymine in the other chain, and guanine similarly with cytosine. A single DNA molecule (one double chain) may carry, e.g., ca. 15,000 of such pairs. It is now generally assumed that the information which must guide synthetic and other processes in the cell is determined by the order of the four basic groups along the double chain. Although there is as yet no full certainty about the "code," it has been supposed that each consecutive set of three such groups can play the part of a "letter"; this will lead to about twenty distinguishable "letters." The number twenty is of importance in connection with the circumstance that protein molecules are aggregates formed out of about twenty different amino acid residues. The directive to build a particular amino acid residue into a protein at a certain location would then be deduced from combinations of three basic groups at a certain location in a DNA molecule.[109]

Estimates have been made of the amount of "information" that in this way can be stored in the DNA molecules in the nucleus of a cell. It seems probable that each DNA molecule will correspond to a single "gene," as the carriers of genetic information in the chromosomes of the cell nucleus have been called. It is possible that the nuclei of human cells may contain one hundred thousand genes, each gene corresponding to a DNA molecule with fifteen thousand basic pairs. With each set of three pairs counting for a "letter," one would arrive at the equivalent of about five hundred million "letters." Taking a printed page of a book as containing about three thousand letters (including spacings and signs of interpunction), this might be equivalent to about one hundred and sixty thousand pages.[110]

As regards the reproduction of the DNA molecules needed in cell multiplication and for the production of germ cells, it is assumed that the two parallel chains can separate (probably step by step), and that each one picks up material (already present in its neighborhood) from which it can build up an appropriate complement to itself, so that again it becomes a double chain. This mode of "copying" ensures that the proper order of the groups is retained in each of the two double chains formed by this process.

Much attention is being given to the way in which the information contained in the DNA molecules is applied in the synthesis of protein molecules (assuming that amino acid groups of various kinds already are available). A system of auxiliary substances is involved in the transmission of information, denoted as "messenger RNA" (RNA indicating ribonucleic acid), soluble or "adapter RNA," and others.[111] The auxiliary material, amino acid groups, sugars, phosphates, etc. needed in the syntheses must have been supplied by various enzyme-regulated cycles of processes going on in the cell.

§ 81.

Apart from information directing the synthesis of enzymes and other proteins, there must be present information concerning a host of further data. Among other things, proper timing is needed: syntheses must occur in a certain order, and particular life cycles must be regulated.[112] It is assumed that starting and stopping is regulated by the presence of inhibitors, and de-inhibitors, or stimulators, etc., several of which are known.[113] The timing must be a reaction partly upon the amounts of substances already produced in the cell, partly upon exterior phenomena such as changes of temperature, of salinity, of light and darkness, etc., but little is known concerning the processes involved.

There must also be instructions concerning the architecture of the system: products cannot just be dumped anywhere but must be brought to specific locations, and structures must be built up as a support for other materials;[114] e.g., the proper location of walls within and around cells must be ensured. As noticed in the preceding chapter, life may have begun in systems with a more or less definite structure supported by crystalline material; the use of fluid material may have been a later invention. This leads us to the topic of the transportation of material resulting from synthetic processes. For a part transportation may be left to diffusion as a result of Brownian motion. Actual flow can be a result of accumulation of material at a certain spot pushing other material aside. But this still puts before us the question of forces when we try to imagine how newly synthesized molecules are freed from the support where the reactions have taken place, how they "press" against molecules already present, etc. It cannot be quite a passive process: there must be some activity at certain spots. There can be, of course, active deformation of molecules as a result of relocation of electrons, leading to attractions or repulsions between certain groups of atoms. Such deformations, when occurring in chains or other groups of connected molecules, can lead to the motion of structural parts in a cell. Flow systems have been observed in cells, of a nature which baffles many attempts at explanation, and the problem arises whether there are instructions for these motions.[115]

With all this, the set of instructions must have a large amount of versatility since there must be an ability to cope with many kinds of changes in the environment. There must also be the ability to cope with the fact that the movements occurring in the cells often seem to be rather haphazard and erratic: they certainly are not nicely periodic as oscillations in a physical system. Finally, it has been found that cells and cell systems have enormous powers to repair damage; thus, the information system must be able to cope with errors.[116]

There has not yet been found a method for estimating the total amount of information which will be needed to ensure the proper growth of a living organism from germ cell to a living being. The problem is utterly complicated and thus far cannot even be stated in a clear form since we do not know how much can be left to purely physical (or chemical) effects, or how much variation is tolerated in the execution of the program. It will be of great importance for the discussion of basic biological problems if data concerning this amount of information can be obtained.[117] In that case we can consider the problem of whether the amount needed is comparable with the amount that can be stored in the DNA molecules, or whether there is a wide disparity between the two amounts. The problem also involves the question whether the information present in the DNA molecules may contain redundancies, and how far redundancies can be useful in order to prevent "misunderstanding" and to cope with possible errors occurring in the growth process.

§ 82.

We face the problem that either the available information is sufficient to guide the physical and chemical processes involved in the growth of a cell in all details, as would be the case in a completely automatized factory; or the instructions available in the DNA code indicate only a set of more or less abbreviated data, each of which needs additional interpretation through a nonmechanical, nonphysical agent, that is, through conceptual activity.

The first point of view is often taken as a guiding line in biochemical research. However, although great advances are being made and great possiblities for extension of knowledge in this respect are still ahead, the descriptions of processes of biochemical synthesis and metabolism, as well as those of processes of growth and reproduction, leave many gaps open. They can be compared with descriptions of industrial processes giving information on machinery, etc., but relying on the active participation of intelligent workers, foremen, engineers, and so on, to put the machinery into operation and stop it again, to have an eye on the transfer of material, to interpret instructions and blueprints, and, if necessary, to correct errors in the orders. The descriptions which are found in biochemical literature do not exclude the possibility of intervention of conceptual activity; on the contrary, most of them must rely upon some kind of auxiliary processes for the many details which are not covered by the description.[118]

An author who has explicitly stated his belief that organisms on the whole do *not* store information by mechanistic means is Elsasser, as has been mentioned earlier (see note 85). Waddington in his book *The Ethical Animal* seems to approach the idea that there is more than mechanically stored information.[119]

Many objections can be brought forward against the idea that the development and growth of a living organism should be completely programmed by the store of information in the DNA molecules (plus perhaps information in other molecules). In the first place there is the question: "From where did the information arise? Who or what arranged the program?" The answer that the program has been derived from the structure of previous living beings leaves open the question how complicated structures can arise from simpler ones, and how information content can increase. The answer "through natural selection" is unsatisfactory and certainly cannot hold at the physical (atomic or molecular) level. Moreover, there is the difficulty of the statistical nature of the physical laws at the atomic level, which precludes full programming at that level. Finally, the assumption that growth is completely programmed leads to the idea that all processes within a living organism are results of programs, so that organisms would be automata, and no way is left for bringing into the picture any form of valuation, choice, or other conceptual activity.

We prefer the point of view that the information present in the DNA molecules is of a summary character, and that it needs interpretation through conceptual activity in the organism, which activity is transmitted from process to process in a direct subjective way. The acceptance of this point of view is not a whimsical fantasy. I am convinced that it will lead to a new attitude in looking at results of observations and experiments, and that it will often induce us to group data and problems in ways different from those followed until now.

§ 83.

The introduction of conceptual activity as a factor in the processes of life is not a simple matter. It cannot be invoked as a panacea to stop all gaps in our knowledge. Although we have recognized a certain freedom as an essential element, we must look for more or less definite forms of strategy fitting together into an organized whole probably with a more or less hierarchical arrangement. Ideas from the theory of certain games may be of use in this connection. Thus, along with the search for codes guiding the synthesis of proteins in living cells, one must also attempt to analyze the intervenient steps from the point of view of strategies, each with its own pliability, rather than always looking for mechanical methods of operation. Certain "letters" or "words" in the language contained in the DNA molecules may refer to particular strategies or substrategies with the understanding that there is room for improvisation in the application of each strategy.[120]

As indicated in the preceding chapter, the main motivation for the strategies must be the aim to avoid dead ends in cyclic sets of processes, although other aims probably have arisen in the course of evolution, for instance, aims connected with esthetic effects. We have assumed that the basic form of conceptual activity must be found in influencing choices between situations which are considered as equally probable on the basis of quantum laws. It is necessary to amplify this idea by assuming that there are cooperative forms of conceptual activity affecting the reactions of large (sometimes very large) complexes of atoms more or less "in a single grip."[121] That this involves the assumption of "foci" of "wisdom" in living bodies has been mentioned in note 86. The term "focus" here is an abstract term: it does not refer to groups of atoms which can be located observationally. We must also warn against the naive idea that in these foci there should be operative a more or less adequate representation of what is going to happen or of the consequences thereof, in any form which *we* would connect with it. In so far as there is a concept, we can better term it a "myth," thus making use of a vague analogy with the role played by myths in human societies, where myths operate through representations far away from any "objective" picture of facts.

It will be impossible to reach down to these representations by means of methods of physical observation. At most we may be able to guess by analogies. Keeping in mind Bohr's warning (see the end of § 65), we conclude that it will not be possible to observe any elementary activity on the atomic

level. But we may become able to discuss the results of a
collection of similar processes and compare their outcome in
a living organism with the outcome we might have expected
from an analogous purely physical situation according to the
predictions of quantum theory. We may find that there is less
dispersion and more definiteness in the living organism. This
will be the closest approach on the microscopic scale that we
can reach toward the functioning of life as different from
mere statistical randomness.

A topic which may afford a basis for research concerning
such effects of greater definiteness is the problem of *structural imperfections*. In inorganic crystals the lattice structure
is never perfect (see § 53). Structural errors occur by chance
as the result of random processes operative during the growth
of a crystal, and something is known about their frequency.
If the synthesis of proteins, etc., in living cells were a process
affected by the same laws as inorganic crystallization, we
might expect similar errors in the resulting products. At present there is no method for detecting structural imperfections
in the products built up in the living cell, nor do we know
how far imperfections can be tolerated in the molecules serving as structural elements in a living being. We are confronted
here with an important problem, which, like that considered
at the end of § 81, may be amenable to quantitative analysis.
If it is found that the amount of errors normally occurring
in anorganic crystals is too large for the protein molecules
which must serve in a living structure, an indication would
be obtained for the effectiveness of a nonphysical activity.

§ 84.

An indication for conceptual activity can perhaps also be
found in the behavior of cells which come into contact with
one another. This behavior has been extensively investigated
by Weiss, who uses the term "mutual recognition" for the
evidence of discrimination which comes forward from the observational data.[122] In various cases, for instance, in wound

healing and in transplantation experiments, cells are observed to move, and in this process they make contacts with one another. Cells of the same type, when reaching each other, draw close together and remain joined; this need not immediately imply the formation of static bonds, but the cells continue to glide over one another, changing their relative positions until an apparently satisfactory and stable pattern has been reached. On the other hand, if cells of different types come together, there is no indication of a positive reaction to each other's presence, and they separate by withdrawal of those parts of their borders that had been in touch.

When cells of a living organism have artificially been separated by breaking down the adhesions between them and then have been brought into an environment which can maintain their life for an extended period, they are often found to reaggregate into a structure of the original type. Cells can also "locate" their proper destination in the body even if they are deprived of their customary routes for getting there. Thus, there is association and segregation among cells, resulting in the formation of ordered patterns which are actively insured and guarded and restored after disturbances by a system of mutual conformances and nonconformances with which the various cell types are endowed. Muscles reached by nerve cells send a specifying influence back into the nervous centers with information on what muscle of what name lies at the end of what line.[123]

Weiss stresses the importance of specificity of interacting cells as a real and basic control of cell behavior. Various mechanisms are considered to explain the phenomenon of recognition, which perhaps may be based upon conforming charge distributions, conforming molecular groupings, or as yet unsuspected mechanisms.[124]

While admitting the importance of chemical or physical effects in these processes of recognition, I venture the hypothesis that "recognition" is accompanied by some concept of "this is it," however vague that may be. It must involve a notion of something that is "all right," that "had to be done" or "had to be found," with a vague anticipation that it may lead to further possibilities. Such a concept would be rooted in a subjective feature of the organism constituted by the cell. The terms used by Weiss and Waddington in their discussions of the problem of recognition seem to show that they are struggling with ideas of this kind, while still feeling themselves bound to search for more physical concepts. It looks almost as if Weiss uses the term "specificity" as a substitute for the notion of subjectivity.

I believe that we must go further, and that we must start from the assumption that *each cell has an individuality of its own.* These individualities may be greatly suppressed in multicellular organisms by dominating influences which force large groups of cells into a state comparable to robots, but special circumstances will call their individual subjective aspects into activity again. It is important to introduce the notion of conceptual activity as an efficient factor in the complexes of reactions shown by cells. Even if this is accepted only as a provisional link in our reasoning, it can point to new ways of approach for the understanding of cellular activities and of their integration into a working whole.[125]

§ 85.

The discussions of the previous section lead us to the following conclusions:

1. The information or set of instructions codified in the DNA molecules of the cell nucleus should be considered as a set of strategies rather than as a set of fixed programs. These strategies have a certain pliability, and their application can be adapted to circumstances. Some strategies may have turned into more or less fixed programs with loss of pliability. Strategies and programs can refer to all kinds of activities in the cells, metabolism, synthesis, movements, etc.

2. The assumption that it is strategies which are codified rather than fixed programs requires the assumption that dis-

criminating activity, that is, conceptual activity, comes into play in their application.

3. Strategies can be brought into action simultaneously or separately under the influence of master strategies. There must be forms of conceptual activity on various levels. Reigning over these forms of conceptual activity, each cell has a certain subjective form for itself which guides its reactions to what is happening within and around it.

We may imagine that in the period of perhaps some billions of years during which life was preparing for its future cellular form on earth a great many strategies were tried out in cyclic sets of processes and in complexes of such sets, and that at the same time a coding system for them was developed. It can become a task for biological research to find out which "elementary strategies" or "unit strategies" can be recognized, and whether these may be connected with particular "words" in the DNA language.

The assumption of conceptual activity implies that there is an efficient influence of the continuity of subjective form in sets of processes. This means that there is transmission of information which is not coded completely in the chemical system, information which in some way sets the purpose to retain freedom. Life is the outcome of the persistence of subjective forms carrying such purposes.

The idea has been expressed in the biological literature that additional information not contained in the chemical structure of the germ cells may come from the environment since every living system must be considered in never ending reaction with its environment. It is then necessary to ask what kind of information is meant. If the supplementary data coming from the environment are such as can be ascertained from the physical properties of the environment according to the principles of physics, the available data are limited by the statistical character of the outcome of any observation. Such data cannot bring us further since the most intimate reactions in living beings depend upon decisions at those spots where the physical laws leave indeterminacy. Moreover, we then have lost the idea that a purpose is carried along since the idea of retaining some freedom in reactions cannot be deduced from physical properties of the environment.

If, on the other hand, it is argued that the influence of the environment need not go through the physical observational process with its unavoidable loss of data, a new principle would be invoked which so far has never been put forward in an explicit form. It would mean that the forms of development observed in living beings are guided by relations which cannot be tested by any experimental method. Evidently we then have introduced a metaphysical point of view, and we have admitted that life involves more than the domain of physics. Although the form might be different, we would approach the point of view defended in this essay.

§ 86.   The appearance of mutations

Geneticists have come to the result that the origin of a mutation must be found in the substitution of a different amino acid residue in one of the enzymes that are produced in a cell since a change in an enzyme will lead to changes in cellular reactions and thus in processes of growth. It is further assumed that a substitution in an enzyme occurs as a result of a change in one or more of the basic groups in a DNA molecule. The mechanism of the replication of DNA molecules through the separation of the two chains, each of which collects the necessary material to build a complementary partner, will ensure that once a change has been introduced it will be reproduced correctly in the "daughter" DNA molecules.

This picture of a mutation is sometimes presented as the key to the understanding of the process of evolution. It induces us to direct great attention to the "language" contained in the DNA molecules as a representation of the various proteins that must be synthesized in the cell. It is evident that "cracking the code" — as the current expression is — will be of enormous interest for our understanding of the processes in the cell. It is sometimes even suggested that we may become able to change the order of the groups in the DNA molecules artificially by means of chemical reactions, so that there may be found a possibility of directly influencing the production of new mutations. It must not be forgotten, however, that all methods of chemical investigation thus far are carried out by introducing certain substances into the environment in which the cells or their nucleic material are embedded, and it is left to the molecules themselves to react upon these substances, to exchange part of their material for other material, etc. A particular method of investigation makes use of viruses, which apparently "attack" the genetic material of cells; but also this is more or less working "in the bulk." One cannot attack a single molecule, and it is doubtful whether this ever may be possible without attacking life itself and killing it.

The picture of a mutation in the form indicated here leads to questions on various levels. In order to make possible the reproduction of DNA molecules either without change or with changes, there must be available a sufficient "pool" of the various groups out of which these molecules are assembled. As mentioned before, it is supposed that the necessary material is produced in synthetic processes occurring in the cell under the guidance of appropriate enzymes. Thus, the picture as sketched here can be operative only when there has already been reached a high level in cellular evolution. There is no picture so far of the detailed processes by which the primary synthesis of long DNA chains proceeds. Can one assume that forces such as are operative in the case of anorganic crystallization are sufficient to ensure the proper structure?

When it is assumed that the synthesis of the DNA molecules proceeds by putting into a proper order groups which already have been made available beforehand, the idea that a "mistake" can occur and that a wrong group may appear at a given location looks acceptable. The fact that mutations can be induced by submitting cells to powerful radiation perhaps can be explained by assuming that first some DNA molecules are damaged, and that next, when they split into two halves, the damaged parts associate themselves with wrong groups.

The change in an enzyme, which is considered to be the result of a change in the language of the DNA molecules, will lead to changes in cellular reactions. The question arises: "Will life still be possible with these changes?" The general opinion is that in many cases this will not be possible, and that many mutations must be considered as lethal. Only in a few cases a "viable" result makes its appearance. But it is unknown what is involved in the production of a viable mutation out of the change of an enzyme. One must suspect that it needs internal adjustments. Then the problem arises: "Do these adjustments come out automatically, or is it that some direction is given?"

The descriptions in the literature, while pointing to features of great importance, leave many gaps to which no answer has been found and which appear particularly difficult when one keeps to the mechanistic picture. I propose that we should consider a mutation primarily as a *change in strategy*. This change may be induced by the relocation of certain groups in DNA and in enzymes, which change, if not destructive, can be met by an appropriate change in the plan of development of the organism. The words "change in strategy" and "change of plan" again bring to expression that the organism has a subjective form, and that conceptual activity at a variety of levels is involved in its reactions. While mostly induced by what we would consider as chance, it is a reaction to this chance directed by certain aims, primarily by the aim to resist being driven into a dead end. Many tentatives of the subjective form may fail, and a viable mutation is something of a major achievement. When success has been attained and has become more or less stabilized, so that the viable mutation starts to appear in great numbers, natural selection can operate on it. The stabilization of the mutation, however, is de-

179

pendent upon more than only the change in the code incorporated in the DNA molecules: a complex of reactions following upon this change must have been stabilized as well.

§ 87.

I return to the basic notion of the principle of natural selection, which is that differences in character of the various species involve differences in survival value, and that selection comes into operation as a result of the latter differences. This confronts us with the question: "Can we assume that each difference in character *involves a definite difference in survival value?*" Various authors have recognized that we are facing a problem here. Olson, for instance, mentions that there are "small features which show patterns of origin, persistence, and trends, often directional for some span of time, in spite of the fact that there is no apparent way of relating them to specific adaptation."[126]

There are many instances of variety in pattern, by far more conspicuous than those considered by Olson, where it is extremely difficult to suppose that each separate pattern has its own specific survival value. This refers to such classes of living beings as Diatoms, Foraminifera, Radiolaria, and others. To take the case of Diatoms: Several thousands of species have been described, each with its own distinctive pattern, each breeding true to type (otherwise they could not be used as guide fossils). Of course there must have been mutations to produce the variety of patterns. However, while we may assume that the Diatom type as such has a specific survival value in comparison with other classes of algae, and while there also may be differences in this respect between discoidal forms and spindle-shaped forms, etc., it seems improbable that each separate pattern which is shown by the manifold discoidal forms has its own distinctive survival value. In other words: It is highly improbable that any special pattern, say that of the species of the genus Arachnoidiscus, has emerged in competition for survival with other discoidal forms slightly

differing from the Arachnoidiscus type. If one would assume
this for all the now existing types of Diatoms, one would be
required to suppose that nature in the preceding geological
ages has experimented, so to say, with tens of thousands of
possible forms, out of which about two thousand to three
thousand have finally remained. This would raise the question:
"What would the competing forms have been like? Forms with
more radii or with less radii, in symmetric patterns or with
imperfect symmetry? Why should the number of radii affect
survival value?" Nowhere has there been found any indication
for such a hypothesis.

Among the factors which determine the details of a pattern
we certainly must count purely physical effects.[127] Symmetry
often may be a result from physical effects. The laws of diffusion will play a part; sometimes these can lead to rhythmic
patterns when diffusion takes place simultaneously with chemical reactions in colloidal material. Surface tension is another
important physical force. (The effects of atomic arrangement
which become visible in the forms of anorganic crystals, however, may be too far down from the scale of visible patterns,
and, for instance, the rule of rationality which prevents crystals from having exact fivefold symmetry does not operate in
the patterns exhibited by living beings.)

Nevertheless, even admitting that physical effects are responsible for part of the symmetry, it is impossible to explain
the whole gamut of forms, symmetric and nonsymmetric,
from physical effects alone. *The gamut is far too rich for that.*
The forms observed depend not only upon the physical effects but also upon the location of the points where this or
that physical effect started to work and on the instant of time
at which it was brought to work. We must look for something
which governs location and timing.

Given a basic type of living being, I believe there is latitude
for a kind of patterning effect which is *"at play"* somewhere
within the genetic system, which induces the action of certain
physical forces at some points and that of other forces at
other points or other instants of time, and which, in combi-

nation with the effects of these forces, leads to the observed patterns. This patterning effect, operating within the possibilities left open by the statistical rules embodied in the physical laws, is a form of conceptual activity directed by a sense of values.[128]

In the cases considered here, in the manifold patterns exhibited by Diatoms, Radiolaria, Foraminifera, mollusk shells, butterflies, and other classes of living beings, the "sense of values" somehow must be connected with beauty. This is not meant to indicate that there is an activity which "foresees" the resulting pattern and evaluates it on the same esthetic basis as a human artist would do. The evaluation must be connected with other features, more primitive, more directly related to the atomic situation on which it operates. In the classes of living beings referred to there unfolds for us a series of attempts at pattern-arranging not connected with survival value but aiming at esthetic results.[129]

§ 88. *Adaptation as an instance of conceptual activity*

Let us now consider the adjustments which are necessary in order that a mutation arising from a change in a gene may lead to a being that can live. A first point is that, granted that the new organism has no internal constructional misfits which would prevent living, it will have altered potentialities; hence, it must find a new way of life amidst the surroundings into which it is born. The necessary adaptations may go in the direction of efforts already made by the predecessors of the new type, but they can also present new problems, particularly when the modification of the bodily structure is important.

The example which is closest to us is that of man's brain, as has been pointed out by Alfred Russel Wallace.[130] The last phases of bodily evolution which gave to man his present brain size and brain structure brought potentialities which man could develop and which he has been developing ever since. While brain size as a general achievement was a factor in the competition for existence among the prehuman forms, and while, once the present brain type was acquired, there was competition between the resulting human forms concerning the successful application of the new faculties, we cannot assume that there has been a competition for existence bearing upon the formation of such and such particular cell connections involved in the potentialities of our brain system. Wallace pointed to the fact that all men on earth, notwithstanding the primitive circumstances under which many peoples are living, have brains which, when proper opportunities and education are given, can reach up to almost the highest faculties of our present civilization. It is therefore highly probable that all these faculties have been present immediately in the earliest forms of real man in a package, so to say, although the early men had no occasion to make full use of all that was latent in them.

This forces us to assume that there has been a biological development in the nervous system and in the brain, which provided an instrument of high potentialities *before it was put to full use in the struggle for life.* If natural selection, in the sense in which we have applied this term before, operated during the growth of the brain, the structure which resulted showed potentialities which far outran the issues of the original struggle for life.[131]

The pattern of nervous connections which developed during that earlier struggle for life may have some analogy with the systems studied by Rosenblatt as "perceptrons" (see Appendix to Chapter 5). There apparently have evolved a number of successive "layers" of associator cells, and, while there was some general underlying scheme in the connections between them, the details of the connections were more or less haphazard and not "planned." They may even be different from individual to individual. But with the structure there was given the potentiality of learning, which — as in the perceptron — may have involved adjustment of transmission factors along the connections. The adjustment is probably something that is not transmitted in a hereditary way and must be learned by each young individual anew; we may suppose, however, that gradually there has evolved a potentiality for learning more and more rapidly. It is difficult to distinguish at this point between transmission through education and transmission through organic structure (including chemical effects): it might be that the increase of capacity for learning has something to do with a change in some organic adjustment which is transmitted by the mechanism of heredity.

Julian Huxley, Waddington, Berrill, and others have pointed out that evolution in man now has become a cultural process elaborating the potentialities for understanding and cooperation between men, as well as the potentialities for probing further into the mysteries of what surrounds us. This cultural process is a direct extension of the biological evolution. It stresses the fact that a certain organic structure was prepared before all its potentialities had been tested; and at the same time it stresses that conceptual activity, after having accompanied the development of organic structure, now has reached a point where it can immensely elaborate the potentialities of that structure. In its early stages the conception did not foresee that it would ultimately make possible the appearance of the artist, the scientist, the philosopher. The only primitive conception may have been the awareness that a large type of brain would open more possibilities, although we have no idea of the form in which such a conception may have been clad. Roughly we may make a comparison with the fact that, while it can be foreseen that the construction of an enlarged IBM machine will open the possibility of more extensive calculations, it may also open up new domains of mathematics unknown to those who constructed the machine.

§ 89.

What has been discussed in the preceding section must be applicable to other mutation phenomena, or rather to chains of mutation processes. As a second example we may consider the eye in so far as it is the instrument for the perception of a *field of vision.* For the present purpose the distinction between the composite eye of insects and the vertebrate eye (which is also found in the Cephalopoda) is not of primary interest: the point at issue is the difference between light sensitive organs and an organ for vision. Perhaps the insect eye affords the simpler case.

We do not know which steps have succeeded one another in the relevant evolutionary history, but we can imagine that the following stages may have been features of selective importance in the struggle for existence: (*a*) the development of sensitivity for light in special cells; (*b*) the increase of sensitivity by the addition of a lens, which entailed that maximum sensitivity became restricted to a more or less definite direction; (*c*) sensitivity for light coming from several directions, as a result of the appearance of more than one light sensitive organ. Such steps may have been the outcome of "chance" mutations, although these words rather cover up the mysteries than explain their nature. However, the evolution from sensitivity for light coming from a few directions toward the acquisition of a field of vision is a step of different order. This cannot have been the result of a stage by stage process, each stage adding a few more directions, and each being subjected to natural selection through a difference in survival value.

As a more pertinent alternative I would suppose that there exist certain growth processes which, once they have led to the appearance of a few similar units, may continue to be active and produce a large number of similar units, say of single tubes each with a light sensitive nerve cell and a lens, juxtaposed with more or less spherical symmetry so as to form an organ of the type of the composite insect eye. It must be assumed that at the same time connections have been formed between the nerve cells, of the somewhat random nature of those found in the perceptron, with intermediate layers of associator cells and ultimately leading toward a set of response units. *Some form of conceptual activity must have been connected with the response units,* which was able to induce an adjustment of the transmission coefficients *in such a way that pattern recognition became possible.* Again a form of play may have formed a transitional stage before a more permanent system of connections and of pattern recognition evolved. At any rate, it is only when pattern recognition had become an established habit that an instrument appeared which could become an asset in the struggle for existence since it brought enhanced survival power. (A further extension of pattern recognition must have taken place when binocular vision became possible as a result of the location of two eyes at the front of the head, as occurred in certain mammals. What happened then is again an instance of conceptual activity, which started to recognize distance and depth in the field of vision. Later this must have influenced muscular movements.)

My point, consequently, is that there occur processes of growth and processes of multiplication of elementary organs which, after having originated in connection with mutations of selective value, can continue to operate without being subjected at once to commensurate selective effects. Continuous growth can be noxious, but here the point at issue is that sometimes it may lead to structures which ultimately find a useful role in the life of the organism and provide an unforeseen playground for new adjustments.[132]

Thus, I see three phases of importance: (i) *growth* more or less independent from the issues of natural selection; (ii) *adjustment of constructional details* in the growing structure so that it will not make life impossible but on the contrary can be put to some use;[133] (iii) *adaptation of behavior* on the basis of the new faculties and elaboration of new forms of interaction with the environment. While conceptual activity of some form must play a part in phase (ii), and perhaps even in phase (i), it certainly must be effective in phase (iii) since this phase involves choices, decisions, and the storage of memories in situations never before encountered for which no standardized reflections were available. In such a case as the evolution of vision, we may say that a new dimension

186

has been opened for the struggle for existence, which requires new forms of adaptation.

Adaptation, when taken in the sense presented here, is not a mere passive result of natural selection deciding a posteriori which form of behavior gives the largest survival value. While it is true that natural selection is an ultimate arbiter, there is an active process working at many earlier stages, involving conceptions, the solution of problems, new discoveries of possibilities. This active adaptation would be my interpretation of the phrase "response" to the "challenge" of the environment.[134]

The two forms of adjustment, internal during growth and external as adaptation, are results of a single tendency; hence, they must be closely interwoven. It is probable, therefore, that the external adaptation can have reactions upon the internal conceptual activities, so that it also may have influence upon further mutational processes.[135]

I hold that the conceptual element involved in this active adaptation is an expression of creativity in the sense in which this term was defined in Chapter 1. This creativity is an element in evolution which can lead to a progression toward more highly organized forms, that is, forms with more potentialities for diversified activities ("can" and not "will," as there occur backslides with a reduction of potentialities). In this train of ideas *each species or each separate biological type must be considered as the realization of a purpose in the realm of life.*[136] It will be recognized that various aspects of the relations between purposes, as discussed in § 60 of the previous chapter, have their counterpart in relations between species.

It is to the recognition that each biological species is the realization of a purpose that I look *for the explanation of direction in evolution.* Directed evolutionary advance is not an exclusive result of blind forces, not even with the help of mysteriously invoked potencies of "natural selection." It is the result of a fundamental feature in the universe which makes use of that which it encounters in "chance" occasions and *reacts to it with purposes*. Natural selection is only an ultimate fiat: it operates on the results of purposive activities.[137]

§ 90.

We can summarize the preceding considerations as follows:

(*a*) Mutations can arise from reactions to random events.

(*b*) Mutations involve extensive adjustments both during the growth of bodily structure and in behavior, that is, in the response of the new structure to its environment.

(*c*) Both internal and external adjustment involve conceptual activity. The adjustment is not a matter of pure chance. A mutation leading to the appearance of a new biological type must be considered as the realization of a purpose.

(*d*) A reaction (feedback) from the adjustments in the growth process to the memory and to the coding system is needed to ensure the development of a posterity retaining the character of the mutation.

(*e*) There must also be feedback to the memory and to the coding system from the conceptual activity operating in the adjustment of behavior.

(*f*) The feedback partly leads to coding occurring through chemical features built into the DNA molecules, which features can be directly transmitted to the offspring. Along with this there is transmission of information which is not coded in the chemical features.

(*g*) It follows from (*e*) and (*f*) that there can be hereditary effects arising from the response of the living being to its environment.

(*h*) Conceptual activity in the adjustments involves creativity. It is this feature to which we ascribe the progressive character of the major lines of evolution.

(*i*) Conceptual activity and creativity are directed in principle to an increase of potentialities for activity. They are not exclusively restricted to ensuring a maximum of survival for the new type. There are other factors than mere survival which play a part in the evolutionary process and which may aim at esthetic effects, for instance.

(*j*) Natural selection is a fiat upon the appropriateness for survival of internal adjustments and of adaptations of behavior involved in a mutation. It is not in itself a principle which explains the directions that are observed in evolution.

(*k*) What is greatly needed for the investigation of the problems discussed in this chapter is a quantitative approach to two problems: (1) How much information is required to guide the growth of a living being from germ cell to maturity and how much information can be stored in the DNA molecules of the genes, in order to make a comparison of the two amounts of data? (2) How much precision is necessary in the synthesis and in the reproduction of molecules to prevent the normal functioning of the organism from being impaired, in comparison with the amount of errors to be expected as a result of statistical fluctuations and quantum uncertainty in anorganic crystallization?

There exists no proof that natural selection can explain the evolution of living organisms as a result of "blind forces," that is, when it is based on the assumption that the only effects coming into play are those described by physics for atomic and molecular structures. No reference to the "relentless control" exerted by natural selection has ever proved that it can make probable that which is highly improbable according to the laws of physics (compare note 81). It does not make sense to invoke natural selection as a factor operating between molecules or radicals, produced by anorganic reactions, however complicated these may be. There never has been presented a sufficient analysis of the problems involved. Whatever changes may be needed in details of the foregoing assumptions, I hold that no road can be found leading to an understanding of life which does not introduce some form of conceptual activity, and that all suggestions for an explanation of life on a purely mechanistic basis are worthless. A discussion of natural selection which does not start explicitly from the existence of life with its faculty for sensing purposes subconsciously invokes some effect of this kind or is blind to the gaps which are left open.[138]

Biology is the study of life as a manifestation of inventiveness and creativity, demonstrating itself in growth and development, in its multitude of forms, in its spread over all forms of habitat, in the achievement of beauty, enjoyment, freedom, and consciousness. Development requires the establishment of traditions as support for its persistence, and much of biological study is appropriately devoted to the understanding of these traditions as exhibited in behavior, in pattern and organization, in metabolism, in reproduction. However, the essence of life is initiative breaking existing traditions, increase of freedom, and making and breaking of new traditions in ever-growing richness of possibilities.

RETROSPECT AND FINAL OBSERVATIONS

I will now briefly review the leading thoughts developed in the preceding chapters.

We started by introducing certain notions presented as a set of ultimate principles to be used in the construction of a unified picture against which our experience can be projected. The construction cannot be explained by referring it to still another picture since that other picture would then be the ultimate one: it must obtain its meaning through the relations introduced between the terms applied in the exposition, as well as through a comparison with the relations that we find around us. For our purpose the most important of the latter are: on the one hand, the results of physics and its related sciences; on the other hand, the subjective phenomena which we experience within ourselves, in the belief that they derive from effects functioning in all forms of life. We may find a somewhat analogous procedure in the method followed in metamathematics, and one can say that we introduce certain "objects" and certain "operations." Objects and operations in a metamathematical system are not defined by references to more basic notions, but must find their content in the relations assumed between them. The definitions to be given consequently run forward and backward between the same terms, which support one another through the connections expressed in these definitions.

The "objects" which we have distinguished are the following:

1. *Facts;*
2. *Forms of relatedness* (forms of definiteness).

We have introduced one "operation": *conceptual activity.*

The definitions run:

I. Conceptual activity is the experience of facts with emphasis on certain preferred forms of relatedness, leading to the establishment of a new fact which gives expression to the selected relationship.

II. Facts are the results of instances of conceptual activity which have come to their conclusions. In their turn, facts constitute material for new experience.

III. The recognition of forms of relatedness in experience is the essential feature of conceptual activity. Forms of relatedness can only be known and understood through the part they play in conceptual activity. Every aspect of the universe which involves the recognition of a form of relatedness implies conceptual activity. Each fact which is experienced, is experienced with forms of relatedness.

The reason for the introduction of the metaphysical principle involved in the notion of conceptual activity was to supply a *principle of discrimination and of organization* which is not found in physics. Conceptual activity is essentially *giving meaning to something* and thereby giving it relevance. It is the conception of a distinction which by its creation becomes effective. This is the basis for all structure, the first beginnings of which are found in the notions of quality, quantity, location in spatial relationship, and location in temporal relationship. Mechanistic pictures of the universe, as the picture developed in physics, are the formulation of chains of relationship or rules of succession between events. They necessitate empirical specifications of the situation or of the objects to which one or other of these rules can be applied. To make a full description of the universe, an abstract principle is needed which must fulfill the role of a qualifier from which the necessary distinctions can follow. The introduction of conceptual activity is therefore fundamental in our outlook on all that happens in the universe. It is the basis of all functioning.

Its introduction at the same time makes the picture of the universe wide enough to include the subjective aspects of the phenomena of life.

Conceptual activity is a process which drives itself to a result. Since every conception can give relevance only by leaving a background beyond that to which meaning is given, there never can be complete satisfaction: the background continually calls for new conceptual activity. Consequently, conceptual activity is *rhythmic*. The separate instances of conceptual activity are called *processes*. Their general aspects have been discussed in Chapter 1.

The stepwise or "atomic" character of conceptual activity is the basis for atomicity and quantization in physics. On the other hand, it provides the occasion for judgments since "to give meaning to something" is the same as "to conceive a judgment of values." Thus, atomicity and the effectiveness of valuation are directly connected.

The ultimate reality of the universe is considered as a multiple and never ending complex of steps or processes developing out of one another. Each process is a mode of functioning which arises out of the experience of existing facts and which by its completion passes into a new fact. Each process is an instance of conceptual activity: it is the experience of facts with an emphasis on certain forms of relatedness recognized in the experience and preferred as that which shall be expressed in a new fact. The phrase "preferred forms of relatedness" introduces the notion of *subjectivity*: it is the forms of relatedness preferred by whatever acts as a subject on a certain occasion. Conceptual activity appears at a certain focus and binds together that upon which it focuses.

There are infinitely many forms of relatedness. They furnish infinitely many potentialities for connections between facts. Examples are: relations of order and arrangement, quantitative relations, forms of physical relationship. Not less fundamental are esthetic relations and ethical relations. These are not considered as accidental byproducts of the other forms but as essential forms of relationship in their own right.

As stated before, forms of relatedness can be known and understood only through the role in which they appear in processes and in facts that can be experienced. It is not assumed that there exists a definite system of esthetic and ethical relations which can be known in complete form with full certainty. The point made is that subjective experience involving esthetic or ethical notions, notwithstanding the elusiveness of these notions, must be considered as important for our knowledge of the universe.

The recognition of definite forms of relatedness in experience, in preference to other possible forms (that which we have called the subjective emphasis on certain forms in preference to other forms), is the essential feature of conceptual activity.

Through their entrance in conceptual activity, the preferred forms of relatedness represent *potentialities for connections between future facts*. It follows that some recognition of future possibilities is an essential feature of conceptual activity (the quantification "some" is inserted because full recognition of future possibilities does not exist). Thus conceptual activity involves *anticipation* and *aim*. This is the teleological element accepted in the picture. It is the basis for the recognition of values, and the activity of selecting certain forms of relatedness in preference to other forms can be denoted as an evaluation of possibilities.

The recognition of values may not be construed as directed toward ultimate "final" ends: its range of vision (to use this term) is limited to a near future. Whether or not there exist "final" ends is beyond our recognition. We can recognize relations only in the experience we have, and, while we extrapolate and generalize, this never can bring absolute knowledge or absolute certainty.

The fundamental doctrine concerning conceptual activity is that *each instance of conceptual activity* (each process) *has a certain freedom in giving emphasis to particular forms of relatedness*. This doctrine of conceptual autonomy is the expression of a fundamental belief in *creativity as a basic fea-*

ture of the universe. There will never be an end to creative advance so long as it is impossible to express all forms of relationship in the outcome of a single process.

The scheme presented so far is a scheme of abstract relationship. It makes no sense to ask whether there is anything which acts as "carrier" of conceptions or of forms of definiteness. Neither the concept of matter nor that of living beings has as yet been reached. It is conceptual activity which serves as basis for all phenomena. The situation encountered in any philosophical attempt to construct a set of fundamental concepts is not essentially different from that which results when, for instance, a postulational development should be given of quantum theory. Here the abstract notion of the wave function must be introduced without having anything upon which it can be made to rest; mathematical equations must be set up for which one cannot invoke ideas concerning particles or concerning forces, for these do not yet exist in the scheme. It is only in later stages of the completely abstract development that relations are obtained which by means of appropriate postulates can be brought into connection with the results of observations. One may also consider the similar situation in the general theory of relativity and gravitation where "coordinates" are introduced to support an abstract notion of "space" or "space-time" before anything can be said about motions of tangible objects or about measurements. The usual presentations of these theories suppose that the reader is somewhat acquainted with the ideas to be developed: they seldom take the pain to build up a complete system of postulates and axioms; nor do most readers feel the necessity for a properly constructed edifice since interest mainly goes to application.

Perhaps we may ease the situation somewhat by assuming that the notions which have been introduced describe some kind of "field" intended to give room for the idea of value along with relations referring to space and time. The field of space and time and evaluations is to serve as a canvas upon which to project all relations in which we find ourselves involved. In some respects it may be helpful to consider the universe as filled with conceptual activity manifesting itself in an immense complex of processes, continually advancing and building up ordinary "space-time" by its continual progression, so that space-time relations are a result of conceptual activity. They come out partly as a result of fundamental relations, partly as a result of the course conceptual activity has taken. Two of the fundamental relations have been mentioned previously. One is that conceptual activity focuses itself each time upon a limited region of the universe, limited both as regards extension (with regard to "space") and as regards duration (with regard to "time"). The other is that a temporal direction has been introduced: we have spoken of the experience of existing facts, and of potentialities for connections between future facts; hence, there is a distinction between past and future. Various points which are involved in the elaboration of these principles have been discussed in Chapter 2 and in the Appendix to Chapter 4.

After this digression we return to the main line of thought. The freedom of selection in conceptual activity, postulated before, is limited by the doctrine that *there is a certain persistence of the emphasis and of the selection which occurred in the immediately preceding instance of conceptual activity.*

Each process has experience from an immediate predecessor not only through the fact in which that process has resulted but also through a continuity of subjective form of the conceptual activity in that process. There may be some transmission of subjective form from processes further in the past, but in many series of processes this transmission rapidly dwindles to ineffectiveness with increasing distance.

The persistence is the germ of *tradition* in emphasis. It makes possible the transmission of forms of relatedness through extensive complexes of processes. The possibility of transmission leads to the appearance of *societies of processes,* considered in Chapter 3. Societies of processes bring increased strength of persistence in the selected forms of relatedness and permit great intensity in the expression of these forms. Societies lead to the establishment of definite *lines of tradition* in which forms of relatedness are transmitted from step to step with little or no alteration.

In most societies each newly emergent process experiences the majority of the other members of the society in its past exclusively as facts, whereas it has direct subjective experience only from its immediate predecessor or from a small group of predecessors. Thus, the subjective aspect of the experience can become insignificant in comparison with a massive objective experience received from the facts presented by the majority of the members of the society. As a consequence of their belonging to a society, all these facts have certain features in common. This similarity can have the result that there is little or no conceptual activity of significant effectiveness in each newly emergent process. We may then say that conceptual activity becomes *dormant* in these societies. This means that transmission through the experience of a massive collection of facts of similar character has grown so strong that the awareness of possibilities for the selection of new forms of relatedness has diminished to practically nothing. Hence, there is no awareness of anything which would mean freedom, and traditions develop into rigid laws holding in these societies. *These rigid traditions form the basis of the physical laws and of physical causality.*

It is here that physics comes into the scheme together with all scientific knowledge in general, that is, knowledge based upon the observation of repeatedly occurring, completed facts. Physics and its related sciences constitute the analysis of persistent traditions in the relations between facts resulting from societies of processes. The picture does not give an absolute character to the physical laws: as traditions, although extending over immense periods, they are subjected to the possibility of changes which may lead to the establishment of new traditions. That we can observe these laws is a result of the circumstance that conceptual activity is also active within ourselves, so that we share in the experience of past facts and in the formation of conceptions concerning this experience.

The societies which are the carriers of the physical laws constitute matter. The term is used here so as to include both matter in the ordinary sense, and fields (wave fields, electric fields, etc.), and more generally anything the behavior of which is governed by definite laws. Various aspects of the laws of physics have been considered in Chapter 4.

The notions of self, of being a person, of intention or purpose, of message as distinct from noise, and of awareness do not count in the physical laws. Experience has taught that the formulation of these laws also requires the exclusion of esthetic and of ethical relationships.

The fact that the physical laws in many respects show a statistical character demonstrates that in each transmission of forms of relatedness by mere tradition certain determinative features are lost. As there is no coordinated conceptual activity in the societies considered here which could provide the possibility of making correlated decisions with regard to the lost forms of relatedness, there appears randomness with respect to these forms in the outcome of processes occurring under these circumstances. Thus, for certain forms of relationship all possible results have the same weight (as indicated in § 51, the words "the same weight" require that a method be introduced for the distinction between "different" results). From what is known from physical theory (as the interpretation of observational results), this randomness generally appears with respect to one half of the data which would be needed in a complete description of the behavior of a system in terms of coordinates and canonically conjugated momenta (quantities related to the velocities). The circumstance that one half of the observable variables can obtain definite values while the other half is left to randomness is connected with the fact that in the transmission of forms of relatedness by mere tradition, with the exclusion of the subjective aspect of conceptual activity, there is loss of information concerning something that is going on in the processes themselves (see § 47).

We can state this also in the following words: As there is neither self-awareness in societies in which conceptual activity has become dormant nor a direct connection between our self-awareness and that of processes taking place in those societies, knowledge concerning these processes can only be obtained by making observations from the outside. Such observations give information exclusively concerning the outcome of completed processes. No observational procedure can provide data about the forms of relatedness which disappear in the transmission by mere tradition from facts. In every observation information is lost. This must be the ground for the indeterminacy relations of quantum physics. The result is that in the atomic domain only statistical predictions can be made concerning the outcome of subsequent processes and of subsequent observations.

Coming to living beings, we are forced by *the fact that there exists life* and that we experience life within ourselves and recognize life in other beings to postulate that *there exist societies in which conceptual activity remains effective,* or, as we may say, remains *awake* instead of becoming dormant. In these societies direct transmission of subjective form is effective, and conceptual activity retains freedom, so that at least on certain occasions it exerts a more or less coordinated influence directed toward preferred forms of relatedness.

The effectiveness of conceptual activity postulated here can become apparent only through contrast with existing traditions; otherwise it loses itself in randomness. Its primitive form is *play,* which is an activity aiming at the expression of certain selected forms of relationship in the results of a set of successive processes. Such sets at first will have been of finite extent. Play is the introduction of new traditions, usually of limited scope, which are combined with or partially replace existing traditions. In many cases the play will come to an end; this necessitates the assumption that new starts are made again and again. In § 75 we suggested that there may exist societies of processes with effective conceptual activity connected not with atomic matter but perhaps with wave fields, which societies evolved along with the evolution of the universe of galaxies and stars. The conceptual activity in such societies may have induced forms of play in societies of other types containing atoms and molecules.

A decisive step in the development of play was the discovery of *cyclic sets of processes*, to which attention has been given in §§ 70 through 73 of Chapter 5. This made possible the accumulation of subjective experience concerning situations which were met again and again. It promoted the development of a notion that a certain freedom of decision was to be continually found within the cyclic set. The possibility of pursuing different courses while moving repeatedly through the same set must have kept conceptual activity awake instead of letting it become dormant. It must be here that the bifurcation originated in the evolution of societies, leading in one direction to the fixation of traditions and to societies where conceptual activity became dormant, and in the other direction toward societies where conceptual activity remained awake and found a way for continued effectiveness in cycles of processes. The distinction between the two lines of evolution may have evolved gradually and probably has been subject to many oscillations from one type to the other. This again requires the assumption that in earlier societies lines of transmission of subjective form must have remained open, and that conceptual activity had some freedom.

In societies based on cyclic sets of processes in which conceptual activity remains awake, successive processes are bound together by relations which conserve subjective form and find their determination from more data than those available to outsiders through the type of observation that forms the basis for the analysis of physical relationship. This has the consequence that quantum indeterminacy does not prevail to the same degree as we observe in systems where conceptual activity has become dormant: from time to time there is evaluation of possibilities, and there is some coordinated decision;

in other words, not all possibilities or all configurations obtain the same weight. In the societies now under consideration there is transmission of forms of relatedness along lines which we cannot discover with the aid of our methods of physical observation.

In these societies the development of play must have strengthened an awareness for the possibility of acting as an organism, as an entity distinct from its environment. This involves an integration of various lines of transmission. The assumption of the possibility of such an integration is a logical sequel to the assumption concerning the presence of special forms of connection between the subjective aspects of sets of processes. The awareness of being an entity distinct from its environment led to *the aim of making the play persistent,* of preventing that it should come to a dead end and peter out. With this aim we approach the *origin of life* in the more specific sense. The evolution of individualization and that of the tendency toward persistence are closely connected: both are consequences or expressions of the integration, and one cannot say which is the primary feature.

The evolution indicated here, with its strengthening of coordinated subjective transmission, can be described as the *evolution of memory.* This is a part of the subjective form transmitted from process to process and influencing conceptual activity in each new process. The manifold repeated experience in cyclical sets of processes accumulating in the memory provides conceptual activity with a tool which enables it to delegate patterns of conceptual activity to subordinate and more or less detached forms of conceptual activity. This may make possible an acceleration of the steps of the dominant conceptual activity. It also provides a possibility for accepting new evaluations and new forms of relatedness which can lead to the choice of new pathways or "new strategies" in the cyclic systems. This has been discussed in § 71. One of the results can be the choice of partially deterministic pathways by which certain portions of the development are fixed. The choice of such deterministic portions becomes most important when they lead on to a situation where a more extensive set of possibilities for choice is found: greater scope for choosing a continuation of the set of processes gives chances to make the play persistent in the face of a wider margin of disturbing changes in the environment. It can also lead to amplification of cycles and to the choice of new cycles or sets of cycles as a basis for operation on an extended scale. This we have termed the appearance of a *mutation,* and it involves a correlated array of changes in sets of processes. It is a step toward the exploration of new forms of life. Such developments usually will go together with a strengthening of the dominant form (or forms) of conceptual activity and a strengthening of the subjective notion of being an organism.

From what we know about living organisms it can be concluded that part of the transmission of patterns (as apparent in sets of processes) has become codified through the building up of chemical structures. It remains a problem to find out how much has been codified in that way, and what part must be played by conceptual activity to supplement the code by making subjective decisions or to interpret the code. Development has gone toward the formation of cells with their elaborate metabolic apparatus and their supporting structures, while most of the codification has been delegated into special genetic material; but this is a topic beyond our discussion. It seems that data concerning patterns and strategies are also stored in parts of the structure other than the recognized genetic material, and again there is the problem: "How much is stored 'mechanically' (or chemically), and what is left open to subjective decision?" It has been mentioned that investigations concerning the total amount of data that can be stored in the genetic material and comparison with the amount of data going into the growth and development of a living organism may give important information concerning the nature of life.

Several lines of development have led to the emergence of living beings with great receptiveness for forms of relatedness. In certain types this has led to the appearance of what we call *consciousness of purpose.* This must have been an outcome of the storage of representations of forms of relatedness in the memory in such a way that they can be easily retrieved. It must have been an evolution toward the recognition of a wide domain of possibilities and thus toward greater powers for action. Through the acquisition of such powers greater freedom has become possible: with regard to actions upon the environment more channels are open for choice.

Along with the purpose to ensure persistence other purposes have emerged in living organisms, of which a very conspicuous one is that of producing *patterns which have an esthetic value.* In the evolution of life upon the earth this must have occurred much earlier than the appearance of consciousness. To produce patterns which have a certain esthetic value is to give expression to a tendency for beauty. This is a form of "power of conception," and it must count as one of the freedoms which life has won.

In Chapter 6 we have discussed various aspects of the problem of natural selection as it is involved in the evolution of life. "Natural selection" is an expression for the "permissivity" of the environment with regard to the experimentation of conceptual activity. In its aggregate effect natural selection has had a great influence upon the emergence of forms of life which have been able to develop on the earth. But as a "motive power" in evolution it provides only a part of the story. The other part is the fundamental tendency toward new evaluations, toward experimentation, which is inherent in conceptual activity and which is at the basis of the phenomena of mutation. Mutations may be induced by chance effects, but in order to lead to something viable, arrays of adjustments and adaptations are necessary. Conceptual activity reacts upon chances which are recognized as "having some interest" or as "promising" and again and again attempts to find a course for making use of them.

The principles chosen as a basis for our philosophical picture have for a large part been taken from man's personal experiences. It is from inner life that we are acquainted with the urge to give expression to sensations and to thoughts. While sensations and thoughts arise as reactions to all that moves us, we know how the form of the sensation and the way in which it is expressed are influenced by our biological nature as well as by our social environment. We are aware of the support that can be given by tradition since traditions represent decisions which have already been made. We feel how experience can be intensified by our being part of various types of groups. We also know the danger of fossilization of traditions, against which our initiative must wage a never ceasing battle.

We have trusted the reality of these inner experiences and have considered them as experimental data to be treated with the same attention as the data concerning material happenings which man has collected in such wide variety. By taking them up into our philosophy the possibility has been found for the construction of a unified picture in which our knowledge concerning the physical behavior of matter is tied together with the evaluations and emotions that form the other side of our mind.

We consequently recognize that the zest which is living within us has sprung from a fundamental urge in the universe identical with the creative forces active everywhere in nature. As a result we see something that is akin to us in the aspects of nature around us, something that can speak to us in matter and its motion as well as in the forms of life. For one who is aware of this there is comradeship not only in his fellowmen: he can see comradeship in a much wider part of the world, and he is mindful that this commands our attention, our care, our sympathy. To him the beauty of the earth, of its living creatures as well as of crystals, of mountains, of moving water and the clouds, the stars, the sounds as well as the silence of nature may give expression to the urge of creativeness which pervades the entire universe.

To live is not merely to reproduce patterns. To live is a never ceasing attempt to make use of possibilities and to recognize new possibilities. A major feature of life is to grasp new forms of relationship and thereby to come into possession of new information. Part of this information becomes codified; another part is carried along in a subjective form which acts as a permanent source for new information and new experimentation. It will never be possible to explain life completely by means of a mathematical scheme, notwithstanding the fact that mathematical formalization can be applied to much that has been achieved. A crucial topic for study in biology must be the genesis of new information, the way in which it finds application, and the freedom of choice which a living organism can reach by its means. Such freedom can lead to advances in evolution through the rearrangement of processes which it may permit, similarly as the rearrangement of a mathematical proof can open new pathways in mathematical reasoning and discovery. Judging from what we experience within ourselves, we believe that forms of enjoyment are connected with this freedom. One would like to know what part is played by such enjoyment in the life of other beings as well as in the evolution of new living forms.

Life is a never ending struggle against that which otherwise would appear as mere statistical chance and chaos. It is an unceasing attempt to create order in domains in which values have been perceived. To live is to render that which has been received in a form different from what it was: to render it enriched by the values which conceptual activity has attached to it and has expressed in it. Conceptual activity is a manifestation of creativeness, and it will never be possible to predict which forms it ultimately may take. Life will always direct itself to new frontiers and ask new questions.

REFERENCES AND NOTES

The main books in which A. N. Whitehead has exposed his philosophic ideas in systematic form are the following ones:

Science and the Modern World (New York: The Macmillan Company, 1925, with numerous reprints); also published as a Mentor Book in various printings since 1948;

Process and Reality, an Essay in Cosmology (Cambridge, England: Cambridge University Press, 1929; also published in New York: The Macmillan Company, 1929, with differences in page numbers and in a few other respects); a paperback edition, derived from Macmillan's, has been published as a "Harper Torchbook" by Harper & Brothers, New York, 1960;

Adventures of Ideas (Cambridge, England: Cambridge University Press, 1933); also published as a Mentor Book by the Macmillan Company in 1955;

Modes of Thought (Cambridge, England: Cambridge University Press, 1938).

Quotations from these books will be given first with the page numbers of the original editions as listed here; then, for the first three books, between parentheses with an asterisk, with the page numbers of the paperback editions.

Part III, "Philosophical," of *Adventures of Ideas*, pp. 223–305 (177*–239*) can serve as a helpful summary of the ideas presented in *Process and Reality*.

Of the many books which have been written on Whitehead's philosophy by other authors, I mention only: *Victor Lowe, Understanding Whitehead* (Baltimore: The Johns Hopkins Press, 1962). Perhaps I may refer to p. 250 of Dr. Lowe's book. I have not consulted other books; most of them are occupied with aspects of Whitehead's philosophy which seemed to be less relevant with regard to the purpose I have in mind.

It is not possible to list all other books which have had influence upon the exposition given in this essay. Some of the more important are:

H. Bergson, *Les Deux Sources de la Morale et de la Religion* (Paris: Félix Alcan, 1932); quotations have also been taken from *L'Evolution Créatrice* by the same author (Paris: Félix Alcan, edition of 1930);

J. C. Smuts, *Holism and Evolution* (London: Macmillan & Co. Ltd., 1936); also Smuts' Presidential address before the British Association, "The Scientific World Picture of Today" (London, 1931) should be mentioned;

L. Mumford, *Technics and Civilization* (New York: Harcourt, Brace and Co., 1934);

L. L. Whyte, *The Next Development in Man* (London: The Cresset Press, 1944);

N. J. Berrill, *Man's Emerging Mind* (New York: Premier Books 1957); *Sex and the Nature of Things* (New York: Pocket Books, Inc. 1955);

C. H. Waddington, *The Ethical Animal* (London: Allen and Unwin, 1960).

References to these books, as well as to other books and to papers, will be given where necessary. I would also mention numerous thoughts diffused through the later works of H. G. Wells. A quotation from *First and Last Things* is given in note 71. Thoughts taken from E. Douwes Dekker have been mentioned in note 6.

Two publications by myself concerning the subject of this essay have appeared in the Netherlands:

Over de Verhouding tussen het Entropiebegrip en de Levensfuncties (*On the Relation between the Concept of Entropy and the Phenomena of Life*), Verhand. Nederl. Akademie v. Wetenschappen (Amsterdam), Div. Phys. Sciences, Section I, vol. XVI, No. 3 (1943), pp. 1–39; and

Ervaring en Conceptie (*Experience and Conception*) (Arnhem: van Loghum Slaterus, 1956).

Notes to Chapter 1

(Numbers in parentheses following the number of the note and preceded by the § sign refer to the section of the text)

1. (§ 1) A. N. Whitehead uses various terms to denote the fundamental steps in the development of the universe.

   "Event": "An event is the grasping into unity of a pattern of aspects," *Science and the Modern World,* Chap. VII, p. 174 (121*). See also Chap. XI, p. 254 (177*).

   "Actual occasion of experience," "actual occasion," or simply "occasion," *Science and the Modern World,* Chap. X, p. 227 (158*), *Adventures of Ideas,* p. 226 (178*).

   "Actual entity," "Actual Entities (also termed Actual Occasions), or Final Realities, or Res Verae," *Process and Reality,* p. 29 (32*), category (i). See also the last paragraph of p. 122 (135*, next to last paragraph).

2. (§ 2) Concerning the "objective immortality of facts" see *Adventures of Ideas,* p. 247 (194*) and *Process and Reality,* pp. ix, 40 (ix*, 44*), and elsewhere.

   The discussion of societies of processes, developed in Chapter 3, will show that most experience derived from past facts is obtained in complexes of facts, resulting from the many processes of large societies which for long stretches of their existence reproduce facts with great conformity, that is, presenting almost identical forms. From this it would seem to follow that the assumption of absolute immortality of facts is not *per se* necessary, although the assumption is important from a philosophical point of view. Even if facts would finally vanish (dissolve into nothingness), there will at any instant always be sufficient facts nearly repeating previous facts and thus furnishing material for experience of the same relations. Ultimately the two assumptions, absolute immortality of each fact once it has been established and gradual vanishing of facts, may lead to different consequences, but at the present moment we have no data to make a definite decision between these alternatives.

3. (§ 2) The "finite universes" of various physical cosmological theories are mathematical models of a partial aspect of what is around us.

4. (§ 4) *Process and Reality,* p. 118 (131*): "The breath of feeling which creates a new individual fact has an origination not wholly traceable to the mere data." See also *Adventures of Ideas,* pp. 327–328 (254*), sub (c).

5. (§ 4) Concerning creativity see *Process and Reality*, p. 28 (31°); *Adventures of Ideas*, p. 230 (181°).

6. (§ 6) The quotations are from *Process and Reality*, pp. 405 and 327, respectively (438°, 354°). I also quote from *Adventures of Ideas*, p. 245 (192°–193°), although this is meant to illuminate another aspect of the universe: "The Universe is dual, because, in the fullest sense, it is both transient and eternal. The Universe is dual because each final actuality is both physical and mental. The Universe is dual because each actuality requires abstract character. The Universe is dual because each occasion unites its formal immediacy with objective otherness. The Universe is *many* because it is wholly and completely to be analysed into many final actualities — or in Cartesian language, into many *res verae*. The Universe is *one*, because of the universal immanence. There is thus a dualism in this contrast between the unity and multiplicity. Throughout the Universe there reigns the union of opposites which is the ground of dualism."

The concept that "all is in all" has been expressed by many philosophers of various ages. In the form "Alles in alles" it was a favorite maxim in the works of the Netherlands author E. Douwes Dekker (1820–1887), in particular in his *Ideen*, written under the pseudonym "Multatuli" (published originally by G. L. Funke, Amsterdam, in irregular issues since 1862). Two other thoughts of Multatuli have found a place in this essay. One is contained in the sentence (Introduction, p. 9): "It appears immediately as a total effect, no matter how accidental or minute certain driving or resisting forces may look when we introduce them into our equations." The other occurs at the end of the Retrospect: "To live is to render that which has been received, in a form different from what it was: to render it enriched by the values which conceptual activity has attached to it and has expressed in it."

7. (§ 6) The quotations are from current translations of the Brihadaranyaka Upanishad and the Chandogya Upanishad; see, for instance, *The Wisdom of Hindu Mystics: The Upanishads, Breath of the Eternal* (New York: Mentor Religious Classics, 1957), p. 111 and p. 73, respectively.

It appears from R. Otto's book *Mysticism East and West* (New York: The Macmillan Company, 1932, reprinted in "Collier Books," 1962) that a comparison of the ideas both of the German Meister Eckhart (thirteenth century) and of the Indian thinker Sankara (who lived around A.D. 800) with Whitehead's philosophy may be of interest. Both older philosophers struggled with the relation between absolute Being and the many "creatures" or phenomena. It is the specific merit of Whitehead that he brought together in a single dynamic principle the two aspects of Being: that of presenting an ultimate foundation, and that of realizing itself in an endless complex of processes — the two together expressing the fundamental principle of creativity.

8. (§ 7) Compare *Process and Reality,* p. 328 (355°): "In none of these feelings, taken in their original purity devoid of accretions from later integrations, does the subjective form involve consciousness"; and p. 378 (408°): "Consciousness flickers; and even at its brightest, there is a small focal region of clear illumination, and a large penumbral region of experience which tells of intense experience in dim apprehension. The simplicity of clear consciousness is no measure of the complexity of complete experience. Also this character of our experience suggests that consciousness is the crown of experience, only occasionally attained, not its necessary base."

9. (§ 7) Concerning the term "appetition" see *Process and Reality,* pp. 43 and 301 (47°, 323°).

10. (§§ 8 and 49) This is not completely true, although it still is the most widely accepted position. The conviction that all determining influences come from the past, and that there are no purposes operative in physical occurrences, was embodied in Galileo's and Newton's mechanics. It formed the basis for all developments in physics and mechanics during the entire nineteenth century. While the theory of relativity and quantum theory have wrought great changes in the picture of physics and have broken down the concept of complete determinism, it still remains true that the standard forms of the working equations of physics describe a development from an earlier situation (taken as the given situation) toward a later one dependent upon the data pertaining to the earlier one.

From time to time other ideas have been brought forward which discuss the possibility that the development of a physical system may be determined in part by conditions to be expressed in terms of the future behavior of the system. These speculations have their origin in unsolved mathematical problems connected with certain features of the customary equations. A recent example is a paper by G. N. Plass on "Classical Electrodynamic Equations of Motion with Radiative Reaction" in *Reviews of Modern Physics, 33,* 37–62 (1961); this paper refs back to a paper by J. A. Wheeler and R. P. Feynman, "Interaction with the Absorber as the Mechanism of Radiation," in *Reviews of Modern Physics, 17,* 157–181 (1945) (which authors in their turn refer to still earlier speculations). In these papers a hypothesis is investigated according to which an electrically charged particle may influence the motion of other charged particles both by effects which propagate away from the first mentioned particle to reach other particles at a later instant, and by effects which should have reached the other particles at an earlier instant of time, that is, in the past. The observational result that most phenomena around us give evidence only of effects reaching other particles after, and not before, the emission, seems to come out as a statistical result connected with the circumstance that we usually have to do with large assemblages of particles, in which case, according to the theory developed, the effects moving into the past are canceled out.

So far no definite opinion can be given concerning the place which such speculations may gain in the development of physics. For the moment they are presented as mathematically admissible forms of connection submitted for judgment by other physicists. In part the formulas proposed are an expression of certain inadequacies of the present day formalism. The notion of an absolutely sharp infinitesimal instant of time, on which most of the differential equations of physics are based, is probably a fallacy: there is something in time which is subjected to quantum conditions but which is not yet fully understood. The introduction of a relation with the future (or of "signaling into the past") is an attempt to describe certain background relations which are left out of sight in the abstractions of the current physical picture.

The introduction of physical theories accepting a connection with the future may point to the acceptance of some form of anticipation related to the anticipation introduced into the text. Thus it may be that coming developments in physics will bring a widening of the physical picture which may have some room for ideas concerning the basic structure of happenings in the universe as have been considered in the text.

There remains, nevertheless, the important difference that physics does not recognize the notion of a conception as an effective agent, acting in a valuation. For this we refer back to the text above (last paragraph of § 8).

11. (§ 10) As the fundamental urges associated with conceptual activity are functioning far below the level of consciousness,

this must also hold for the primitive forms of the ethical aspect involved in these urges.

When in higher organisms the ethical aspect begins to reach the level of consciousness, it appears as a feeling "this must be done." This is aptly illustrated by H. Bergson in *Les Deux Sources de la Morale et de la Religion*, pp. 19–20: "Pensons donc à une fourmi que traverserait une lueur de réflection et qui jugerait alors qu'elle a bien tort de travailler sans relâche pour les autres. Ses velléités de paresse ne dureraient d'ailleurs que quelques instants, le temps que brillerait l'éclair d'intelligence. Au dernier de ces instants, alors que l'instinct, reprenant le dessus, la ramènerait de vive force à sa tâche, l'intelligence que va résorber l'instinct dirait en guise d'adieu: il faut parce qu'il faut. Cet 'il faut parce qu'il faut' ne serait que la conscience momentanément prise d'une traction subie." ("Let us therefore think of an ant having a moment of reflection in which it would occur to her that it is too bad to work for others without rest. Her desires in the direction of laziness, however, would have only a few moments' duration, just the time of a lightning flash of intelligence. At the last of these instants, when instinct gets the better of the intelligence and forcibly brings her back to her task, intelligence (on the point of being absorbed by instinct) would say 'it must because it must,' as a kind of taking leave. This 'it must because it must' would be nothing else than an instantaneous consciousness of being drawn back by force.")

Bergson comes back to this example, *ibid.*, pp. 94–95, in a further development of his discussion of the sentiment of moral obligation.

12. (§ 11) It is of interest to refer to the following statement occurring in Chapter II of Part I of *Process and Reality*, p. 26 (29*): "Final causation and atomism are interconnected philosophical principles."

13. (§ 11) Following Niels Bohr the term "complementary" has been used to indicate two aspects of any happening which supplement each other and which are also each other's limitation. It is impossible to render the full character of any happening in an objective description, and a pair of complementary pictures gives the best approximation that is attainable. Bohr originally introduced the term in quantum physics (compare § 44), but both he himself and other scientists have suggested its extension as a philosophical term.

I observe that it is doubtful whether the quantum theoretical notion of complementarity fully can be taken over in the philosophy presented here. In Whitehead's philosophy every process is an operation which starts from a totality of experience, selects certain aspects from this experience as material to be expressed, and rejects other aspects. It is doubtful whether one can imagine a process A' which would express all aspects rejected by a process A and reject all that which was expressed by A, so that A' could be termed the "complement" of A. It seems hardly possible that such a notion will have a real meaning in view of the unlimited possibilities for the selection and for the grading of data and for expressing forms of definiteness. Even if it were possible to imagine a process A' fully complementary to a process A, the idea of full complementarity will not be applicable to the facts in which the results of the two processes are expressed. Consequently, in general it makes no sense to introduce the assumption that each possible relation can find expression either in the outcome of a process A or in the outcome of the "complementary process A'."

There is no general distributive rule. Processes are operations which cannot be divided or dissected. Nor can they be joined together with retention of their own characters. It is only within certain societies of processes (see Chapter 3), where the outcome of each individual process is strongly influenced by traditions existing in the society, that simplifications can occur in the character of the process as an operation upon experience which may make possible the application of a practical definition of complementarity. Its scope is then restricted in view of a limited domain from which experience is derived. This is the case when we consider the societies that are carriers of the laws of physics. In certain cases the restriction even may go so far that the distributive relation may find application. This would depend upon the character of the society of processes which is considered.

A statement that the logic of quantum theory may need the rejection of the distributive law is not in contradiction with the philosophy presented here, since this philosophy leaves greater room for variety in relations or in absence of relations.

14. (§ 12) The internal development of a process is the subject of Part III of *Process and Reality*, pp. 307–397 (329*–428*), entitled "The Theory of Prehensions." We quote from its opening section, p. 309 (334*–335*): "The philosophy of organism is a cell-theory of actuality. Each ultimate unit of fact is a cell-complex, not analysable into components with equivalent completeness of actuality.

"The cell can be considered genetically and morphologically. The genetic theory is considered in this part; the morphological theory is considered in Part IV, under the title of the 'extensive analysis' of an actual entity.

"In the genetic theory, the cell is exhibited as appropriating, for the foundation of its own existence, the various elements of the universe out of which it arises. Each process of appropriation of a particular element is termed a prehension. The ultimate elements of the universe, thus appropriated, are the already constituted actual entities, and the eternal objects. All the actual entities are positively prehended, but only a selection of the eternal objects. In the course of the integrations of these various prehensions, entities of other categoreal types become relevant; and some new entities of these types, such as novel propositions and generic contrasts, come into existence. These relevant entities of these other types are also prehended into the constitution of the concrescent cell. This genetic process has now to be traced in its main outlines."

It must be observed that the elaborate analysis of the genetic process in Part III is difficult to follow. It has not been attempted to introduce this material into the present essay.

15. (§ 12) See *Process and Reality*, p. 29 (32°), category (v), "Eternal Objects, or Pure Potentials for the Specific Determination of Fact, or Forms of Definiteness," and category (ii), "Prehensions, or Concrete Facts of Relatedness." The development of the concept occurs passim (see the index of *Process and Reality*) and in particular in Part III, already quoted in note 14.

A helpful exposition is given in *Science and the Modern World* in the first part of Chapter X, "Abstraction," pp. 226 ff. (157° ff.). This should be read in connection with the first part of Chapter II, "Mathematics," pp. 29 ff. (20° ff.).

When we look over the part that is played by the forms of relationship or forms of definiteness, it appears that it is not *per se* necessary to consider all of them as eternal, as is implied in Whitehead's term "eternal objects." The conclusions to be developed later on, in particular concerning the part played by initiative in life (see Chapter 5), are compatible with the assumption that *new forms of relatedness can be the result of conceptual activity* and as such make their appearance in the evolution of complexes of processes. Once conceived, they will stay on as possibilities for relationship, and new processes have either to include them or to reject them. One may assume that, once conceived and thus created, they will remain for ever.

16. (§ 12) We quote from Chapter II of *Science and the Modern World*, p. 39 (27°): "the discovery of mathematics is the discovery that the totality of these general abstract conditions, which are concurrently applicable to the relationships among the entities of any one concrete occasion, are themselves interconnected in the manner of a pattern with a key to it."

17. (§ 12) Perhaps we must admit more possibilities, such as:
   (i) Acceptance.
   (ii) Rejection.
   (iii) Keeping a proposition in suspense for later decision.
   (iv) Modification of a proposition and adaptation to the case at hand.

   This will save us from the necessity of being bound already here to a two-way logic which recognizes only acceptance and rejection and would make a rigid distinction between "true" and "false." Compare *Process and Reality*, p. 270 (291°).

18. (§ 13) See *Process and Reality*, p. 29 (33°), category (viii), "Contrasts, or Modes of Synthesis of Entities in one Prehension"; further pp. 322–324 (349°–350°).

19. (§ 14) *Process and Reality*, p. 482 (517°): "The nature of evil is that the characters of things are mutually obstructive."

20. (§ 15) Compare *Process and Reality*, p. 117 (129°) for the description of the attainment of a specific satisfaction in an actual entity. See also *ibid.*, p. 353 (381°): "This 'aim at contrast' is the expression of the ultimate creative purpose that each unification shall achieve some maximum depth of intensity of feeling, subject to the conditions of its concrescence."

Notes to Chapter 2

21. (§ 16) Compare *Process and Reality*, p. 36 (40°): "(vi) *The Category of Transmutation*."

22. (§ 17) This postulate is formulated most clearly in *Adventures of Ideas*, p. 235 (185°) § 14, Conformation of Feeling: "There is a continuity between the subjective form of the immediate past occasion and the subjective form of its primary prehension in the origination of the new occasion. In the process of synthesis of the many basic prehensions modifications enter. But the subjective forms of the immediate past are continuous with those of the present." The preceding sentence states:

"This doctrine balances and limits the doctrine of the absolute individuality of each occasion of experience." And p. 236 (185°): "This continuity of subjective form . . . is the primary ground for the continuity of nature." This is followed by "Thus non-sensuous perception is one aspect of the continuity of nature."

The idea is taken up in the notion of "immanence" pp. 241, 252 (190°, 197°–198°).

Passages of *Process and Reality* referring to the same idea are: p. 162 (176°), connected with *Adventures of Ideas*, p. 252; p. 346 (374°–375°): "In so far as there is negligible autonomous energy, the subject merely receives the physical feelings, confirms their valuations according to the 'order' of that epoch, and transmits by reason of its own objective immortality. Its own flash of autonomous individual experience is negligible for the science which is tracing transmissions up to the conscious experience of a final observer. But as soon as individual experience is not negligible, the autonomy of the subject in the modification of its initial subjective aim must be taken into account"; and p. 352 (380°–381°): "Thus the first phase of the mental pole is conceptual reproduction, and the second phase is a phase of conceptual reversion. In this second phase the proximate novelties are conceptually felt."

As is seen, the postulate was more or less implicit in the discussions of *Process and Reality*, while it obtained an explicit formulation in *Adventures of Ideas*. I have thought that it would be appropriate to give it a prominent position.

23. (§ 17) Compare *Adventures of Ideas*, p. 232 (183°): "In human experience, the most compelling example of non-sensuous perception is our knowledge of our own immediate past," and what follows upon this sentence. We may equate here "non-sensuous perception" with the often used term "extrasensorial perception."

See also what is said on "perception in the mode of causal efficacy" in *Process and Reality*, p. 169 (184°), § VII.

24. (§ 18) See *Process and Reality*, p. 48 (52°): "There is a prevalent misconception that 'becoming' involves the notion of a unique seriality for its advance into novelty . . . . In these lectures the term 'creative advance' is not to be construed in the sense of a uniquely serial advance." Further p. 401 (433°–434°): "The actual entity is seen as a process; there is a growth from phase to phase; there are processes of integration and of reintegration . . . . This genetic passage from phase to phase is not in physical time . . . physical time expresses

some features of the growth, but *not* the growth of the tures."

The distinction between the physical or exterior time-scale and interior duration is stressed by H. Bergson, e.g., in *L'Evolution Créatrice,* pp. 11–12: "L'univers dure. Plus nous approfondirons la nature du temps, plus nous comprendrons que durée signifie invention, création de formes, élaboration continue de l'absolument nouveau." ("The universe has duration. The more we shall penetrate into the nature of time, the more we shall understand that duration means invention, creation of forms, continuous elaboration of what is completely new.") See also *ibid.,* pp. 356–357; and in *La Pensée et le Mouvant* (Paris: Félix Alcan, 1934), pp. 188 and 234. It must be observed, however, that it is not easy to put Bergson's ideas concerning this subject in sharply circumscribed forms.

While I took over the term "duration" from Bergson's "durée," it should be noted that in *Process and Reality* Whitehead uses the term "duration" in a different sense and defines it as a complete set of actual occasions (i.e., processes) such that all the members are mutually contemporary one with the other, *op. cit.,* pp. 175–176 and pp. 453–456 (190*–191*, 486-490*). In consequence of this, a duration in Whitehead's sense is a cross section of the universe, *ibid.,* p. 175 (190*).

25. (§ 19) In *L'Evolution Créatrice* H. Bergson remarks on p. 174: "Les concepts sont en effet extérieurs les uns aux autres." ("The concepts are indeed exterior relatively to each other.") However, Bergson is speaking here of something which is different from the matter treated in the text.

26. (§ 21) See *Process and Reality* pp. 84 and 173 (95*, 188*) concerning "contemporary actual entities" or "contemporary occasions"; and *Adventures of Ideas,* pp. 251, 253, and 255 (197*, 198*, 200*). I have used the term "coexistent" instead of "contemporary" in order to avoid a reference to time.

27. (§ 22) See *Adventures of Ideas,* p. 256 (201*): "Thus in any two occasions of the Universe there are elements in either one which are irrelevant to the constitution of the other."

28. (§ 23) *Ibid.,* p. 253 (198*).

29. (§ 23) *Ibid.,* p. 255 (200*): "It is not true that whatever happens is immediately a condition laid upon everything else."

30. (§ 24) The term "nexus" is used by Whitehead; see *Process and Reality,* p. 29 (32*), category (iii), and pp. 26 and 134–135 (30*, 147*–148*); *Adventures of Ideas,* p. 258 (203*).

My definition differs somewhat from the one given by Whitehead since I would forgo the use of the word "immanence" at this place.

31. (§ 26) Concerning "contiguity" see *Adventures of Ideas*, pp. 259–260 (203°–204°). In *Process and Reality* the term is considered in relation to a more mathematically framed theory of cosmic order: Part IV, "The Theory of Extension," pp. 399 ff. (429° ff.). See, for instance, p. 434 (468°).

Notes to Chapter 3

32. (§ 27) See *Process and Reality*, pp. 46–48, 123–129, and 134 ff. (50°–52°, 136°–142°, 147° ff.); *Adventures of Ideas*, pp. 260–267 (204°–209°). The definition given in the text follows for the main part that in *Adventures of Ideas*, p. 261 (205°), which is somewhat more extensive than the one given in *Process and Reality*, p. 124 (137°).

33. (§ 27) In *Process and Reality*, p. 127 (140°) this is formulated somewhat differently as follows: "A society does not in any sense create the complex of eternal objects which constitutes its defining characteristic. It only elicits that complex into importance for its members, and secures the reproduction of its membership."

34. (§ 27) *Adventures of Ideas*, p. 262 (205°): "The real actual things that endure are all societies." *Process and Reality*, p. 138 (152°): "Molecules are structured societies, and so in all probability are separate electrons and protons. Crystals are structured societies. But gases are not structured societies in any important sense of that term; although their individual molecules are structured societies."

35. (§ 28) *Process and Reality*, p. 125 (138°): "there is no society in isolation." See also *ibid.*, pp. 139–140 (153°–154°).

36. (§ 29) *Ibid.*, p. 137 (151°).

37. (§ 30) "Identical particles cannot be distinguished by means of any inherent property since otherwise they would not be identical in all respects. In classical mechanics the existence of sharply definable trajectories for individual particles made it possible in principle to distinguish between particles that are identical except for their paths, since it was believed that each particle could be followed during the course of an experiment. This is not possible according to the conceptions of quantum mechanics whenever it occurs that the "particles" come so close together that the wave packets by which they

are described, will overlap" (quoted substantially from L. Schiff, *Quantum Mechanics*, Chap. IX, Section 32, first paragraph, p. 216 of the edition of 1949). The doctrine has certain consequences for the theory of interaction of particles, e.g., in the theory of collisions.

38. (§ 33) With reference to "personal order" and "corpuscular society" see *Process and Reality*, pp. 47 and 48, respectively (50*, 52*).

39. (§ 35) Concerning the accidental character of the present laws of nature and concerning the particular cosmic epoch in which we find ourselves see *Process and Reality*, pp. 126–128 (139*–141*), and pp. 134 ff. (147* ff.).

The idea has been stated very sharply by Whitehead in *Modes of Thought*, pp. 211–214: "None of these Laws of Nature gives the slightest evidence of necessity. They are the modes of procedure which within the scale of our observations do in fact prevail. I mean, the fact that the extensiveness of the Universe is dimensional, the fact that the number of spatial dimensions is three, the spatial laws of geometry, the ultimate formulae for physical occurrences. There is no necessity in any of these ways of behaviour. They exist as average, regulative conditions because the majority of actualities are swaying each other to modes of interconnection exemplifying those laws. New modes of self-expression may be gaining ground. We cannot tell. But, to judge by all analogy, after a sufficient span of existence our present laws will fade into unimportance. New interests will dominate. In our present sense of the term, our spatio-physical epoch will pass into that background of the past, which conditions all things dimly and without evident effect on the decision of prominent relations.

"These massive laws, at present prevailing, are the general physical laws of inorganic nature. At a certain scale of observation they are prevalent without hint of interference. The formation of suns, the motions of planets, the geologic changes on the earth, seem to proceed with a massive impetus which excludes any hint of modification by other agencies."

Whitehead continues: "To this extent sense-perception on which science relies discloses no aim in nature.

"Yet it is untrue to state that the general observation of mankind, in which sense-perception is only one factor, discloses no aim. The exact contrary is the case. All explanations of the sociological functionings of mankind include 'aim' as an essential factor in explanation. . . . In fact we are *directly* conscious of our purposes as *directive* of our actions (italics by Whitehead). Apart from such direction no doctrine could in any sense be acted upon. The notions entertained mentally would have no effect upon bodily actions. Thus what happens would happen in complete indifference to the entertainment of such notions.

"Scientific reasoning is completely dominated by the presupposition that mental functionings are not properly part of nature. Accordingly it disregards all those mental antecedents which mankind habitually presuppose as effective in guiding cosmological functionings. As a method this procedure is entirely justifiable, provided that we recognize the limitations involved. These limitations are both obvious and undefined. The gradual eliciting of their definition is the hope of philosophy.

"The points that I would emphasize are, first that this sharp division between mentality and nature has no ground in our fundamental observation. We find ourselves living within nature. Secondly, I conclude that we should conceive mental operations as among the factors which make up the constitution of nature. . . ."

See also *Science and the Modern World*, pp. 112, 115, and 122 (78*, 80*, 85*).

In connection with this it may be observed that H. Bergson in *L'Evolution Créatrice* makes the observation that the intellect is characterized by a natural lack of understanding for life: it feels itself at ease primarily when it has to deal with anorganic matter (p. 179: "L'intelligence est caractérisée par une incompréhension naturelle de la vie," and p. 213: "l'intelligence se sent surtout à son aise en présence de la matière inorganisée").

40. (§ 37) The contrast between the two types of societies is discussed by Whitehead in *Process and Reality* on pp. 140–143 (154*–157*). We quote from p. 140 (154*):

"Thus the problem for Nature is the production of societies which are 'structured' with a high 'complexity,' and which are at the same time 'unspecialized.' In this way, intensity is mated with survival.

"There are two ways in which structured societies have solved this problem. Both ways depend on that enhancement of the mental pole, which is a factor in intensity of experience. One way is by eliciting a massive average objectification of a nexus, while eliminating the detailed diversities of the various members of the nexus in question. This method, in fact, employs the device of blocking out unwelcome detail. . . ." and from p. 141 (155*): "The second way of solving the problem is by an initiative in conceptual prehensions, i.e. in appetition. The purpose of this initiative is to receive the novel elements of the environment into explicit feelings with such subjective forms as conciliate them with the complex experiences proper to members of the structured society. Thus in each concrescent occasion its subjective aim originates novelty to match the novelty of the environment."

The bifurcation in development between the two types of societies will be considered later in Chapter 5. In § 73 it is pointed out that societies with cyclic sets of processes apparently have provided the fertile soil from which the second type could evolve. It should be noted that societies of the second type always contain many subsocieties of the first type, which they need as a means for stabilization.

Notes to Chapter 4 and Appendix

41. (§ 40) H. Bergson, *L'Evolution Créatrice*, p. 203, uses the expression that matter, in so far as it can be considered as an undivided totality, should be taken as a "flux" rather than as a "thing," in order to gain a point of view which shall decrease the distance between that which is inert and that which is living. I think that my expression, "matter is a habit," will appear to be more fruitful.

42. (§ 41) There are several references in *Process and Reality* to connections between the "philosophy of organism," as Whitehead calls his doctrine, and quantum theory. See, for instance, pp. 109, 131, 164, 360, and 437 (121*–122*, 145*, 179*, 389*, 471*). Compare also for "rhythms" and "vibrations" pp. 109, 131, 210, 228, 265, 392, and 395 (122*, 145*, 228*–229*, 247*, 285*, 423*, 426*); and for "vectors" pp. 163 and 249 (177*, 268*), and elsewhere. There can be an important idea in Whitehead's statements on this topic, but they are vague and will require much elaboration before a connection can be established with the results of physics (compare what is observed at the end of § 47 on the problem of elementary particles).

A number of preliminary questions which present themselves in this connection have been discussed by A. Shimony in a paper "Quantum Physics and the Philosophy of Whitehead," presented before the Boston Colloquium on the Philosophy of Science, March 3, 1964, to which I have prepared a series of comments. My opinion is that we must disregard those of Whitehead's statements which are not tenable in view of the development of physics (Whitehead was not a physicist himself), but that this in no way impairs the basic assumptions of Whitehead's philosophy which reach much deeper than physics. For Shimony's paper and my comments see *Boston Studies in the Philosophy of Science*, R. S. Cohen, ed., vol. 2 (New York: Humanities Press, 1965), pp. 307–342.

I would here also refer to a paper by the late Professor D. van Dantzig, "Some Possibilities of the Future Developments of the Notions of Space and Time," *Erkenntnis*, 7 (1938), 142–146. In a lecture given in 1938 in Delft (Netherlands) van Dantzig expressed the idea that "the life history of a particle, an electron or a photon for example, would not be given by a continuous succession of states, but would consist of a series of separate phenomena," for which he proposed the term "flashes." In that lecture van Dantzig referred to Whitehead's term "events" as a comparable notion.

43. (§ 42) Compare H. Bergson, *L'Evolution Créatrice*, pp. 356–357: "Savoir, c'est-à-dire prévoir pour agir, sera donc aller d'une situation à une situation, d'un arrangement à un réarrangement. La science pourra considérer des réarrangements de plus en plus rapprochés les uns des autres; elle fera croître ainsi le nombre des moments qu'elle isolera, mais toujours elle isolera des moments. Quant à ce qui se passe dans l'intervalle, la science ne s'en préoccupe pas plus que ne font l'intelligence commune, les sens et le langage: elle ne porte pas sur l'intervalle, mais sur les extrémités." ("To know, that is to say, to foresee in order to act, thus will be to move from one situation to another situation, from one arrangement to a rearrangement. Science may consider rearrangements which are more and more close together; it thus will increase the number of instants which are isolated, but it is always isolating instants. As regards what happens in the interval, science does not give attention to it, she overlooks it, in the same way as do common understanding, the senses, and language: science is not concerned with the interval, but only with the end points.")

44. (§ 45) Concerning the noncausal behavior of an atomic system as a result of external observation we refer to H. A. Kramers, "Die Grundlagen der Quantentheorie," in "Hand- und Jahrbuch der chemischen Physik" (Leipzig, 1933), Band I/1, pp. 4 and 5: "Der Kern dieser neuen Auffassungen liegt vor

allem in einer Kritik des Beobachtungsbegriffs, und die früheren Schwierigkeiten hatten besonders ihren Grund darin, dass man sich durch Extrapolation der klassischen Begriffe ein Weltbild zu schaffen suchte, nach dem man widerspruchslos von einem 'objektiven', wirklichen Geschehen in Raum und Zeit reden konnte. Die Diskussion der empirischen physikalischen Gesetze has uns tatsächlich gelehrt, dass eine solche Extrapolation unerlaubt ist, dass vielmehr eine jegliche Messung mit einer objektiv nicht beschreibbaren, also — wenn man will — irrationellen Wechselwirkung zwischen dem Beobachtungsapparat und dem Beobachteten behaftet ist." (Translated by D. ter Haar under the title *Quantum Mechanics* [Amsterdam: North-Holland Publishing Company, 1957], p. 3: "The nucleus of these new ideas is a critique of the concept of observation and the earlier difficulties were mainly due to the fact that by extrapolating the classical concepts one tried to obtain a description of the universe in which one could talk of 'objective' real events in space-time. However, the discussion of the empirical physical laws has shown us in fact that such an extrapolation is not permitted and that every measurement is connected with an interaction between the measuring apparatus and the observed system which cannot be described objectively and which is thus, as it were, irrational.")

Compare also: John von Neumann, *Mathematische Grundlagen der Quantenmechanik* (Berlin: Springer, 1932), p. 222 (translated by R. T. Beyer under the title *Mathematical Foundations of Quantum Mechanics* [Princeton, N.J.: Princeton University Press, 1955], pp. 417–418).

Another author on this topic is: P. Jordan, *Anschauliche Quantentheorie* (Berlin: Springer, 1936), p. 285.

It must be observed that there are some physicists who do not accept the intrinsically statistical character of the laws of physics as defended by Bohr, Heisenberg, Jordan, von Neumann, and many others. Compare D. Bohm, *Causality and Chance in Modern Physics* (New York: D. van Nostrand, 1957), and the review in *Physics Today*, 10, No. 11, 30–32 (November 1957).

My own creed is to accept the statistical character of the laws of physics completely and to assume with Whitehead that any particular result comes out as the result of a remnant of conceptual activity dwindling to ineffectiveness. In ordinary physical happenings there is no coordinated effect of conceptual activity, and the statistical rules hold fully; where a result of different nature appears, we have not to do with a mechanism but with the activity of a living being.

45. (§ 46) The only case where the outcome of an experiment can be predicted with certainty is when the experiment is the immediate repetition of the same experiment performed just before upon the same system.

46. (§ 48) As an example, consider the throwing of dice. When a single die is thrown, the number obtained can vary from 1 to 6 with a mean value $(1 + 2 + 3 + 4 + 5 + 6)/6 = 3.5$. Fluctuations up to 2.5 on either side of the mean value will occur in some of the throws, that is, variations up to ca. 71% of the mean value.

Now suppose that some quantity is determined by the sum of the results of 1000 throws of a die. One must expect that the result of 1000 throws will be in the neighborhood of 3500, that is 1000 times the average value found above. Most probably the sum will differ somewhat from 3500, and when the process of making 1000 throws is repeated many times, the sum will fluctuate around 3500. There will be, however, a negligible chance that in one series of 1000 throws all throws will produce 1 (which would lead to a sum of 1000), or that all throws would give a 6 (so that the sum would be 6000). On the contrary, in each series of 1000 throws there will be many higher and many lower numbers, and calculation as well as observation shows that the fluctuation to be expected in the sum on both sides of the mean value 3500 will be of the order of $(1000)^{1/2}$ = about 31 times the mean fluctuation of a single throw. Hence it will be of the order 31×2.5 = 78, which is not much more than 2.2% of the mean value 3500. The relative fluctuation thus has decreased more than 30 times. The decrease becomes still more marked when the number of throws combined in a single series is made larger and larger.

There exist more complicated relations when the phenomena are not completely independent of one another (as is the case with the successive throws of a die), but the nature of the relationship remains the same.

47. (§ 49) The dominating influence which the Western World has given to physical time in the regulation of its activities has made us "slaves of time." Compare, for instance: L. Mumford, *Technics and Civilization* (New York: Harcourt, Brace and Company, 1934), pp. 12–18 on "The Monastery and the Clock," in particular p. 15: "The clock, moreover, is a piece

of power-machinery whose 'product' is seconds and minutes: by its essential nature it dissociated time from human events and helped create the belief in an independent world of mathematically measurable sequences: the special world of science."

Extending the gist of Mumford's point, I mention that L. L. Whyte, in *The Next Development in Man* (London: Cresset Press, 1944), pp. 125–133, discusses the effects upon society of the overriding tendency toward thinking in quantitative terms which is characteristic of the last two centuries. I quote from p. 127: "Quantity, for all its efficacy as an instrument of research, contains no general principle of form, of order, or of organisation. All magnitudes have equal status before the laws of elementary arithmetic, whose operators recognise no distinction between one value and another. Similarly in its social application the quantity concept sets no limit to the pursuit of wealth, the manipulation of the symbols of the markets, or the desire for expansion in any field."

Returning to the concept of time, we note that biologists and physiologists have called attention to the fact that living beings have their own "biological time-scales" widely different from the physical time-scale.

From the mathematical point of view it should be noted that in certain forms of Schrödinger's equation for the development of the wave function in the quantum theory of complicated atomic systems the time variable can have an individual character for each particle separately. Certain unsolved questions hover around this point.

48. (§ 49) It is this result from the theory of relativity which has led Whitehead to the introduction of the notion of co-existence, as defined in § 21.

49. (§ 51) A peculiarity of the method of counting "different" internal configurations according to the rules of quantum theory is that particles of identical nature — electrons, atoms of the same kind, and others — are not counted as different individuals when they can react with one another. When two electrons "collide," that is, when they approach each other so closely that they influence each other's motion through the forces between them and then again go away from each other, according to these rules it is impossible to say "which is which" after the collision. (Compare note 37.)

50. (§ 51) It is found that the number of configurations corresponding to a state which — for the same number of molecules, the

same total volume, and the same total energy — differs mark-edly from the equilibrium state is so much smaller than the number of configurations corresponding to the equilibrium state that one can calculate the equilibrium entropy just as well from the total number of configurations compatible with the three external data.

This brings us back to what was said already in the text: all configurations have the same probability; however, since the great majority (by a very large factor) of these configura-tions corresponds to the equilibrium state, only this state can be seen by the outside observer.

Since each configuration represents a possible distribution of the molecules in space and a possible set of velocities, we may also consider them as *realizations* of the possibilities open for the gas. Thus we can say: All realizations are equally probable, and by far the largest number of them gives the equilibrium state.

51. (§ 52) Quantum theory rules out the possibility of absolute rest for any particle, for absolute rest would mean that both position and velocity (and consequently momentum) could be defined and known simultaneously with absolute precision. Thus, even at the lowest energy level there is a kind of oscil-lation of such intensity that Heisenberg's principle holds. The lowest energy level defined by this principle is sometimes called the "zero point energy." Although mathematically de-scribed as an oscillation, it represents only a single "configura-tion."

52. (§ 52) In the calculations necessary to find the number of possible configurations attention must be given to the volume allowed to the system. When the total energy remains the same but the volume is increased more and more, the effect of variety in position will count for more, and the equilibrium state ultimately will be the gaseous state.

When a system finds itself in a given space but has such contact with its environment that it can exchange energy with the latter, the variety of configurations possible in the surrounding matter must be taken into account in the appli-cation of the entropy principle. When the surroundings are extensive and are kept at a constant temperature, the system ultimately will acquire that same temperature. The state of equilibrium of the system is then characterized by the maxi-mum value of the difference between the entropy of the system proper and the quotient of its energy by the temperature. If the entropy of the system is denoted by S, its energy by U, and the temperature by T, the quantity which must have the greatest possible value is $S - U/T$. An equivalent statement is that for given volume and given temperature the so-called free energy $U - TS$ must be a minimum. (A related consideration occurs in note 73.)

Still another formulation is used in the case of a system which is in contact with its environment in such a way that not only can it exchange energy, but that also it can change its volume, under conditions in which the surroundings subject it to both a determined temperature and a determined pressure. (See note 84.)

53. (§ 53) For data concerning structural errors in crystal lattices we refer to: *Imperfections in Nearly Perfect Crystals*, ed. W. Shockley and others (New York: Wiley & Sons, Inc., 1952); *The Defect Solid State*, ed. T. J. Gray and others (New York: Wiley & Sons, Inc., 1957); H. G. van Bueren, *Imperfections in Crystals* (Amsterdam: North-Holland Publishing Co., 1961). As regards dislocations, knowledge up to about 1954 is summarized in a paper by J. M. Burgers and W. G. Burgers, "Dislocations in Crystal Lattices," in *Rheology: Theory and Applications*, ed. F. R. Eirich, Vol. I (New York: Academic Press Inc., 1956), pp. 141-199. Many other papers have been devoted to the subject, new forms of dislocations have been discussed, and the important feature has come forward that spiral dislocations have an essential importance for crystal growth. On this latter subject see: A. R. Verma, *Crystal Growth and Dislocations* (London: Butterworths Scientific Publications, 1953); and W. Dekeyser et S. Amelinckx, *Les Dislocations et la Croissance des Cristaux* (Paris: Masson et Cie., 1955).

W. G. Burgers once stated the idea that the system of dislocations in a crystal characterizes the "personality" of the crystal, since each individual crystal has its own distribution of dislocations which influences various properties of the crystal.

54. (§ 56) See *Process and Reality*, pp. 392–395 (423*–426*), and for a related idea, p. 265 (285*). We have criticized Whitehead's ideas on this matter in note 42. It does not seem attractive to consider vibrations with frequencies of 10^{15} and upward per second as basic processes, each driven by a conception and coming to a conclusion before a new one starts. Moreover, although oscillations and periodic orbital motions

often play a part in the theoretical formalism of physics, this does not mean that they are always really there: the mathematical expressions are abstractions.

We can free ourselves of this difficulty if we take account of a statement made in § 37: When we have to do with societies of processes which persistently repeat the same pattern, the amount of conceptual work needed in each successive period becomes vanishingly small once the tradition is well established. Hence, if we exclude the first few periods at the start of a series, we can say that for the rest no conceptual activity is connected with the repetition, and the whole chain of repetitions becomes a feature in a single process of wider nature. This allows us to consider the undisturbed oscillations of the electromagnetic field of a photon or the stationary state of an atomic system as items in a single process.

55. (§ 56) This was proved by John von Neumann, *Mathematische Grundlagen der Quantenmechanik* (quoted in note 43), Kap. VI, Der Messprozess (pp. 222–237); (in Beyer's translation pp. 417–445).

The subject was presented in another form by H. Everett III, in what he called the "relative state" formulation of quantum mechanics, *Reviews of Modern Physics, 29*, 454–462 (1957). The essence of what was brought forward by Everett was already contained in a paper on "Information in Quantum Measurements" by H. J. Groenewold, *Proc. Roy. Netherl. Academy of Sciences* (Amsterdam), B55, 219–227 (1952).

It is possible to give a combined account of the ideas of all three authors, bringing them into a single picture; see J. M. Burgers, The Measuring Process in Quantum Theory, *Reviews of Modern Physics, 35*, 145–150, and 1032 (1963).

56. (Appendix to Chapter 4) The introduction of conceptual activity is, of course, the link with the doctrine of Chapter 1.

57. (Appendix to Chapter 4) For comparison I quote the translation of the opening verses of the Gospel according to John by James Moffat (*The Bible, a New Translation*, New York and London: Harper & Brothers, 1922 and later years): "The Logos existed in the very beginning, the Logos was with God, the Logos was divine. He was with God in the very beginning: through him all existence came into being, no existence came into being apart from him."

The following passage from *Process and Reality* is relevant to this doctrine, p. 345 (373*–374*): "What is inexorable in

God, is valuation as an aim towards 'order'; and 'order' means 'society' permissive of actualities with patterned intensity of feeling arising from adjusted contrasts. In this sense God is the principle of concretion; namely, He is that actual entity from which each temporal concrescence receives that initial aim from which its self-causation starts."

58. (Appendix to Chapter 4) A result of this discussion is that there is no need to incorporate fundamental numerical data into Whitehead's picture in order to account for the present values of the constants of physics.

Notes to Chapter 5 and Appendix

59. (§ 58) The first quotation is taken from John Perret, "Biochemistry and Bacteria," in *New Biology*, no. 12 (London: Penguin books, 1952), p. 79. I presume that the words "organic" (here referring to a particular class of chemical compounds) and "isothermally" can be omitted; although they hold for the forms of life known to us on earth, other forms might be possible under changed conditions.

The second definition was given by K. Smith, in *American Scientist, 46,* 415 (1958), with a reference to a paper on "Psychology and the Concept of 'Life'" by the same author in *Psychological Review 58,* 330–331 (1951).

60. (§§ 58 and 76) Statements on the nature of life or on the origin of life.

Melvin Calvin, "Chemical Evolution and the Origin of Life," in *American Scientist, 44,* 248–263 (1956): "The whole burden of this discussion will be to try to show you that it is possible to devise schemes within the scope of modern science that will lead to the development of defined systems — by a system I mean a confined region in space — which can have the attributes that we now recognize as belonging to living materials, without having to postulate a cataclysmic, improbable event at any one time. . . . "The term 'evolution' has been most commonly used and developed by the biologists, and has a fairly clear-cut definition in their language. It has been used to describe the changes and development of various forms of life as they have been read in the paleontological record and interpreted in the light of modern genetics and biochemistry. It calls for the possibility of random variation amongst systems together with a mechanism for selecting amongst those random variations. This, in essence, is what the term 'evolution,' as I understand it, means in biological language. What I would like to do is to extend the very same terms into nonbiological systems and show that they apply, and that their application to a nonliving system will give rise, in the normal course of events, to confined systems in space which we could call living cells." (p. 248.)

N. H. Horowitz, "The Gene," *Scientific American, 195,* 78–90 (October 1956): "We can imagine the spontaneous origin of some chemical substance capable of reproducing itself, of mutating and of directing the production of specific catalysts in its environment. It would not be long before this substance, trying out new molecular arrangements by blind mutation, began to evolve along lines favored by natural selection. In time all the complexity that is now associated with living matter might well develop." (p. 90.)

George W. Beadle, "Molecules, Viruses, and Heredity," *Bulletin of the Atomic Scientists, 15,* 354–360 (1959): "We can now define life in objective terms — ability to replicate in the manner of DNA (deoxyribonucleic acid), and to evolve through mutation and natural selection. Biochemists may, before long, be able to duplicate in test tubes the conditions under which 'living' molecules arose on earth a few thousand million years ago. Understanding of the nature of life is thus replacing mystery." (p. 360.)

F. Hoyle, *Frontiers of Astronomy* (New York: Mentor edition, 1957), Chapter 6, section on "The Origin of Life," pp. 98–99: "At what stage may life be said to appear? This depends on what we mean by life. As more becomes known about life it is increasingly clear that there is no hard and fast dividing line between what is alive and what is not alive. It is to a considerable extent a matter of choice where the line is drawn. . . . We say that a dog is alive to denote the fact that the material of the dog is in a special condition, differing markedly from that of the material of a stone. But the properties of both the dog and the stone are different manifestations of the behaviour of matter.

"Perhaps the most convenient definition of the origin of life is at the stage where some structure (built out of the highly complex molecules) becomes capable of using itself as a blueprint for the building of similar structures." [The reader will notice the ambiguity of the words "using itself."]

H. J. Muller, in *Evolution after Darwin,* III (Chicago: University of Chicago Press, 1960), "Discussion Panel One: The Origin of Life," p. 71: "I think that, in the course of discussing the origin of life, we shall necessarily come closer to a definition of what life is, so that it is not necessary to define it now. I think the most fundamental property distinguishing a living thing — and that can therefore be used to define life — is its ability to form copies of itself. We call this "reproduction"; but such copies must also include innovations — mutations — that distinguish a given living thing from its parents. It is this property of not merely reproducing itself but also reproducing its mutant types that inevitably led the first multiplying objects through the three-, four-, or five-billion-year course of evolution by which all present-day living things, including ourselves, have gradually taken shape under the directing influence of natural selection. Natural selection could not go on without the necessary basis of an ability or faculty of the material to copy not merely itself but its variations. That, I think, is the heart of life, and such material, when it arose, is rightly called 'living.'"

Somewhat later in the same Panel Discussion Muller said (*ibid.*, p. 93): "My answer is that those who define life as I do will admit that the most primitive forms of things that deserve to be called living have already been made in the test tube by A. Kornberg."

All these statements suffer from a great vagueness. They are no more than unproved wishful guesses even from a physical point of view. Moreover, they do not give any attention to the problem: "What does life really mean? How has it come about that there is a distinction between an organism and its environment?" Calvin, Horowitz, and Muller refer to the "directing influence of natural selection," but in a seemingly innocent way this is invoking a mystery. The physical sciences do not know individuality, do not recognize persons, do not recognize death; on the other hand, the reference to natural selection assumes that individuals are already existing, and that the terms "survival rate" and "death" can be applied to them. The immense distance between the properties exhibited by living beings and those observed in nonliving matter is covered up in a few words, and it is suggested that there is no need for questions here.

There are biologists who make more careful statements. I quote from H. Gaffron, in the same Panel Discussion, p. 72: "Matter can practically always be defined in terms of physics, chemistry, and biochemistry. This certainly is not enough to define life."

Subsequently Gaffron observes that it is unfortunate that experiments leading to the production of organic substances through electrical discharges are brought into high schools and secondary schools as a demonstration of the origin of life, "because, contrary to the notions now becoming popular, it does not solve the problem of life. These substances are quite dead. From the point of view of a misleading oversimplification it would have been even better if we had not found anything as easy to do, because then the difficulty of the true question would not have been obscured at the very beginning." (*Ibid.*, p. 78).

61. (§ 58) See James T. Culbertson, "Some Uneconomical Robots," in *Automata Studies, Annals of Mathematics Studies,* No. 34 (Princeton: Princeton University Press, 1956), pp. 99–116. I quote (p. 100): "If we could get enough central cells and if they were small enough and if each cell had enough endbulbs and if we could put enough bulbs at each synapse and if we had time enough to assemble them, then we could construct robots to satisfy any given input-output specification; i.e., we could construct robots that would behave in any way we desired under any environmental circumstances. We will illustrate this point later in the paper. There would be no difficulty in constructing a robot with behavioral properties just like John Jones or Henry Smith or in constructing a robot with any desired behavioral improvements over Jones and Smith." The "cells" to which Culbertson refers in these lines are physical instruments working by means of mechanical or electronic connections.

62. (§ 58) Homer Jacobson, "On Models of Reproduction," *American Scientist, 46,* 255–284 (1958); Harold J. Morowitz, "A Model of Reproduction," *American Scientist, 47,* 261–263 (1959); L. S. Penrose, "Self-reproducing Machines," *Scientific American, 200,* 105–114 (June 1959).

63. (§ 58) In physics the term "cooperative phenomena" is sometimes used to describe phenomena which appear when one has to do with systems consisting of large numbers of particles; see F. Zwicky, "On Cooperative Phenomena," *Physical Review 43,* 270–278 (1933), and other papers.

The theory of these phenomena, however, has not involved the assumption of new principles other than those already known in physics. As Zwicky observes, "no fundamentally new laws must be invented for the solution of the problems of cooperative action of a great number of elementary particles. The difficulty rather lies in our present inability to visualize the simultaneous cooperation of a great number of particles and the lack of mathematical methods to obtain exact solutions of sufficiently general cases of interaction between many elementary particles."

As examples of cooperative phenomena one can mention surface tension, lattice vibrations in crystals, conduction of electricity at low temperatures with the appearance of superconductivity, and others (see note 121).

64. (§ 59) See *Process and Reality*, p. 287 (308°): "no sample is 'random'; it has only followed a complex method."

65. (§ 59) I quote from Whitehead's *Modes of Thought*, p. 101: "In order to observe accurately, (one must) concentrate on that observation, dismissing from consciousness all irrelevant modes of experience. But there is no irrelevance. Thus the whole of science is based upon neglected modes of relevance, which nevertheless dominate the social group entertaining those scientific modes of thought." And p. 211: "Science can find no individual enjoyment in nature: Science can find no aim in nature: Science can find no creativity in nature; it finds mere rules of succession. These negations are true of Natural Science. They are inherent in its methodology. The reason for this blindness of Physical Science lies in the fact that such Science only deals with half of the evidence provided by human experience. It divides the seamless coat — or, to change the metaphor into a happier form, it examines the coat, which is superficial, and neglects the body which is fundamental.

"The disastrous separation of body and mind which has been fixed on European thought by Descartes is responsible for this blindness of Science."

See also *Essays in Science and Philosophy* (New York: Philosophical Library, 1947), p. 26, where Whitehead says: "Our scientific systems will suppress all understanding of the ways of the universe which fall outside their abstractions." (Another quotation from *Modes of Thought* pertaining to this topic is given in note 39.)

66. (§ 61) The concept of Holism is set forth by J. C. Smuts in his book: *Holism and Evolution* (London: Macmillan and Company, 1936); see in particular Chapter V, "General Concept of Holism," pp. 84 ff.

The following quotation (p. 88) shows that there is a parallelism between Smuts' thoughts and those of Whitehead and of the philosophy presented here: "The view-point of Evolution as creative, of a real progressive creation still going forward instead of having been completed in the past, of the sum of reality not as constant but as progressively increasing in the course of evolution, is a new departure of our own time, and it is perhaps one of the most significant departures in the whole range of human thought. Not only has the old static view of reality with its fixed elements and species disappeared, the new dynamic view of Evolution does not merely negate the old static view, it has gone much further. Evolution is not merely a process of change, of regrouping of the old into new forms; it is creative, its new forms are not merely fashioned out of the old materials; it creates both new materials and new forms from the synthesis of the new with the old materials." And further, p. 89: "Hence arises the view of Evolution as creative of the new, as an epigenesis instead of an explication, as displaying novelty and initiative, as opening up new paths and rendering possible new choices in the forward march, as creating freedom for the future and in a very real sense breaking the bondage of the past and its fixed predeterminations."

My feeling is that in the elaboration of his ideas Smuts sometimes has personified his concept of holism, as if it were the directive agency. I would keep it more vague, as one of the effects resulting from the basic creativity. There may be other forms in which creativity can express itself.

67. (§ 63) See *Process and Reality*, p. 142 (156*).

68. (§ 63) Spontaneous reactions sometimes can endanger the persistence of a society, as is the case with "lethal" mutations. When such reactions appear repeatedly, we may speak of a pathological behavior. Nevertheless, the spontaneous reaction originally aimed at an adaptation toward a new equilibrium of contrasts. Its damaging effects must be ascribed to results which were not foreseen in the conception leading to the spontaneous reaction.

69. (§ 63) See *Adventures of Ideas*, p. 266 (208*): "It seems that, in bodies that are obviously living, a co-ordination has been achieved that raises into prominence some functions inherent in the ultimate occasions. For lifeless matter these functions thwart each other, and average out so as to produce a negligible total effect. In the case of living bodies the co-ordination intervenes, and the average effect of these intimate functionings has to be taken into account."

70. (§ 64) The idea that life creates matter can also be found in H. Bergson, *L'Evolution Créatrice*, pp. 260–261, but much

more vaguely expressed and without attention to the aspect of matter as a carrier of traditions. Bergson points to the restricted outlook which arises from the notion that "all matter should be eternal."

71. (§§ 65 and 69) See *Process and Reality*, p. 147 (161°): "The conclusion to be drawn from this argument is that life is a characteristic of 'empty space' and not of space 'occupied' by any corpuscular society. . . . Life lurks in the interstices of each living cell, and in the interstices of the brain. In the history of a living society, its more vivid manifestations wander to whatever quarter is receiving from the animal body an enormous variety of physical experience." And p. 148 (162°): "So far as the functioning of the animal body is concerned, the total result is that the transmission of physical influence, through the empty space within it, has not been entirely in conformity with the physical laws holding for inorganic societies. The molecules within an animal body exhibit certain peculiarities of behaviour not to be detected outside an animal body. In fact, living societies illustrate the doctrine that the laws of nature develop together with societies which constitute an epoch. There are statistical expressions of the prevalent types of interaction. In a living cell, the statistical balance has been disturbed."

(See also *Adventures of Ideas*, p. 266 (208°), already quoted in note 69.)

The idea that molecules and atoms are not identical everywhere has been stated very clearly by H. G. Wells, in *First and Last Things. A Confession of Faith and Rule of Life* (London, G. P. Putnam's Sons, 1908, reprinted in "The Thinker's Library"), from which the following passage may be quoted: "I have doubted and denied that there are identically similar experiences; I consider all objective beings as individual and unique. It is now understood that conceivably only in the subjective world and in theory and the imagination, do we deal with identically similar units, and with absolute commensurable quantities. In the real world it is reasonable to suppose we deal at most with practically similar units and practically commensurable quantities. But there is a strong bias, a sort of laborsaving bias, in the normal human mind to ignore this, and not only to speak but to think of a thousand bricks or a thousand sheep or a thousand Chinamen as though they were all absolutely true to sample. If it is brought before a thinker for a moment that in any special case this is not so, he slips back to the old attitude as soon as his attention is withdrawn. This type of error has, for instance, caught many of the race of chemists, and atoms and ions, and so forth of the same species are tacitly assumed to be identically similar to one another.

"Be it noted that, so far as the practical results of chemistry and physics go, it scarcely matters which assumption we adopt, the number of units is so great, the individual difference so drowned and lost. For purposes of inquiry and discussion the incorrect one is infinitely more convenient.

"But this ceases to be true directly we emerge from the region of chemistry and physics."

72. (§ 65) Niels Bohr, "Light and Life," *Nature, 131,* 421–423, and 457–459 (1933); the quotation is from p. 458.

Somewhat further down Bohr adds: "On this view, the existence of life must be considered as an elementary fact that cannot be explained, but must be taken as a starting point in biology, in a similar way as the quantum of action, which appears as an irrational element from the point of view of classical mechanical physics, taken together with the existence of elementary particles, forms the foundation of atomic physics. The asserted impossibility of a physical or chemical explanation of the function peculiar to life would in this sense be analogous to the insufficiency of the mechanical analysis for the understanding of the stability of atoms."

At the end of this article Bohr makes the following observation (pp. 458–459): "However, in this connexion, I should like to emphasize that the considerations referred to here differ entirely from all attempts at viewing new possibilities for a direct spiritual influence on material phenomena in the limitation set for the causal mode of description in the analysis of atomic phenomena. For example, when it has been suggested that the will might have as its field of activity the regulation of certain atomic processes within the organism, for which on the atomic theory only probability calculations may be set up, we are dealing with a view that is incompatible with the interpretation of the psycho-physical parallelism here indicated. Indeed, from our point of view, the feeling of freedom of the will must be considered as a trait peculiar to conscious life, the material parallel of which must be sought in organic functions, which permit neither a causal mechanical description nor a physical investigation sufficiently thorough-going for a well-defined application of the statistical laws of atomic mechanics. Without entering into metaphysical speculations, I may perhaps add that any analysis of the very concept of an explanation would, naturally, begin and end with a renunciation as to explaining our conscious activity."

I do not follow this passage and do not see what Bohr had in mind when he used the word "will" in this text. In the philosophy which I am trying to develop the idea of "willing something," like that of "consciousness," appears only as a result of the integration of many basic processes; they do not belong to the realm of elementary phenomena. This is probably in agreement with Bohr's remarks. Neither does the concept of "will" enter into my picture as something coming from without, from a realm unconnected with material phenomena. However, what I am attempting to point out is that there are influences which are not described in the language and the concepts of physics but which nevertheless have a decisive effectiveness and which derive from phenomena in the universe just as basic as those responsible for the appearance of matter.

73. (§ 66) It might be objected that there is always a tendency for a physical system to pass to the state of lowest energy. However, as mentioned in the first sentence of the paragraph, the case considered in the text refers to a set of configurations all belonging to the *same energy level*, so that there are no differences in energy. The energy here must be calculated by taking into account both the configuration of the system and that of the environment; the energy in general will be distributed over both.

In statistical theory sometimes a different way of counting is used which is applicable when the system and the environment can be considered as separate in such a way that it becomes possible to speak of the energy of the system without making reference to the environment. No attention is then given to the configurations of the environment, and the latter is considered as a reservoir of energy in constant fluctuation, to which energy can be transmitted from the system (if this passes to a state of lower system energy) or from which energy can be transmitted to the system (if this passes to a state of higher system energy). The condition is now introduced that the environment has a constant temperature, which in effect is a condition concerning the magnitude of the energy fluctuations in the reservoir. The weight of a configuration of the system is then provided with a factor of the form $\exp(-U/kT)$, where U is the energy of the system in that configuration, T the absolute temperature of the environment, and k is Boltzmann's constant, mentioned in § 51. The presence of this factor indicates that in the circumstances taken in view the higher the energy of a configuration, the smaller its weight, which means that such a configuration has a correspondingly smaller chance of appearance. It will be evident that this will bring about a bias for the appearance of configurations of low system energy.

Since living systems find themselves in an environment which is nearly at a constant temperature, it may be asked whether these considerations apply to them. Certainly they do (we come back to some equations connected with these relations in note 84). But with these considerations we cannot reach an explanation of the immense diversity in reactions shown by living beings and in their structures: the variety is much wider than what can be measured on a single energy scale. Hence the tendency to move toward configurations of the smallest energy content, observed in anorganic nature, does not help us to explain life.

74. (§§ 66 and 72) By acting upon distinctions which are not counted in physical theory, *conceptual activity introduces new information* (compare the last part of § 51). This has influence on the value to be assigned to the entropy. The simple formula mentioned in § 51, according to which the entropy is given by the logarithm of the total number of configurations (multiplied by the Boltzmann constant k), holds only when all configurations have equal weight. It must be replaced by a more complicated formula when the weights are unequal. It is not necessary to give the precise expression, but an example may serve as illustration. If in a certain case conceptual activity leads to the selection of a particular configuration as a unique form, that configuration no longer will be a member of a set of configurations of equal weight but will form a category for itself with only one single realization. It has then obtained, so to say, zero entropy. This would be an extreme case, resulting as it were from the perfect vision of an artist who picked out the unique representation of that which he considered to be of the highest value. More often we must expect that some subclass of configurations will obtain a preferred meaning within a larger class. In any such case the assignment of unequal weights reduces the entropy. In this sense we may say that *the effect of conceptual activity appears as entropy decrease.*

G. E. Hutchinson, in *The Itinerant Ivory Tower* (New Haven: Yale University Press, 1953), p. 24, in reviewing a discussion by L. G. M. Baas Becking of my view on this subject, stated that this illustration is more likely to throw light on the nature of works of art than on the nature of living matter. My point, taken from Whitehead, is that creativity is the most important aspect of all functioning of life, and that all forms of creativity are interrelated; thus, an illustration taken from art may give a clue to phenomena of life. (The original publication to which Baas Becking referred was my paper "Over de Verhouding tussen het Entropiebegrip en de Levensfuncties," mentioned on p. 207.)

To state my point of view again: Increase of entropy is a habit, a very powerful habit, exhibited by all complexes of processes which are governed by a set of traditions and which occur in a sufficiently large number of realizations so that an entropy can be defined by counting the number of configurations which are subordinated to a given macroscopic specification. However, by assuming the effectiveness of conceptual activity, the possibility is opened that new valuations from time to time become preponderant. When this occurs, we are dealing with a unique situation to which either the method of counting equivalent configurations cannot be applied, or where the number of equivalent configurations is markedly reduced through the introduction of new distinctions. There is then a rupture in the counting of equivalent configurations: a new start must be made since configurations formerly accepted as equivalent have ceased to be equivalent. The new way of counting initially reduces the entropy. Later on, when a chain of processes has got well under way and is again ruled by a new set of traditions, the habit of entropy-increase can reestablish itself.

The amount of entropy reduction may be tiny in comparison with the large increase of entropy in what are considered to be the "normal" chains of processes, and it may be unobservable for our experimental methods. Nevertheless, it constitutes an instance of that coordinated spontaneity which forms the essence of life.

75. (§ 67) The ideas developed in §§ 67 through 73 arose from discussions with Dr. T. L. Lincoln at the Institute for Fluid Dynamics and Applied Mathematics of the University of Maryland. It was his idea that many features which can be studied in games like chess afford analogies able to elucidate features of organic evolution. See: Thomas L. Lincoln, "The Morphology of Search: Evolution in Complicated Board

Games and in the Organization of Biological Systems," manuscript submitted under Naval Contract NONR 595-17, to be published. (See also note 120.)

A brief indication may be given of the way in which games can illustrate some concepts involved in the description of life. While games have rules defined either by a mathematical formalism or by a physical system, it is characteristic of games that the rules do not define the course of the game completely: at each "move" a set of possibilities is left open to the player(s) of the game. The game is governed by a purpose, viz., to win, or perhaps better formulated from our point of view "not to be defeated." It is the task of the player to attempt at each move to foresee to some extent the consequences of the possibilities before him, and to make the choice which appears to be most promising in view of this purpose of the game. The idea of a game consequently involves nonphysical features in two respects: (a) in the existence of a purpose; (b) in the necessity of anticipating and evaluating alternatives in relation to that purpose. In general not everything will be known concerning the possibilities of the situation, so that only an incomplete evaluation can be made. The presence of this uncertainty is of much importance in many games. Thus, there is analogy with the part performed by conceptual activity in sets of processes: conceptual activity is the attempt to evaluate possibilities in view of a certain purpose when it drives a process to its conclusion.

In some games it is possible to work out descriptions of the moves that are open to the player at the successive stages of the play and to determine the consequences of these moves. With the aid of such data various problems can be solved mathematically, for instance, the average chance of winning the game when a player starts from a given initial move; or the chance of never being defeated when the player has an adversary concerning whom partial information is available. Chess is too complicated for calculations extending over a large number of moves, but even here data are available concerning the comparative value of certain strategies which can be of help to the chess player (compare the article mentioned in note 93).

From the point of view of comparing the playing of a game with the behavior of a living being which is "playing" against its environment, the interesting thing is the amount of decision on the part of the player which must go into the play and the possibility before him of making a variety of choices.

This is the analog of the part performed by conceptual activity in the model of a living being, considered in §§ 69 ff. For the study of life it is the relation between the part ensured by "mechanization" and the part that must be left to conceptual activity which is of importance. Current research in biochemistry and biophysics is usually directed toward finding out what is regulated "mechanically" by physical or chemical structures; the investigation is then directed toward finding the rules and determining the statistical averages. While the biologist recognizes the great importance of finding the rules, *his main concern should be to find out what is not regulated in that way,* that is, to find out what are the points where freedom of action and choice is possible, what are purposes toward which the choice can be directed, and whether there are possibilities for enlarging the scope of the freedom. Rearrangement of strategies sometimes may lead to situations in a play where the player can find before him various ways appropriate for winning, which will allow him to choose between alternatives. Extensions of the game can then be planned with additional purposes, or various games can be combined when they have been matched to one another. The amount of freedom that can be obtained from a certain strategy can open possibilities for avoiding defeat in a game against an adversary who incessantly changes his own strategies. It can also afford possibilities for new forms of play and for introducing esthetic points of view, for instance, by combining the game with various forms of display (as in a tournament).

Life is directed toward freedom; it is submitting to rules only in so far as this will be useful for obtaining a wider range of action and for moving into new directions. The pursuit of esthetic points of view is one of these directions.

These considerations form the background for the discussion in §§ 67 through 73. In §§ 67 and 68 the model is defined, and its "physical" properties are considered; from § 69 onward attention is given to the part which can be played by conceptual activity within the setting of this model.

76. (§ 67) One of the principal exponents of the theory that life has arisen through the action of light on chemical substances present in the primitive atmosphere or in the ocean of the earth is A. I. Oparin in his book *The Origin of Life* (translation published by Dover Publications, Inc., New York, 1953).

For a discussion of the ideas brought forward by Oparin, by J. B. S. Haldane, and by others, see A. J. Kluyver and C. B.

van Niel, *The Microbe's Contribution to Biology* (Cambridge: Harvard University Press, 1956), pp. 159 ff.; and G. Ehrensvärd, *Life, Origin and Development* (translation published by the University of Chicago Press, 1962), Chapters VIII ff., pp. 99 ff.

Various experiments have given support to the hypothesis that organic substances even of some complication can be formed by the action of light. See, for instance, H. Gaffron, "The Origin of Life," in *Evolution after Darwin*, I, (quoted in note 100), pp. 39–84, in particular p. 70.

77. (§ 67) The idea was mentioned to me in 1955 by the physicist Dr. Ronald Fraser, editor of the "ICSU Review" until 1963.

78. (§ 67) C. Reid, Quantum Phenomena in Biology, *Science*, *131*, 1078–1084 (April 15, 1960), in particular the diagram given on p. 1081, col. 3. Reid refers to previous work by other authors.

79. (§ 67) The picture of a branching tree is applied in a paper on the foundation of quantum mechanics by H. Everett III, quoted in note 55 (see in particular p. 459, col. 2). The distinction between system and environment as made above is not used in that sense by Everett, who is interested in implications which are not of importance here.

80. (§ 68) We have assumed that the system, when it returns to state *a*, is in the same state and same configuration as it was originally, so that there is no "imprint" on the system. It might be possible that somewhere in the environment a kind of "groove" could have been formed when the system passed through the series of steps leading to the reappearance of state *a*, and such a "groove" might guide the system when it performs the next cycle. The groove may even become deeper by repetition and thus become more effective after a certain number of cycles. A river making its own valley by erosion could be taken as an example. Another example seems to be presented by certain models described by Gordon Pask, where electric currents deposit thin threads of metal along the current path in a colloidal electrolytic solution (see G. Pask, "The Natural History of Networks," in *Self-Organizing Systems* [New York: Pergamon Press, 1960], pp. 232-263, in particular pp. 246–248).

I do not believe that such cases can be used as a general basis for the explanation of what happens in living organisms. They entirely depend on a particular milieu and often contain elements which first must be made and assembled by a human experimenter. It is true that one can look for effects of the nature of Pask's "threads" within organized biological systems, that is, within organisms; but at this stage we are not yet so far and are considering only the very first steps of something that may lead up to organized systems.

81. (§§ 69 and 90) By influencing the assignments of weights so as to avoid dead ends, the subjective form can bring directiveness into the reactions of the system and in this way counteract an important principle holding for physical systems at equilibrium: the *principle of microscopic reversibility*. This principle states that in a system of matter in equilibrium any reaction between atoms, molecules, or other particles occurs just as often as the reverse reaction. It was enunciated by R. C. Tolman in *The Principles of Statistical Mechanics* (Oxford: Oxford University Press, 1938), p. 163: "Hence we can now conclude, under equilibrium conditions, that any molecular process and the reverse of that process will be taking place on the average at the same rate, provided, of course, that we use equal ranges in the molecular phase space in defining the two processes. This result may be called the *principle of microscopic reversibility at equilibrium*" (italics by Tolman). The condition "that we use equal ranges in the molecular phase space" can be replaced by the following one: "that we consider transitions between fully specified configurations as they are defined according to quantum theory."

Growth and development of living beings take place under conditions which are very near to equilibrium. When a physical system is in a state slightly different from equilibrium, statistical theory predicts a slight unbalance between molecular processes and their reverse processes, which unbalance will lead to a reapproach to equilibrium in which the balance is restored. This is the subject of the theory of "irreversible thermodynamics," for which L. Onsager developed certain relations deduced from the principle of microscopic reversibility. When there is a continuous flow of energy through a physical system, it will assume a steady state somewhat different from equilibrium. But there has not been found an example of a physical system which from itself would show a development as is found in living systems.

Any theory of growth and development in primitive living systems must define its position with respect to the principle of microscopic reversibility and must face the problem that physical theory will predict disintegration just as fast or maybe slightly faster than growth. I do not know of any discussion of this point by authors who attempt to describe the early stages of the appearance of life. A reference to the complicated nature of every living being does not help when the problem is that of the origin of such beings; neither does a reference to the notion of "natural selection," which has no application in physics.

82. (§ 70) The importance of turbulence has been discussed by G. E. Hutchinson in a communication "Turbulence as Random Stimulation of Sense Organs," *Transactions 9th Conference on Cybernetics, March 1952* (New York: Josiah Macy Foundation, 1953), pp. 155–158.

83. (§ 70) This suggests that the urge to stay alive was an invention made at some later time during the development of the playing. It turned the play into an earnest business and gave concreteness to the notion of life as a recognizable phenomenon.

In passing it may be observed that the notion of "play" leaves room for features such as ruthlessness, cruelty, destructiveness, and even includes the possibility of self-destruction. I believe that these features must be considered as rather basic: they are not the results of later aberrations. However, once the notion of "to keep going" had been developed, there was the possibility for the emergence of another feature also inherent in the fundamental conceptual activity: the development of tenderness applied to certain aspects of life.

84. (§ 71) See, for instance, A. J. Kluyver and C. B. van Niel, *The Microbe's Contribution to Biology* (Cambridge: Harvard University Press, 1956), Chapters 1 and 2, in particular p. 55: "the energy resulting from the coupled dehydrogenation and hydrogenation is not liberated as heat, but, according to current terminology, is stored in the newly formed 'energy-rich phosphate bond';" and further p. 68 on the universality of electron transfer, where it is stated that the essential feature of the coupled dehydrogenation and hydrogenation is the transfer of an electron which in the cytochromes brings about a change of the iron atom from the trivalent to the bivalent state.

Data on the amounts of energy involved in biologically important reactions are given in H. A. Krebs and H. L. Kornberg, *Energy Transformations in Living Matter; a Survey* (Berlin: Springer Verlag, 1957).

Some thermodynamical considerations may be of interest.

Since one can assume that all biologically important reactions take place at constant pressure and constant temperature, the free energy involved is determined by the so-called Gibbs function, $G = U - TS + pV$, where $U =$ internal energy; $T =$ absolute temperature; $S =$ entropy; $p =$ pressure; and V = the volume of the system. When it is possible to guide the reaction in such a way that it occurs in a reversible form, the maximum amount of work that can be performed (e.g., against electrical forces, or as muscular work, or against an osmotic pressure, or in the synthesis of some chemical product) is determined by the decrease of the (Gibbs) "free energy" G. When reactions are coupled in such a way that the free energy liberated by one reaction is usefully applied in another reaction or by performing work, we can say that the coupling tends to minimize the loss of this free energy.

Another important function is the so-called enthalpy, $H = U + pV$, which measures internal energy corrected for the work that must be done against the external (constant) pressure. When a reaction occurs in an irreversible way, so that no useful work is performed, it develops heat to the amount of the decrease of the enthalpy. This heat is then conducted or radiated away in the environment and is lost.

The following relation holds: $G = H - TS$. As has been mentioned in § 51, we can write: $S = k \ln W$, where k is Boltzmann's constant, and W is the number of configurations which are compatible with the state of the system (the logarithm is the natural or Napierian logarithm). We now introduce $Z = W \exp(-H/kT) = \exp(-G/kT)$, which quantity is the probability function for a system in equilibrium with an environment serving as a reservoir of energy (heat) and kept at constant temperature T and pressure p. In an ideal case where a reaction is so arranged that the free energy does not change during the transition, for instance, from state a to state b, there is no loss of free energy, and we would have $G_a = G_b$, which implies $Z_a = Z_b$. To see what this means, one must note that if $H_a > H_b$, which states that the transition is accompanied by a decrease of enthalpy, we find $W_a > W_b$, indicating that state b has a smaller number of configurations compatible with it than has state a. This can be interpreted by saying that in this case decrease of enthalpy can be used to reach a state which has a smaller number of configurations, in other words, to make a more specific choice. On the other hand, if $H_b > H_a$, we must have $W_b > W_a$: the second state

(state b) must have a larger number of configurations in order that the system can reach this state, which is characterized by a higher value of the enthalpy.

When a system has a set of states all of which have the same value for Z, these states can be in equilibrium with one another. This means that the fluctuations always present in the environment will have just as much chance to drive the system, say from state a to state b, as from b to a, so that there is complete reversibility. The fact that many reactions in living organisms tend to approach such a state of affairs means that the living organism attempts to keep its contacts with the environment such that many transitions can occur just as easily forward as backward. Such a state of affairs leaves room for play of conceptual activity, which can then direct a series of reactions by influencing weight factors not accounted for in the physical description.

85. (§§71 and 82) This point has been extensively discussed by W. M. Elsasser in *The Physical Foundation of Biology* (New York: Pergamon Press, 1958), p. 145: "We summarized these experiences by enunciating the principle that organisms on the whole do not store information by mechanistic means"; and p. 151: "If the outstanding property of organisms is that they do not store large masses of information in a small space, then a closer scrutiny of the empirical conditions associated with potential storage might provide us also with a clue to the processes that supplant storage."

To this we add from Elsasser's Introduction (p. 19): "On the other hand, in order to formulate the theory of epigenesis we had to postulate that the information content of an organism does actually increase tremendously in the process of embryonic development. Any causal relationship which involves an increase of information content in the system investigated as time goes on will be designated as *biotonic* (Elsasser's italics). Thus embryonic development is characterized by a preponderance of biotonic causality." Although Elsasser's ideas may not coincide with those presented in my text, the assumption of an effect of biotonic causality may have a certain parallelism to what I have called effects of conceptual activity.

On pp. 174–176 Elsasser discusses the role of the environment and considers the question whether the new information may be coming from the environment. His conclusion is that the information content of organism is in very large part *endogenous* (Elsasser's italics). A smaller part is exogenous.

The idea that some information might come from the environment has been expressed also by others; we come back to this in § 85.

86. (§§ 72, 74, and 83) With the appearance of a dominating conceptual activity, forms of conceptual activity operating at lower levels are still continually going on. This can be concluded from the numerous adjustments which cells can make within our body, for instance, in processes of repair of damage by means of forms of perception of which our dominant conceptual activity has no idea (compare § 84). We must recognize that at many levels, even within individual cells, there is operative a certain "wisdom" directed toward some creative achievement.

This word "wisdom" is used by C. H. Waddington in *The Ethical Animal* (London: Allen and Unwin, Ltd., 1960), Chapter 16: "Biological Wisdom and the Problems of Today." I quote from pp. 63–64: "As soon as one places the problem of free will in juxtaposition with that of consciousness, it becomes apparent that it cannot be solved either by any manipulation of our existing physico-chemical concepts, since these include no hint of self-awareness, or by any analysis of the language used in formulating the situation, since no linguistic analysis can annul our experience of self. We need ideas which depart more radically from those of the physical sciences; something perhaps akin to the thought of philosophers such as Spinoza or Whitehead, who have suggested that even non-living entities should not be denied qualities related to the self-awareness and will which we know, in much more highly evolved form, in ourselves."

Another quotation from Waddington is given in note 119. See also note 125.

87. (§ 72) The fact that life cannot thrive upon equilibrium heat motion or upon Brownian motion indicates that the effect of conceptual activity cannot be compared with that which Maxwell once envisaged for a set of "demons" (see J. C. Maxwell, *Theory of Heat* [London: Longmans, Green, and Company, 1888 and later reprints], p. 328, on "Limitation of the Second Law of Thermodynamics"). Maxwell imagined that demons might separate the faster molecules from the slower ones in a gas in equilibrium without doing work upon them simply by appropriately opening or closing a hole in a partition between two halves of the vessel in which the gas is contained. If the demons should permit the faster molecules to go to one side of the partition and the slower ones to the other side, a difference of temperature would appear between the two

halves of the vessel. The order in the system would increase, and as a consequence there would be a decrease of entropy. It would mean that "available energy" would have been generated out of random energy.

It has been shown by Szilard that if the "demons" should have to make *measurements* in the physical sense in order to ascertain the velocities of the molecules, they would act similarly as a physical apparatus: the measurements would be observations and produce disturbances (see § 43). Szilard proves that these would increase the entropy of the gas by at least as much as the entropy would decrease by the separation of fast and slow molecules, so that there never can be a gain. See L. Szilard, "Ueber die Entropieverminderung in einem thermodynamischen System bei Eingriffen intelligenter Wesen" ("On the Decrease of Entropy in a Thermodynamical System by the Action of Intelligent Beings"), *Zeitschr. f. Physik*, 53, 840–856 (1929). Szilard's argumentation, while perfectly correct in itself, does not affect our considerations on the effect of conceptual activity since we consider conceptual activity as different from and more fundamental than physical measurement.

88. (§ 73) Concerning the idea of life as a system of cycles, see G. Ehrensvärd, *Life: Origin and Development* (quoted in note 76), p. 148, and the diagrams discussed in Ehrensvärd's Chapter III (pp. 24–52), which illustrate various subcycles.

89. (§ 73) It may be interesting to refer to a book by Jane Jacobs, *The Death and Life of Great American Cities* (New York: Random House, 1963) and to her conception of a city as a living being involving many intricately interwoven relationships belonging to the realm of "organized complexity" (see pp. 432 ff.).

90. (§ 73) Compare *Process and Reality*, p. 115 (127°) on "The Order of Nature" and the statement "(i) That 'order' in the actual world is differentiated from 'mere givenness' by introduction of adaptation for the attainment of an end." This supports the view that order cannot be explained on its own, and that it involves relations pointing to a future.

91. (§ 75) Some ideas on the possibility of forms of life quite different from those known to us on earth have been expressed by H. Bergson in *L'Evolution Créatrice*, pp. 277–279. On p. 279 Bergson speaks of the nature of life which might have existed "in our Galaxy before the condensation of matter had taken place, if it should be true that life may have started

its flight at the same moment at which, by some inverse movement, nebular matter appeared."

92. (§ 75) One might venture the thought that the continually increasing number of living beings on the earth has gradually "absorbed" all manifestations of conceptual activity in our neighborhood, so that by now it has become too much "diluted" outside living beings to have further observable effects. I mention this thought as something which may come forward from a letter written many years ago by the biologist L. G. M. Baas Becking (deceased in 1963), in which the question was raised: "If we continually go on multiplying ourselves, will there always be enough 'material for forming new souls' for all of us?"

93. (Appendix to Chapter 5) See, e.g., G. E. Shannon, "A Chess-playing Machine," in *The World of Mathematics*, vol. IV, edited by J. R. Newman (New York: Simon and Schuster, 1956), 2124–2133.

94. (Appendix to Chapter 5) See W. Ross Ashby, *Design for a Brain* (New York: John Wiley and Sons, Inc., 1952). Ashby constructed a machine called a "homeostat" which exhibits a way of reacting by "trial and error" strongly reminiscent of the behavior of a living being. Similar apparatus containing millions or billions of reacting elements could show richly varied and complicated patterns of behavior. Ashby once indulged in speculations about future possibilities and dangers of such machines, hinting that, once they have started on the path of learning by experience, they might become selfish and direct things to their own ends (see "Design for a Brain," *Electronic Engineering, 20*, 379–383 [1948]). A counterpart to Ashby's speculations are those of Warren S. McCulloch, "Mysterium Iniquitatis of Sinful Man Aspiring into the Place of God," *The Scientific Monthly, 80*, 35–39 (1955), and other publications by McCulloch.

We also refer to A. M. Turing, "Computing Machinery and Intelligence," *Mind, 59*, 433 ff. (1950); reprinted with the title "Can a Machine Think?" in *The World of Mathematics*, vol. IV, edited by J. R. Newman (New York: Simon and Schuster, 1956), pp. 2099–2123.

95. (Appendix to Chapter 5) The following description of a machine (which has been deduced from a short paper by A. M. Uttley, "The Mechanization of Thought Processes," in *Self-Organizing Systems, Proceedings of an Interdisciplinary Conference, 5 and 6 May 1959*, edited by M. C. Yovits and

S. Cameron [New York: Pergamon Press, 1960], pp. 319–322) reminds us of Whitehead's description of the subjective aspect of a developing process (see § 13):

(*a*) The machine must be able to receive signals coming from the external world. The signals are introduced in forms depending upon the type of machine, and the interactions between the external world and the machine are "processed" or "filtered." The machine can be arranged so that the filtering system is changed by the machine itself in consequence of results coming either directly from the signals, or deduced in the computing process, or as a result of an inbuilt mechanism which changes the state of the machine from time to time in order to make new trials.

(*b*) The machine must have a program or a set of programs telling it how to process the incoming signals. This processing can go to great lengths: a master program can start a search for subprograms; the machine can make certain deductions; the machine can match results obtained by computation with sets of model results built into the machine, which means that it can "test hypotheses"; the machine can store results in the memory system, and it can also erase data from the memory system; the machine has outputs for reacting upon the external world as a consequence of its computational results.

(*c*) Finally, the machine must be able to obtain information concerning the changes in the external world which result from its outputs.

Uttley concludes as follows: ". . . we may venture to resolve the 'thinking-matter' problem by suggesting that thinking is a property of matter, matter in its most organized state —the nerve cell. And the word 'consciousness', may, like 'ether', disappear from our scientific language, not by denying obvious facts, but from a deeper understanding of them." Such an assertion is itself a nice instance of "data-processing" by addiction to machinery, which looks as if it is inspired by a desire to do away with the notions of consciousness and self-awareness and which perhaps may also include an unspoken desire not to be bothered by reflections on responsibility for the way in which we handle and present ideas.

96. (Appendix to Chapter 5) John von Neumann, "The General and Logical Theory of Automata," in *Cerebral Mechanisms in Behavior, The Hixon Symposium 1948* (New York: John Wiley and Sons, Inc., 1951); reprinted under the same title in *The*

World of Mathematics, vol. IV, edited by J. R. Newman, (New York: Simon and Schuster, 1956), 2070–2098.

Substantially similar considerations are presented in John von Neumann, *The Computer and the Brain,* edited by Klara von Neumann (New Haven: Yale University Press, 1958).

97. (Appendix to Chapter 5) See, for instance, *Self-Organizing Systems, Proceedings of an Interdisciplinary Conference, 5 and 6 May 1959,* edited by M. C. Yovits and S. Cameron (New York: Pergamon Press, 1960); and "Principles of Self-Organization," *Trans. Univ. of Illinois Symposium on Self-Organization, 8 and 9 June 1961,* edited by H. von Foerster and G. W. Zopf, Jr. (New York: Pergamon Press, 1962).

98. (Appendix to Chapter 5) F. Rosenblatt, *Principles of Neurodynamics. Perceptrons and the Theory of Brain Mechanisms* (Washington, D. C.: Spartan Books, 1962).

99. (Appendix to Chapter 5) Machines can run "mad" and become a direct danger. The case of a power generator which can get into an unstable state is well known. A machine provided with all the possibilities for reaction with its environment as sketched above, when "gone off the track," may resist for some time all attempts to check its course and even could kill its attackers. Machines provided with a large number of potentialities may have forms of instabilities which the constructors did not or could not foresee. Machines can outwit man, as is evident from the possibility of the construction of an automatic chess player.

However, a more subtle danger is found in certain features of the relations between men and machines in a form of symbiosis. There is a kind of congeniality: man is apt to give more attention to directives coming from his machines than one might have expected when one believes in the idea of free will in man (see Bergson's words quoted at the end of note 39). We know the powerful effects which technological advance exerts upon our society: man follows patterns set by the possibilities of his machines and loses sight of other possible courses of action. Example: the psychological influences resulting from the possession of automobiles and the consequent disappearance of interest in many features of our surroundings, which are only felt as obstacles to smooth and fast driving.

The fact that it is sometimes suggested that machines may be built which shall be able to solve social problems — by combining and analyzing all kinds of standardized data, in order to derive "optimal" rules of conduct for men and women — is an indication how far we have gone in our willingness to sell our souls to machines. It is not even considered how the machine-made rules shall be enforced: it seems to be tacitly assumed that somehow we shall just follow them (as, for example, in multiple-choice testing). The way in which jobs are presented in the advertisements of many scientific journals for work on missile systems, etc., all based upon the application of electronic equipment, is a demonstration of how far we are upon the road of considering the beauty of intricate machinery as a prior feature to independent thinking on other problems.

I consider it quite certain that machines with the potentialities envisaged by von Neumann, Ashby, McCulloch will be built. They will command our admiration — which is natural; but they will also command attention of industry and government, and much of our life will be changed in such a way that still more potentialities can be given to machines. Man will no longer ask himself first: "What is the value of life as I have seen it until today? What shall I do to develop my understanding, my sense of responsibility with respect to other life, my freedom of judgment, my joy in what is good and beautiful?" The question will be: "How can we arrange our life and our environment in such a way that the machines can run most smoothly?" Woe to us!

Notes to Chapter 6

100. (§ 76) *Evolution after Darwin*, in three volumes: I. *The Evolution of Life*; II. *The Evolution of Man;* III. *Issues in Evolution*, edited by Sol Tax (Chicago: University of Chicago Press, 1960).

101. (§ 76) H. J. Muller, in *Evolution after Darwin*, vol. III, "Discussion Panel One": The Origin of Life, pp. 82–83. See also on p. 69, under the heading "Topics for Discussion," the statement: "Darwinian evolution is now considered a fact."

102. (§ 77) The stretch of time which may be of importance here is the interval between successive periods of appreciable mutation rate (see the next section). These intervals perhaps can be of the order of 100,000 years.

103. (§ 79) G. A. Kerkut, *Implications of Evolution* (New York: Pergamon Press, 1960) (see also a review by J. T. Bonner, *American Scientist, 49,* 240–244 [1961]).

104. (§ 79) C. E. B. Bremekamp, "Comments on the Doctrine of Evolution," *Proc. Roy. Netherl. Academy of Sciences* (Amsterdam) *C62*, 461–471 (1959).

105. (§ 79) Several authors have expressed the opinion that the various phyla might have originated from what at first would have looked like small differences. But there are no data concerning the nature of the differences which ultimately could have led to the wide divergences which are observed now. This has been discussed by Kerkut (see note 103). The subject has also been discussed by E. S. Russell, *The Diversity of Animals. An Evolutionary Study* (Leiden: E. J. Brill, 1962, published posthumously), in particular in Part III, pp. 96 ff. (examples: Hermit crabs, pp. 106–110; Cetacea, pp. 114–116; Birds, pp. 116–119), and p. 128 on the possibility of saltatory evolution.

　　See also observations on this problem in the paper by T. L. Lincoln mentioned in note 75.

106. (§ 79) Th. Dobzhansky, "Evolution and Environment," in *Evolution after Darwin*, vol. I (see note 100), pp. 403–428, in particular pp. 404–405.

107. (§ 79) Th. Dobzhansky, as quoted in note 106, p. 408.

108. (§ 80) For some summarizing descriptions of chemical activities in cells and on the role of DNA molecules, see e.g., W. D. McElroy, *Cellular Physiology and Biochemistry* (Englewood Cliffs: Prentice Hall, Inc., 1961); V. G. Allfrey and A. E. Mirsky, "How Cells Make Molecules," *Scientific American*, 205, 74–82 (September 1961); and F. H. C. Crick, "Macromolecules and Natural Selection," in *Growth in Living Systems*, edited by M. X. Zarrow (New York: Basic Books, Inc., 1961), pp. 3–8. The literature is extensive and is continually increasing.

109. (§ 80) Some articles on the "genetic code": F. H. C. Crick, "The Genetic Code," *Scientific American*, 207, 66–74 (October, 1962); M. H. Nirenberg, "The Genetic Code II," *Scientific American*, 208, 80–94 (March 1963); J. D. Watson, "Involvement of RNA in the Synthesis of Proteins," *Science*, 140, 17–26 (April 5, 1963); M. H. F. Wilkins, "Molecular Configuration of Nucleic Acids," *Science*, 140, 941–950 (May 31, 1963); R. V. Eck, "Genetic Code: Emergence of a Symmetrical Pattern," *Science*, 140, 477–480 (May 3, 1963); Th. H. Jukes, "The Genetic Code," *American Scientist*, 51, 227–245 (1963).

　　It has been found that genetic information is also transmitted by other structures than the chromosomes. See Ruth Sager, "Genes outside the Chromosomes," *Scientific American*, *212*, 70–79 (January 1965).

110. (§ 80) The numbers mentioned in the text are, of course, very crude. The number of 100,000 genes is taken from G. W. Beadle, "Molecules, Viruses and Heredity," *Bulletin Atomic Scientists*, *15*, 354–360 (1959). Beadle (*op. cit.* p. 355, 2nd col.) speaks of 10,000 to 100,000 kinds of genes and then estimates an amount of information as contained in a library of 1000 volumes.

P. Doty, "Configurations of Biologically Important Macromolecules in Solution," *Reviews of Modern Physics*, *31*, 107–117 (1959), gives an estimate of 50,000 Å for the length of a DNA molecule with a molecular weight of 10 million and carrying two residues every 3.4 Å (p. 113, col. 2). This would give 14,800 pairs of residues per molecule.

D. Mazia, "How Cells Divide," *Scientific American*, *205*, 101–120 (September 1961), states that "fully extended the DNA in a human nucleus could make a thin thread a meter long" (*op. cit.*, p. 105). This would give a total of about 10^9 "letters," which does not differ greatly from the number 5×10^8 mentioned in the text.

111. (§ 80) See for instance H. Quastler, "Chemical Communication Systems in the Cell," *Trans. New York Acad. of Sciences, ser. II*, *25*, 382–395 (February 1963).

112. (§ 81) See for instance J. Bonner, "The Biology of Plant Growth," in *Growth in Living Systems*, edited by M. X. Zarrow (New York: Basic Books, Inc., 1961), pp. 439–452, in particular pp. 448–451.

113. (§ 81) See C. H. Waddington, *New Patterns in Genetics and Development* (New York: Columbia University Press, 1962), pp. 14 ff., "The Control of Gene Activity."

114. (§ 81) This subject is discussed at length in Waddington's book, quoted in the preceding note.

Waddington's discussion of manifold processes of growth and development stresses the part which is played by physical and chemical laws in the building of various structural units, e.g., three-dimensional atomic lattices, fiber structures, sheet structures. Structures of such types are also found in anorganic crystals (in particular in silicates), and that which Waddington calls "unit-generated forms" (*ibid.*, p. 90) can almost be rendered as "forms due to processes of crystallization." The "template-generated forms" considered on p. 119

of the book apparently are the result of crystallization plus detachment. This is not a common occurrence in the usual phenomena of anorganic crystallization and would require a deeper probing into energy relations for its explanation. Perhaps the catalytic activity of crystals of titanium dioxide and of other metallic compounds in promoting certain types of very regular polymerization may constitute an analogy. Similarly, one would like to have a description of the energy relations involved in the separation and duplication of the strands of DNA.

A biologically important problem is how the dimensions of structures are limited. In anorganic crystallization the only limits are those due to exhaustion of material or to the presence of other bodies. In living structures, on the other hand, the various component parts must be connected in such ways that there can be joint action. The change of pattern, the junction between unlike parts, is of no less interest than a pattern on its own.

115. (§ 81) Cellular movements have been the topic of a symposium on the mechanism of cytoplasmic streaming, etc., held at Princeton University, April 1963, which brought a bewildering complex of problems. See the *Proceedings,* edited by R. D. Allen and N. Kamiya, "Primitive Motile Systems in Cell Biology" (New York: Academic Press, 1964).

116. (§ 81) It may be of interest to list some examples of adjustments which can occur in growth processes, in order to remind us of the wonderful potentialities of living cells. It is, of course, impossible to aim at completeness in this respect and the examples have been chosen more or less at random.

Instances of *normally* occurring coordinative activity are found in the following:

(*a*) The embryonic development of higher animals.

(*b*) The accelerated metamorphosis of insects as it occurs in the pupa from caterpillar to butterfly.

(*c*) The formation of composite beings through the union of separate cells, as occurs in Mycetozoa.

(*d*) The formation of composite beings through budding from a single individual, as occurs in many hydroid polyps where both food-gathering and sexually active polyps appear all connected together, while more variegated cases are presented by the order of the Siphonophora. Another striking case is that of certain Bryozoa, where the upper buds grow into normal polyps (here of much greater complication than is the case with hydroid polyps), while at the bottom end of a colony a system of roots is growing, serving to anchor the colony and becoming more extensive in proportion to the growth of the colony.

(e) The conjugation of unicellular organisms to form a single individual with refreshed potentialities for reproduction.

Instances of coordinated activity of cells in circumstances which are more or less *abnormal* are:

(a) The growth of complete plants from cuttings.

(b) The regeneration of lost limbs or other organs (even an eye can be rebuilt in amphibians) from adjoining tissue.

(c) Induction of the growth of organs at an abnormal location as a result of the transplantation of organ-inducing tissue.

(d) Reactions to parasites, such as the formation of galls, and the curious developments in certain plants living in symbiosis with ants.

(e) The regenerative properties of the polyp Hydra viridis (see, for instance: N. J. Berrill, "The Indestructible Hydra," *Scientific American, 197,* 118–125 [December 1957]; A. L. Burnett, "Hydra: An Immortal's Nature," *Natural History, 68,* 498-507 [1959]).

(f) Driesch's famous experiments on the development of eggs of sea urchins: the egg, after fertilization, starts off as a single cell which divides into two cells, four cells, eight, etc. If one directs attention to the first cleavage, it appears that normally one of the two cells formed at this cleavage leads to the development of the left half of the complete animal, while the other cell leads to the development of the right half. However, if after the first cleavage one of the two cells is taken away, the remaining cell still is sufficient for the growth of a *complete* animal (be it of somewhat smaller dimensions): it is not a half animal which develops from it. Thus, each of the two cells formed after the first cleavage of the original egg still has full powers in it, and apparently is provided with an instruction which can be adapted to different forms of application of these potentialities, depending on whether or not it is accompanied by the sister cell. (In the literature I found as reference for these experiments: H. Driesch, *Archiv für Entwicklungs-Mechanik, 4,* 75 and 247 [1898]. The observations have often been repeated and have been amply confirmed, as mentioned by

D'Arcy Wentworth Thompson, *On Growth and Form* [Cambridge, England: Cambridge University Press, 1942], p. 60.)

117. (§ 81) For a beginning of the study of this subject see: *Information Theory in Biology*, edited by H. Quastler (Urbana: University of Illinois Press, 1953), and in particular a paper by H. R. Branson, "Information Theory and the Structure of Proteins," pp. 84–104.

118. (§ 82) I would again mention Waddington's book (quoted in note 113) as an example. With all its admirable descriptions of morphogenetic processes, the question "what happens between the steps?" remains open. On p. 118 under the heading "Instruction-Generated Forms" it is pointed out that instructions are needed as to how various units must be assembled; on p. 119 Waddington states how difficult it is to see what physical forms such instructions should have, and he adds that "it is not easy to see how any amount of detail could be incorporated in any system of this kind which might plausibly be supposed to operate in biological organisms," unless (perhaps) there is a material structure in the immediate proximity of which the new structure is to be formed. But that is only displacing the difficulty.

From a certain angle this book may seem to be a documentation of the insufficiency of the mechanical picture of biological development. What it discusses reminds one of "puzzling reflections in a mirror" (I Corinthians, *The New English Bible*, 13:12).

J. Bonner in the paper quoted in note 112 writes on pp. 448–449: "I suppose that when the bud of our plant receives the floriferous signal from the leaf, what happens is that the signal says to these genes which contain the flowering information, 'Please get busy and make the materials concerning which you have the information. Make the ribonucleic acid and thence the enzymes which are required for floral differentiation.'" Although Bonner may have meant these sentences in a joking manner, they typify the stage of our knowledge and of its gaps.

Quastler in the paper quoted in note 111 gives a fairly detailed description of the communication system in a cell, which must bring the information contained in the DNA molecules to the loci of enzyme production, but again it is a description which leaves open many intermediate stages. It can be understood only if it is assumed that these stages are taken care of by activities which involve discrimination and some know-how of what to do.

119. (§ 82) C. H. Waddington, *The Ethical Animal* (London: Allen and Unwin, Ltd., 1960), also quoted in note 86.

Passages relevant to the topic mentioned in the text, are (p. 96): "The theory of evolution, and indeed the whole of biology, has always provided a battleground from two rather contrasting methods of analysis. On the one hand, there is the tendency towards what may be regarded as, in a broad sense, 'atomicity'—an analysis into entities which are independent of one another in their essential nature, and which have, when they interact, only external relations with one another. The alternative approach expects to find that it is dealing with organized systems, in which the factors determine, at least in part, each other's essential characters, and enter into cyclic interaction-systems involving internal relations." And on pp. 99–100: "The view which I am urging, and I think that which Bateson is putting forward, is much more in tune with the thought of Whitehead than with that of Driesch or Bergson." I add from p. 89: "Now, with such a mechanism—random mutation in selective but unresponsive environments—it would appear difficult to find any principle which would produce any specific direction of evolutionary change. All evolution would appear to be purely a contingent phenomenon, which just happened to go in the way that it did, but for no ascertainable reason. One could admit, of course, that the mechanism of natural selection is one which will, as has been frequently pointed out, produce states of extreme improbability by preserving just those particular chance variations which happen to fit in with the environment and rejecting all others, but there seems at first sight to be nothing which could decide as to which state of improbability will be favoured in this way out of all those which might conceivably be possible."

120. (§ 83) The ideas proposed here again owe much to discussions with Dr. T. L. Lincoln, who introduced the notion of strategy. See the paper mentioned in note 75.

121. (§ 83) It may be of interest to point out that in the anorganic world two phenomena are found where quantum laws influence the cooperation of large numbers of atoms, so that macroscopic results are reached: the superfluidity of liquid Helium II (below $2.19°$ K), and the superconductivity for electricity appearing in various metals at Helium temperatures. See, for instance, F. London, in the Preface of his book *Superfluids* (New York: Wiley and Sons, Inc., 1950):

"There can be little doubt at present that the superfluids are essentially quantum mechanisms, more specifically, quantum mechanisms on a macroscopic scale." I owe this observation to the late Professor H. A. Kramers.

122. (§ 84) See P. Weiss, "Interactions between Cells," *Reviews of Modern Physics*, *31*, 449–454 (1959), in particular p. 451. The subject is also discussed by C. H. Waddington in the book quoted in note 113, pp. 162 ff.; and by A. A. Moscona, "Tissue Reconstruction from Dissociated Cells," in *Growth in Living Systems*, edited by M. X. Zarrow (New York: Basic Books, Inc., 1961), pp. 197–220.

123. (§ 84) P. Weiss, *Op. cit.* (see previous note), p. 450, col. 2, and p. 452, col. 2. See also C. H. Waddington, *New Patterns in Genetics and Development* (quoted in note 113), p. 163.

124. (§ 84) P. Weiss, *Op. cit.* (note 122), p. 454, col. 2. See also C. H. Waddington, p. 166; and A. A. Moscona (note 122), p. 217.

125. (§ 84) The following quotation from G. G. Simpson, *Principles of Animal Taxonomy* (New York: Columbia University Press, 1961), p. 3, is of interest in this connection: "The necessity for aggregating things (or what is operationally equivalent, the sensations received from them) into classes is a completely general characteristic of living things. One should hesitate, although some do not, to apply such words as 'consciousness' or 'perception' to an amoeba, for instance, but it is perfectly obvious from the reactions of an amoeba that something in its organization performs acts of generalization. It does not react to each bit of food, say, as a unique object, but in some way, in some sense of the word, it *classifies* innumerable different objects all within the class of foodstuffs. Such generalization, such classification in that sense, is an absolute, minimal requirement of adaptation, which in turn is an absolute and minimal requirement of being or staying alive."
That which Simpson describes as "generalization" or "classification" is an aspect of that for which I use the term conceptual activity.

126. (§ 87) E. C. Olson, "Morphology, Paleontology, and Evolution," in *Evolution after Darwin*, vol. I, pp. 523–545, in particular p. 539. Olson's examples mainly refer to the dental system of certain mammals.

127. (§ 87) This subject is considered by C. H. Waddington in *New Patterns in Genetics and Development* (see note 113), Chapter 3, "Types of Morphogenetic Process" (pp. 85 ff.). It is the topic of D'Arcy Wentworth Thompson's well known book *On Growth and Form* (2nd ed.; Cambridge: Cambridge University Press, 1942).

(In passing I would observe that also the reaction of an organism to physical forces or other physical effects will occur through the intermediary of some form of conceptual activity. I see an example of this in the biological adagium that "resistance begets resistance," mentioned by D'Arcy Thompson on p. 1018 in the chapter "On Form and Mechanical Efficiency" [pp. 958–1025]. Here the first word "resistance" means "stress produced by exterior forces," and the second "increase of strength through the growth of particular tissue, etc." An interesting case often commented upon is the fact that elements of bone [the trabeculae] arrange themselves in the directions of the lines of principal stress for the most important types of loading of the structure in which they occur [*ibid.*, p. 977, fig. 462]. Other cases are presented by the arrangement of strong fibers in the outer parts of the stems of grasses and related plants, the stems being often hollow in the interior [*ibid.*, pp. 973–974]. My opinion is that the growth of these elements of bone or of fibrous tissue at the place where they are found is not a merely physical or mechanical reaction to a state of stress: there is involved in it some form of "recognition," some notion that it is "worthwhile" to grow at such a spot and in such a direction.)

128. (§ 87) The idea that evolution involves directiveness as a fundamental characteristic of life has been defended by E. S. Russell in the book quoted in note 105; see in particular the conclusive discussion on pp. 137–139.

The idea of directiveness is also defended by P. T. Mora in "Directiveness in Biology on the Molecular Level?," *American Scientist*, 50, 570–575 (1962); and "Urge and Molecular Biology," *Nature 199*, 212–218 (1963). Mora quotes another book by Russell, *The Directiveness of Organic Activities* (Cambridge: Cambridge University Press, 1945).

129. (§ 87) On the subject of beauty see N. J. Berrill, *Sex and the Nature of Things* (New York: Pocket Books, Inc., 1955), p. 129: "the fact that what is primarily and essentially utilitarian so often turns out to have lyric beauty is something to think about. *I believe beauty is inherent in the nature of our uni-*

verse and shows itself where it can—it is not only in the mind of the human beholder" (italics J. M. B.). And pp. 111–112: "I believe . . . that the real nature of a bird is to stand colorful and bright and unafraid; that birds evolved from their reptilian ancestors in security among the trees, and, having a marvelous sense of color, were able in that security to become colorful themselves; and that the colorful gaudiness at first had nothing to do with sex. You see the same sort of thing among the fishes of the coral reefs. The stony jungle of the reef itself affords protection like that of trees—small fish can dart away into shelter where larger, faster fish cannot follow. And in that security color has come to life—there has been no reason to suppress it, no need to simulate invisibility as in the open sea."

The importance of beauty is expressed even more strongly by Berrill in *Man's Emerging Mind* (New York: Premier Books, 1957), p. 223: "We need no faith in supernatural forces. We need only to recognize that our knowledge of the universe through our senses and our knowledge of the universe through our own inward nature show that it is orderly, moral and beautiful, that it is akin to intelligence, that love and hope belong in it as fully as light itself, and that the power and will of the human mind is but a symptom of reality; that we, when we are most human, most rational, most aware of love and beauty, reflect and represent the spirit of the universe."

See also J. C. Smuts, *Holism and Evolution* (quoted in note 65), pp. 218–219: "Apart from the great human development, beauty in Nature tells the same tale. The song of birds, with its primary appeal to sex, but with so infinitely much more in it than the mere sex-appeal [the latter words hold also when the song primarily should be considered as serving the defense of a territory, J. M. B.]; the glorious forms and colouring of birds and beasts and insects, which no doubt rise in and from the struggle for existence, but finally rise above it, and rob it of all its sordidness and drabness; above all, the wonder of plants and flowers, which were meant for the eye of birds and insects, but which contain so infinitely much more than the eye of bird or insect ever beheld or ever can behold—it is everywhere in Nature the same. Everywhere we see the great overplus of the whole. So little is asked; so much more is given. The female only asks for a sign to recognize the male, and to help her to select him and to enjoy him in preference to others. And for answer she gets an overpowering revelation of beauty out of all proportion to her modest request. . . . There is evidently more in all this than the Darwinian factors can satisfactorily explain, and it would be both foolish and unscientific not to recognise this frankly."

Pictures of unicellular organisms of great beauty, such as Diatoms, Foraminifera, Radiolaria, and of many other living forms were collected by Ernst Haeckel in his *Kunstformen der Natur* (Leipzig und Wien: Bibliographisches Institut, 1899–1904). Radiolaria in particular were Haeckel's favorites, of which he had described something like 4000 species in the reports of the "Challenger" expedition for the investigation of the deep seas.

130. (§ 88) Alfred Russel Wallace, in *Natural Selection and Tropical Nature. Essays on Descriptive and Theoretical Biology* (new edition, London: Macmillan and Company, 1891), Chapter IX, "The Limits of Natural Selection as Applied to Man," pp. 186–214 (apparently originally written in 1870, in *Contributions to the Theory of Natural Selection*). On pp. 202–205 there is a section with the heading "Summary of the Argument as to the Insufficiency of Natural Selection to account for the Development of Man."

131. (§ 88) It is even possible that the first appearance of the new type, that is, of the truly human form, may have been at a disadvantage in the struggle for life in comparison with the prehuman type from which it originated, in particular, during the stage of young individuals. The advantage of the more developed brain will have become evident only later, and the new human being may have been able to overcome its initial disadvantage only as a result of the care of the still prehuman parents, who will have tended their children as long as they were in need of protection. (Wallace noted this point.)

There will have been more cases in nature where the appearance of a new mutation made the young of the species more vulnerable than those of the original type. The new type could then get a foothold only if it appeared with sufficient frequency and if the behavior of the parents underwent the necessary modification to ensure protection for their offspring. The complicated forms of behavior with regard to the care for posterity which are found in many classes of animals have required a lot of adjustments; we cannot suppose that all these adjustments are the result of an interplay between blind variations and survival value.

There is no scheme available to understand the sequence of events which might have brought about the adjustments as the result of blind survival against an overwhelming chance for complete loss of offspring before any result could have become fixed. Too little thought is given to the problems which are involved in the assumption of blind variation and blind effects of survival value. I would refer again to Whitehead's observations, quoted in the second part of note 39 and in note 65. See also E. S. Russell, quoted in note 128.

132. (§ 89) Continued growth may perhaps afford an explanation for what is called "orthogenesis" in evolution theory, and for "hypertely" or "dystely," the appearance of seemingly grotesque and perhaps disadvantageous forms. See Th. Dobzhansky, *Evolution, Genetics, and Man* (New York: Wiley and Sons, Inc., 1955), p. 360, where he quotes H. Cuénot, *Invention et Finalité en Biologie* (Paris: Flammarion, 1941), p. 65.

In connection with the idea that biological types are "purposes," I refer to the end of § 60 on purposes which "overshoot" the mark. "To overshoot the mark" is a common occurrence in applications of human technology; many cases are in evidence. Compare the quotation from Whyte in note 47, on the effect of thinking "in the quantitative mode."

133. (§ 89) The necessity to assume that internal adjustment is connected with each mutation, has been stressed by L. L. Whyte, "Developmental Selection of Mutations," *Science*, 132, 954 (Oct. 7, 1960), and 1692–1694 (Dec. 2, 1960).

134. (§ 89) Several zoologists use the term *"selection pressure"* to indicate an effect of the environment, for instance, an effect of a progressive change in the environment in promoting the appearance of a definite direction of evolution (e. g., E. Mayr, "The Emergence of Evolutionary Novelties," in *Evolution after Darwin*, vol. I, pp. 371 and 374; S. L. Washburn and F. C. Howell, "Human Evolution and Culture," in *Evolution after Darwin*, vol. II, pp. 49–52). In my opinion this term is ambiguous, and I would prefer to use *mutation pressure* to denote the faculty of a species to produce mutant forms having different chances for survival. The mutation pressure can be dormant or active.

When differences in survival rate are marked, we can say that the environment is *permissive* for a more or less definite type of mutants in preference to other types. Sometimes there can be a progressive unidirectional change of some feature of the environment. We may then say that there is a progressive change of permissivity of the environment, and that the appearance of a progressive change of type, such as a reaction upon the change of the environment, is the result of continued mutation pressure within the living type.

135. (§ 89) It is needless to state that such an influence cannot be of the direct kind sometimes naively supposed in the form that a "need was felt" which gave rise to the appearance of a new organ. When effects reach the germ plasma, their route has been devious, and the outcome is unpredictable. But it would be unwise to deny the possibility of hereditary effects derived from reactions to environmental circumstances; we know that there are such effects from radiation.

136. (§ 89) For comparison I quote from H. Bergson, *L'Evolution Créatrice*, p. 276: "chaque espèce se comporte comme si le mouvement général de la vie s'arrêtait à elle au lieu de la traverser" ("each species behaves as if life's general movement had stopped there, instead of continuing onward").

137. (§ 89) Here I would add the following observations concerning some later developments in animals.

Nerve cells have developed as direct connections between sensory apparatus and apparatus for motion or for other activities, in contrast with transmission of signals from cell to cell over long distances. Nervous centers have developed as systems of multiple interconnections endowed with the means for reinforcement of particular connections. The reinforcement procedure makes it possible to grasp and to select particular combinations of sensory stimuli as representations which can be classified and recognized. The field for conceptual activity extended with the growth of these systems of connections.

Consciousness is a specially condensed form of the basic conceptual activity, attaching itself to these representations and introducing the possibility of delay of action, so that an opportunity is gained for the comparison of various courses of action. Consciousness looks away from the general background of conceptual activity, and is mainly directed to these representations.

Nevertheless, consciousness is intimately connected with the background, as is evident from the reciprocal relations between mental state and bodily health as well as from the possibility of what we call "intuition," that is, new flashes of insight coming up from the background and giving a new interpretation to a set of representations. With a particular view to ourselves we may point to the capability of many men and women of expressing in actions, gestures, or attitudes an evidence of their awareness of relations and values far beyond the immediately visible appearances, a fact which is of such great importance in our life. Sometimes we speak of an "uncanny insight" in human relations. It is interesting to go one step further toward "mysticism," when we take this word in the sense in which H. Bergson uses it in *Les Deux Sources de la Morale et de la Religion*, to describe a greatly strengthened contact between the background and consciousness, leading to a more effective intuition and to the deployment of activities giving evidence of being in "unison" with certain general trends in the development of the universe. I quote the following statements: *Op. cit.*, p. 235: "L'aboutissement du mysticisme est une prise de contact, et par conséquent une coïncidence partielle, avec l'effort créateur que manifeste la vie." ("The final reach of mysticism is a taking of contact, and thus a partial coincidence, with the creative effort that is manifested by life"); (*ibid.*, p. 214): "Un mysticisme complet est action, création, amour." ("Complete mysticism is activity, creation, love"); (*ibid.*, pp. 243–244): "Il y a pourtant une santé intellectuelle solidement assise, exceptionelle, qui se reconnaît sans peine. Elle se manifeste par le goût de l'action, la faculté de s'adapter et de se réadapter aux circonstances, la fermeté jointe à la souplesse, le discernement prophétique du possible et de l'impossible, un esprit de simplicité qui triomphe des complications, enfin un bon sens supérieur." ("However, there is an intellectual state of health, firmly based, exceptional, which can be recognized without difficulty. It manifests itself by the desire for action, the ability to adapt and to readapt to circumstances, firmness combined with suppleness, a prophetic ability to distinguish between what is possible and what is impossible, a spirit of simplicity which triumphs over complications, in sum: a superior 'good sense.'") Bergson continues his analysis through the next pages (until p. 251).

While Bergson has in mind mostly those "mystics" who have contributed in one form or another to the progress of mankind, we cannot take away the indefiniteness of the term "being in unison with certain trends in the development of the universe": "mystics" can lead groups of men and women to morally good deeds as well as to bad, or at the least, to unsuitable ones. The point which I am considering is not the outcome but the fact of contacts of great intensity, so that the presence of these contacts is sensed by many other people whose attitudes become polarized. It is a matter for concerted judgment by all men and women to find out whether the objects and the outcome of the movement are good or bad.

We must not reject the possibility that living organisms may possess forms of perception which are unknown to us and which we can imagine only with difficulty. It is perhaps suitable to refer to such phenomena as telepathy and extrasensory perception since it may be that on certain occasions particular forms of conceptual activity could "simultaneously" affect processes which are not contiguous. This might bring about something which would seem to be a transmission of feelings by nonphysical means.

Unknown forms of perception may be involved in the sense of direction which many animals have, in the strange forms of rhythmic behavior exhibited by various living beings, which sometimes follow the moon rather than the sun, in the migratory instinct. It is not to be excluded that what we call "primitive man" may have had some of these perceptive faculties. Some views on these possibilities are brought forward, e.g., by W. H. Hudson, in *A Hind in Richmond Park* (London: J. M. Dent & Sons, Ltd., 1922; reprinted 1951), Chapter IV, pp. 52–55, from which I quote: "And what gives us hope is something still to be found in ourselves—in some, if not in all, of us; vestiges of ancient outlived impulses, senses, instincts, faculties, which stir in us and come to nothing, and in some exceptional cases are rekindled and operate so that a man we know may seem to us, in this particular, like a being of another species. They are numerous enough, and when collected and classified they may form a new subject or science with a specially invented new name, signifying an embryology of the mind."

These faculties are not of a kind which can be brought into a mathematical formulation. I believe that some of the recent statistical investigations on extrasensorial perception are looking at the subject from the most unpromising side. Our present nearly absolute confidence in scientific methods of research and our rejection of other forms of thinking are the results of a particular tendency in our development, a "mechanistic-mindedness" which pervades our thinking and our reactions and is heavily accentuated by the trends of our present social structure. This has directed attention away from our other faculties. It is the reason why we no longer turn to meditation and introspection. It is also the reason why it is so difficult for us to accept the idea that in our cells there is a "wisdom" hidden from our observational methods but nevertheless exerting an all-pervading influence that in many respects protects our life.

138. (§ 90) I add the following remarks:

(I) As an instance of what I consider to be confusion in the use of words, I quote a sentence from an article by G. G. Simpson, "The World into Which Darwin Led Us," *Science*, *131*, 966–974 (April 1960): "The rational world is not teleological in the old sense. It certainly has purpose, but the purposes are not imposed from without or anticipatory of the future." (p. 970, col. 1.) I take the second sentence first. It is important that Dr. Simpson states that the world has purpose, but it is not clear what is meant by this word. That purposes are not "imposed from without" I accept, but the statement "the purposes are not anticipatory of the future" is close to a *contradictio in terminis*. It depends on the article "the" before future: there is no definite future, and there can be nothing anticipatory of this nonexisting future. But the meaning changes when we ask whether purposes can be anticipatory of a future. The answer then must be affirmative: purposes are directed toward some expectation concerning a possible future. The term "purpose" has no meaning when some anticipation of a future is not taken in view.

As to the first sentence, "The rational world is not teleological in the old sense," there is no precise definition of "the old sense"; but in view of what Simpson presents on p. 973, col. 2, concerning vitalism and finalism, the meaning seems to be that the world has not been arranged so as to move toward some definite goal. In this I agree with Simpson. I disagree, however, when one reasons as if movement toward a definite end is the only form of teleology which is thinkable. The basis of Whitehead's philosophy is the idea that in every step of the universe there is some anticipation of a possible future and a decision is made between the possibilities that are still open. This decision is a result of an evaluation, that is, of a purpose, of an end projected in a nearby future. It is, of course, strongly dependent upon the experience which has induced the process. In many treatments of the problem of finalism the authors fail to make a clear distinction between one master end, "God's plan" for the universe, so to say, and anticipation of nearby possibilities with the conception of a limited aim or purpose in view of these possibilities.

I therefore object to the use of the term "supernatural" in this connection (Simpson, p. 973, col. 2, at the end). A belief in "God's plan" could be termed "supernatural"; but the assumption that there are anticipations of possibilities and conceptions of limited extent is presented in Whitehead's philosophy as a feature of nature pervading all that which happens, and not as an "extraneous influence" coming from the void.

A paper by E. Mayr, "Cause and Effect in Biology," *Science, 134,* 1501–1506 (November 1961), in which a reference is made to Simpson's article, does not help to clear up the points which I have indicated. Mayr defines purposeful action as follows (p. 1503, col. 3, at the end): "An individual who—to use the language of the computer—has been 'programmed' can act purposefully." This does not give an answer since it refers "purpose" to "program" and leaves open the question "What is a program? Is a program something else than a set of rules made in view of future actions?" Also there remains the question: "Who or what has set the program?" Mayr's discussion of Aristotle's concept of "teleology" lacks a precise definition, but from what is said on p. 1504, col. 2, and p. 1506, col. 2, it apparently again refers to a superior design or plan. The idea that purposes can be conceived with limited aims without any knowledge concerning what may be the result in a more distant future is not considered at all.

Neither does it help to call in the word "materialism" (see, for instance, H. Gaffron, in *Evolution after Darwin*, vol. I, p. 41) when there is no precise statement concerning what are considered to be the properties of matter. I again object to the juxtaposition of the terms "metaphysical" and "supernatural"; while rejecting "supernatural" influences, I accept that there are effects not described by physics. Life, death, love, thought are terms presenting notions of importance in biology, but none of them belongs to the language of physics.

(II) I would further compare my point of view with a point of view expressed by D. Campbell, "Blind Variation and Selective Survival," in *Self-Organizing Systems* (London:

Pergamon Press, 1960), pp. 205–231. Campbell makes the statement that "a blind-variation-and-selective-survival process is fundamental to all inductive achievements, to all genuine increase in knowledge, to all increases in fit of system to environment" (p. 207, sub. 1); and continues on p. 212: "The phenomenal directness of vision tempts us to make vision prototypic for knowing at all levels, and leads to the chronic belief in the existence of 'direct' and 'insightful' mental processes which it is a major purpose of this paper to deny."

I do not disagree with either the last part of this sentence or with the general idea expressed in the first sentence. Everywhere in the development of the metaphysical picture in these pages it has been stressed that there are no far seeing mental processes, that no single process in a living structure is "insightful" in the sense as is meant in the sentence quoted. "Insight" is gained only through elaborate combinations of processes making use of previous experience. But when Campbell adds (on p. 213): ". . . once the process has blindly stumbled into a thought-trial that 'fits' the selection criterion, accompanied no doubt by the 'something clicked,' 'Eureka' or 'aha-erlebnis' that marks the successful termination of the process . . . ," my point is that he himself now makes use of criteria which are based upon conceptual activity. The occurrence of such a reaction is indeed the most important feature, and it should well be realized that *an "Eureka" or an "aha-erlebnis" is the thing which is outside the domain and the language of physics: it is a metaphysical element.* Such reactions do not occur in nonliving matter, unless one considers machines which man has prepared beforehand to have these reactions. They are typical for living beings.

INDEX

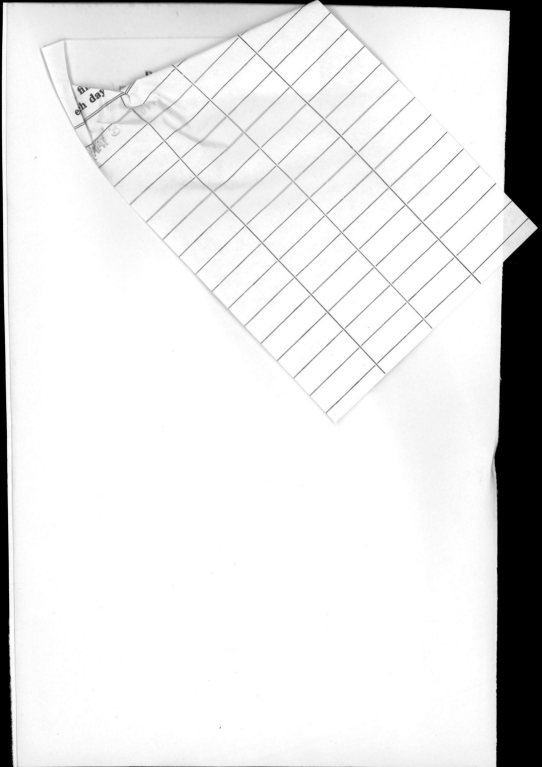